Emotions and Values in Equity Crowdfunding Investment Choices 1

Emotions and Values in Equity Crowdfunding Investment Choices 1

Transdisciplinary Theoretical Approach

Christian Goglin

iSTE

WILEY

First published 2020 in Great Britain and the United States by ISTE Ltd and John Wiley & Sons, Inc.

ISTE Ltd
27-37 St George's Road
London SW19 4EU
UK

www.iste.co.uk

John Wiley & Sons, Inc.
111 River Street
Hoboken, NJ 07030
USA

www.wiley.com

Library of Congress Control Number: 2020943265

British Library Cataloguing-in-Publication Data
A CIP record for this book is available from the British Library
ISBN 978-1-78630-633-3

Contents

Acknowledgments

This book deals with choices in situations of uncertainty, emotional reactions and values. It is derived directly from doctoral thesis work carried out between 2016 and 2018.

I would like to thank Professor Philippe Desbrières, my thesis supervisor, for giving me the chance to commit myself to this PhD, for giving me a great deal of freedom, and also for supporting, encouraging and guiding me by suggesting ideas that I have been also substantially developing or by recommending training which was always timely. Moreover, I am honored by the confidence he has shown in me during these 3 years and I am deeply grateful to him for it.

I would like to thank Mr. Marc Filser for his availability, his support in the financing of an experiment, his review of the experimental protocol, his advice and for edifying avenues for reflection and, finally, for doing me the honor of participating in my thesis jury.

I am also grateful to Professors Véronique Bessière and Armin Schwienbacher for having accepted the demanding role of referee in my thesis jury. Reading their work has fed my reflection and their comments will be sources of enrichment for my future. I hope that they will find the expression of my respectful gratitude here.

I would like to thank the members of Crego for their constructive and kind remarks during laboratory seminars. In particular, I would like to thank Mr. Gérard Charreaux for his always valuable remarks, Mr. Fabrice Hervé for his support and wise recommendations and Mr. Bertrand Belvaux for his suggestions concerning the analysis of the data. Finally, I would like to thank Mrs. Évelyne Poincelot and Miss Kirsten Burkhardt for their pertinent remarks.

I will not forget the professors of my research master's degree in management sciences, some of whom were able to bring abstract concepts or theory to life through their passionate communication.

I would like to thank the members of the CRESE research laboratory at the Université de Franche-Comté for their hospitality and the sound advice from their economists, in particular, Mr. François Cochard and Ms. Karine Brisset.

Many thanks also to the doctoral students Ms. Gaztelumendi and Ms. Bataillard for their diligent participation in pretesting experiments.

I would also like to thank the university staff who collaborated or facilitated the organization of experiments, particularly Ms. Bois-Prinet, Mr. Frédéric Pellerin, Mr. Renaud Aubert, Ms. Chloé Roger, Mr. Guy-Daniel Ligan, Ms. Esla Fachinetti, Ms. Florence Demougeot, Ms. Chittaro and Mr. Millereux.

Finally, I would like to thank my wife, who has personally contributed to the experimentation and has supported me unconditionally in this adventure, as well as my daughter, who was born only a few months before this big move and who, for many weekends, had to put up with a studious father. I dedicate this work to them as well as to my late maternal grandmother, my "mamie", without whom nothing would have been possible.

Introduction

> [...] we neither strive for, nor will, neither want, nor desire anything because we judge it to be good; on the contrary, we judge something to be good because we strive for it, will it, want it, and desire it.
>
> Baruch Spinoza, quoted in Miller (2015)

This introduction begins with a brief introductory statement on the genesis of this research, then continues with a presentation of the context, the justification and exposition of the research object, the methodological approach taken, and the expected contributions of this book before concluding with a presentation of the general plan of this book.

The starting point for this research topic is a simple premise: "behaviors and, more specifically, the choices of investors operating on equity crowdfunding (ECF) platforms were, *a priori*, necessarily marked by a strong emotional dimension." From this first approximate conjecture, the result of a spontaneous interpretation that comes from the psychology of common sense, the next step was to follow a rigorous, scientific approach. First of all, this inductively inferred conjecture required a literature review in the field of entrepreneurial finance.

Research context

ECF is a recent financing method. Therefore, of course, the scientific literature on the subject is not very developed. The first works, which are descriptive, focused on themes such as the success of fundraising campaigns or the motivations of the participants on the platforms. The historical sectors or professions of crowdfunding, donation and reward-based crowdfunding were first explored, and these results were then used as a basis for research into ECF, which is more financially-oriented. In fact, this innovative method of financing, by subscribing to the capital of a young company, involves a host of investors who are a combination of friends and family, business angels and crowdsourcing participants (Onnée and Renault 2014).

The question of the choice of projects by investors is essentially dealt with from the perspective of information theory or signal theory (Akerlof 1970; Spence 1973)[1]. Information asymmetry is particularly strong for companies at the seed stage, where potential investors seek to interpret the available information on the project to detect quality signals (Ahlers *et al.* 2015). The information available to potential investors is protean, consisting primarily of information provided by management, including the project description, a video of the entrepreneurs' pitch, the business plan and all of the fundraising campaign's posts. Secondarily are all the social interactions on the platform (Lin *et al.* 2013; Freedman and Jin 2014). This includes exchanges between investors or questions and answers between investors and managers. The kinetics of the campaign (Hornuf and Schwienbacher 2015b) and the completion rate of the fundraising target (Agrawal *et al.* 2014) are also important quality signals. All this information leads the investor, who is not competent to judge the appropriateness of investments on their own, to imitate, which is a behavior at the origin of the herd behavior which can lead, to a certain extent, to information cascades, i.e. a situation where only the decisions of other agents determine investment choices.

Social interactions can also take place outside the platform, for example, for friends and family who will *in fine* invest on the platform. In this case, literature considers that friends and family have private information that can be assimilated to a quality signal (Agrawal *et al.* 2015). It should also be noted that, although distance is another factor explaining the choice, it is strongly correlated with friends and family.

A second approach is implicit; it consists of inferring the determinants of individual choices from those of the crowd as a whole. Indeed, the choices of the crowd result, according to methodological individualism (Boudon 2004),

1 It should be noted that the concept of a signal developed by these two authors is used in several articles of our literature review in the exclusive sense of information, without there being any associated cost, as the theory suggests.

from the aggregation of individual choices. More precisely, studies of the success of campaigns reveal the choices made by the crowd. However, the main determinants of the success of fundraising campaigns are social in nature. In addition to the herd behavior already mentioned, Mollick (2013) shows that the size of an entrepreneur's social network is a key success factor. However, the social network is merely an extension of the group of friends and family to circles of indirectly connected individuals. Therefore, the explanation for this effect is likely to be twofold: the number of Facebook friends or Twitter followers can be interpreted per se as a quality signal; moreover, when the members of this social network participate in the campaign, the explanation of private information about the leaders and their chances of success, given for friends and family, is also applicable.

Finally, these different explanations for the choice of projects are all based explicitly or implicitly on signal theory, in which the decision-maker is endowed with an instrumental rationality and seeks, by capturing quality signals, to maximize its usefulness, which can be identified by the risk/return ratio for finance. This perspective, which derives from the neoclassical school's postulates of rationality that prevail within the efficiency of financial markets, reduces choice to its cognitive dimension, which excludes any emotional or affective explanation.

Nevertheless, a body of emerging research converges to admit that the choice of projects may be based on reasons other than an exclusive maximization of the expected utility, and even places emotions at the heart of the phenomenon of ECF investments.

Thus, the choice of ECF projects can be connected to the intrinsic motivations of investors. Ryu and Kim (2014) establish this link and show that if the investor is driven by a motivation such as "philanthropy", "recognition" or "relationship", then the reward, i.e. the expected return, has no effect on the choice, contrary to the expected social contribution.

Bessière and Stéphany (2017) believe that crowds act based more on their perceptions than on in-depth analysis; the decision is holistic, intuitive and affect plays an essential role, as does familiarity with risk perception, the latter being altered by the affect heuristic.

In the field of entrepreneurship, several authors examined the effects of entrepreneurial affect (Milovac *et al.* 2015), pitch (Davis *et al.* 2017) and narrative emotions (Wuillaume *et al.* 2016) on investors; their evaluation; and their choices. In addition, Allison *et al.* (2017) studied the phenomenon of persuasion that is at play between entrepreneurs and investors.

In the field of human–computer interaction, Josue and Bahm (2016) propose a method for measuring the emotional impact of pitch videos on sponsors, in line with the results uncovered in the field of marketing regarding the impact of videos on consumer attitudes (Graillot 1996).

The ECF investment framework presents several characteristics that probably make a marketing approach relevant: intrinsic and extrinsic motivations (Hemer 2011), a consumer rather than shareholder logic, linked to limited information and a lack of financial expertise (Bessière and Stéphany 2014), but, above all, a context of persuasion through storytelling, images and video pitches, which are the ingredients of the phenomenon of advertising persuasion studied in the field of consumer theory.

Moreover, beyond the management sciences, in the social sciences and humanities, more specifically, in the fields of the psychology of emotions and judgment and decision-making, the effects of emotional reactions on judgments and decisions are well-established (Zajonc 1980; Frijda 1986; Loewenstein *et al.* 2001; Slovic *et al.* 2002; Kahneman 2003). The neurosciences consolidate the theoretical edifice with the work of Bechara and Damasio (2005) on the somatic marker hypothesis, which constitutes, in a way, the linchpin.

This book falls within the field of behavioral finance, at the crossroads of finance and psychology, but is not confined to these disciplines, because knowledge cannot stop at the clear edge of a definition or disciplinary divides. Thus, an interdisciplinary theoretical framework is used, including concepts, models and theories that are reasonably transferable and capable of improving the understanding of our research object.

Purpose of the research

The purpose of this research is to understand, explain and predict the emotional dimension of project choices by ECF investors, without excluding the cognitive dimension. The particular role of a variable of congruence of the investor's values with those put forward by the project is highlighted, which explains the title of this book. This variable, which is directly related to affective reactions (Schwartz 2006), emerged in the course of the research by means of abductive inference, and was then confirmed theoretically, but also empirically, because of a substantial body of qualitative data. Therefore, from our point of view, the rationality of the investor is complex, an axiological rationality is added to his instrumental rationality, as well as an "affective rationality" that we will define.

This work is exploratory in nature: its aim is to produce an original theory that brings a different and complementary perspective to signal theory. This theory is called the "affective matching" theory; part of its roots lie in the interactionist theory of "*Fit*-IO" for which individuals are attracted to organizations whose values and norms are congruent with their personal values and norms (Chatman 1989; Kristof 1996; Chapman *et al.* 2005). The theory of "affective matching" is also in line with the theories of "cognitive consistency" (Vaidis and Halimi-Falkowicz 2007), and it requires the investor to match the project with which they have a minimum "affective distance" or, equivalently, a maximum "affective matching". The term "affective matching" replaces the term "utility" used in economic decision theory, because the model is not exclusively consequentialist, but nevertheless has similarities with the concept of utility taken from the original meaning of the precursors of decision theory, for which it was a measure of pleasure and punishment (Bentham 1789).

Methodology

Our epistemological approach is postpositivist and the chosen methodology is based on a recursive loop between abduction/deduction/induction types of inference using the body of qualitative data already mentioned (David 1999). An explanatory model is proposed; testing its hypotheses requires the organization of a controlled experiment. Its empirical validation is based on a structural equation model. Additonally, a second model that was developed as an extension of the explanatory model and qualified as an individual predictive model implements the theory of affective matching; testing its predictive quality requires developing an original similarity measure like the distance between vectors.

Expected contributions

The issue of this book is first of all theoretical: this research aims to contribute to the emerging movement of ECF research that advocates a project choice based on the affect and not exclusively on the cognitive. The proposed theory of affective matching and its implementation by an individualized model makes, on the one hand, the prediction of Mangot (2013) – for whom "behavioral finance should not, in the near future, be spared an approach aimed at personalizing behaviors" – a reality and responds, on the other hand, to the call of Pare and Rédis (2011) for the "integration of concepts, and even methods from other disciplinary fields" in order to go beyond the "hypotheses of traditional finance, which are, as has been shown, unsuitable for the new company".

The theoretical questions to which this book will try to provide some answers are as follows:

– Do values and emotional reactions determine the choice of projects in ECF?

– What are the relative influences of these two variables?

– What is the link between values and affective reactions?

– What is the history of affective reactions?

– In the absence of social interactions, does the affective dimension dominate over the cognitive dimension of choice?

– Can an explanatory and predictive model of individual choice be established *a priori* based on knowledge of investor preferences?

– Is such a model meant to be normative?

– What is the investor's rationale?

Beyond the expected theoretical output, this book aims to provide the practitioners of ECF – first and foremost, investors – with a better understanding of their choices and the judgmental biases or heuristics to which they may be unconsciously subjected. The *Autorité des marchés financiers* (AMF), the French organization whose mission is to protect retail investors, will be able to use these results to back up the warnings given to investors.

Fundraising entrepreneurs will be able to usefully draw conclusions about the factors that attract investors, as this shareholder community is sought after for reasons of cognitive input that go beyond financial input. Other applications of the affective matching model, of an industrial nature, are possible and will be discussed in the conclusion.

General structure

This work is organized into two volumes; the first sets out the choices and theoretical foundations on which the second volume (Goglin 2020), which presents our contribution, is based.

This research is organized as follows: the first part (Volume 1) first presents the context of crowdfunding and ECF and then progressively introduces and justifies the object of this research (Chapter 1). A state of the art that intersects several fields of social science research leads to a theoretical framework (Chapter 2). The second part (Volume 2) opens with the modeling and operationalization of the concepts (Chapter 1 of the second volume). The experimental test protocol is then presented (Chapter 2 of the second volume). The last chapter (Chapter 3 of the second volume) tests the hypotheses and initiates a discussion before the final conclusion.

1

Equity Crowdfunding, a New Form of Financing that Raises a Number of Questions

This chapter is divided into three sections. Section 1.1 presents the context in which this research takes place; section 1.2 presents a review of the literature that gradually leads us to the problem set out in section 1.3.

1.1. Equity crowdfunding, a new way of financing companies

In the first section, we present crowdfunding. Then, we will look at equity crowdfunding, its regulatory framework, the crowd of investors and the risks that individual equity crowdfunding investors are exposed to.

1.1.1. *Definition, emergence and state of play on crowdfunding*

1.1.1.1. *Definition*

The word crowdfunding is a neologism first evoked in 2006 by Michael Sullivan[1], a digital experimenter, in an abortive attempt to create a project incubator (fundavlog), for video blogs with a funding feature:

1 See: https://www.goodmorningcrowdfunding.com/evolution-le-crowdfunding-nest-plus-un-simple-phenomene-de-mode/.

> Many things are important factors, but *funding from the "crowd"* is the base of which all else depends on and is built on. So, *crowd-funding* is an accurate term to help me explain this core element of Fundavlog. (Michael Sullivan, August 12, 2006)

Crowdfunding is not a new concept. The public subscription mechanism has long made it possible for private individuals to finance major projects; the Eiffel Tower, for example, has benefited from it.

The innovation of crowdfunding lies in the use of the Internet and social media.

Specialized websites and platforms organize collections and act as an intermediary for the flows (of data and capital) exchanged between investment offers and requests for financing. This indirect crowdfunding concentrates the efforts of academic research, but direct crowdfunding, which is less visible, coexists. It consists of raising funds directly from the crowd, or its community, through a Website, but without the intermediation of a platform (Tomczak and Brem 2013; Poissonnier 2016).

While the definitions of crowdfunding given in literature are heterogeneous, they offer different prisms for reading this phenomenon: process, approach, capital formation strategy, fundraising method or financial mechanism (Germon and Maalaoui 2014). Without claiming to be exhaustive, Table 1.1 chronologically lists several definitions of crowdfunding.

While for Bessière and Stéphany (2017), three notions are essential to crowdfunding (open call, crowd involvement and the importance of social networks), we note that neither social networks nor even crowds are explicitly stated in some definitions. Therefore, the lowest common denominator of these definitions can be formulated as follows: crowdfunding is a source of funding using the Internet.

In addition to these broad definitions, crowdfunding can be divided into different forms or professions: crowdinvesting (for which we will present the equity crowdfunding subcategory in more detail in section 1.1.2), crowdlending, donation and reward-based crowdfunding.

Author(s)	Definition
Lambert and Schwienbacher (2010)	"An open call, mostly through the Internet, for the provision of financial resources, either in form of a donation or in exchange for the future, product or some form of reward to support initiatives for specific reasons."
Bechter *et al.* (2011)	"An approach to raising capital for a project or business by involving a large number of people for small ($1–$100) contributions."
Voorbraak (2011)	"[...] the process of one party requesting and receiving money and other resources from many individuals for financing a project, in exchange for a monetary or non-monetary return on investment."
Ramsey (2012)	"The process of raising money to help turn promising ideas into business realities by connecting investees with potential supporters."
Lynn (2012)	"A relatively new outgrowth of social media that provides funding for a variety of ventures."
Sigar (2012)	"A capital formation strategy that raises small amounts of funds from a large group of people through online means."
Lynn and Sabbagh (2012)	"A new growth of social media that provides an emerging source of funding for ventures."
Powers (2012)	"Crowdfunding is a financial mechanism that allows startup companies to solicit funds from the general public through Website intermediaries."
Wheat *et al.* (2013)	"A new internet-based method of fundraising in which individuals solicit contributions for projects on specialized crowdfunding sites."
Mollick (2013)	"Crowdfunding refers to the efforts by entrepreneurial individuals and groups – cultural, social, and for-profit – to fund their ventures by drawing on relatively small contributions from a relatively large number of individuals using the Internet, without standard financial intermediaries."
Belleflamme *et al.* (2014)	"Crowdfunding involves an open call, mostly through the Internet, for the provision of financial resources either in form of donation or in exchange for the future product or some form of reward to support initiatives for specific purposes."

Table 1.1. *Some definitions of crowdfunding (source: adapted from Germon and Maalaoui 2014)*

In this typology, the first two business lines (crowdinvesting and crowdlending) are essentially in the field of finance insofar, as these investment products generally offer potential profitability. The next two professions (giving and reward-based) are part of a philanthropic logic.

Crowdinvesting allows the provision of financial resources to a company in the form of equity or debt and concerns all issues of securities (Schwienbacher 2015). This recent concept is, therefore, broader than that of equity crowdfunding, which focuses on capital increases by subscription of ordinary shares, preference shares or equity securities (for France). In addition to these securities, crowdinvesting also includes debt securities, such as convertible or non-convertible bonds and mini bonds (for France).

To be entitled to offer participation in financing, in the form of a subscription to financial securities or mini bonds, the platform must have the status of a *conseiller en investissement participative* (CIP, Participating Investment Adviser) or *prestataire de services d'investissement* (PSI, Investment Service Provider). Let us also note the emergence and popularity of loans to real estate developers, to finance real estate programs, notably in the form of bond subscriptions (Hervé *et al.* 2016). Real estate crowdfunding, thus, falls partially into the category of crowdinvesting.

Crowdlending or peer-to-peer lending is experiencing the strongest growth (Bessière and Stéphany 2017). This type of financing is divided into three subcategories: (1) solidarity-based lending platforms, (2) interest-bearing or non-interest-bearing lending platforms for individuals, and (3) corporate lending platforms. Regulatory changes (in particular, the decrees of September 16, 2014, and October 28, 2016) have provided a legal framework that opens up development prospects for the last two subcategories by derogation from the banking monopoly. The status of *intermédiaire en financement participative* (IFP, Participating Finance Intermediary), supervised by the *autorité de contrôle prudential et de resolution* (ACPR, Prudential Control and Resolution Authority), is created for platforms wishing to organize the establishment of relationships between project sponsors and lenders, or donors.

1) Solidarity lending platforms are part of the microfinance sphere; the crowdlending platform acts as an intermediary between individuals, lenders and microfinance institutions.

2) Personal loan platforms allow the crowd to select project borrowers whose creditworthiness is assessed (with a possible credit rating), to grant them a loan without capital security for a term of 6 months–5 years, with an interest rate set according to the term and creditworthiness of the borrower.

3) Business loan platforms offer an effective response for the financing of companies (SARL, SA or SAS[2]) that are facing the demands and delays of banks. Loans are amortizable over a period of 24–60 months, with the interest rate depending on the duration of the loan and the credit risk incurred.

Donation platforms allow Internet users to financially support humanitarian, scientific or cultural projects carried out by associations and foundations. Donations can also be directed to individuals presenting their personal causes and private events between individuals (jackpot) or even to represent the digital counterpart of children's piggy banks. The Internet user does not expect any return, except in a symbolic form (thank you email, membership of an association, etc.). In the case of donations to non-profit organizations, donors benefit from a tax advantage that constitutes a motivational incentive. In France, for cultural reasons, the segment of donations to charities or charitable organizations is less developed than in English-speaking countries (Maalaoui and Conreaux 2014).

On reward-based crowdfunding platforms, the donor receives a non-financial reward that is the quid pro quo for the donation. The in-kind consideration has a value proportional to the amount of the donation and is a strong incentive to participate. For the project promoter, this method of financing is an alternative to loans or investment, and has the advantage of simplicity as it does not require any legal arrangement. When a promise of reward is made, the reward-based crowdfunding operation is a transaction that is de facto similar to a sales contract (Maalaoui and Conreaux 2014). The platforms offering this type of financing are numerous and heterogeneous (general or specialized). Cultural and artistic projects are highly represented in this segment, as are entrepreneurial projects. For the latter, the reward-based crowdfunding campaign is not only a financial contribution, but also works as a market study with consumers. Collecting feedback is valuable because it can be used to refine the positioning of the product, or its time to market (Bessière and Stéphany 2017).

---

2 SARL = *société à responsabilité limitée*, limited liability company; SA = *société anonyme*, public limited company; SAS = *société par actions simplifiée*, simplified joint stock company.

1.1.1.2. *Brief historical perspective on crowdfunding*

While the term crowdfunding was coined in 2006, the concept of crowdfunding is much older. The recourse to public subscription for the financing of major works finds a striking example with the financing of the pedestal of the Statue of Liberty, in 1884, by a public appeal for donations, or with the financing of the Eiffel Tower already mentioned. It is possible to go further back in time by considering the composers Mozart and Beethoven. These composers were already appealing to the generosity of donors to finance their concerts and publications. In France, the Telethon is a fund-raising operation among the general public, for patients suffering from muscular dystrophy; it is apparently similar to crowdfunding without any counterpart (Iizuka 2014). Another concept, called microfinance, is closely linked to crowdfunding insofar, as it can be implemented through solidarity crowdlending.

Microfinance is a way to lend money to low-income people. Examples of microfinance can be found as early as the beginning of the 18th Century, with microcredit groups and cooperatives such as "Ireland's loan funds". This fund, backed by hundreds of savers, provided loans to low-income families in rural areas. Based on this model, more than 300 programs were set up in Ireland in the early 1800s (Maalaoui and Conreaux 2014). Closer to home, Muhammad Yunus, winner of the Nobel Peace Prize in 2006, popularized microfinance through his research projects initiated in the 1970s.

The modern concept of crowdfunding has its roots in crowdsourcing, of which it is an extension (Belleflamme *et al.* 2014). Crowdsourcing is the outsourcing of a production process for a for-profit company, which consists of calling on crowds via the Internet, to contribute (ideas, feedback, solutions, etc.) to the development of the activity (Kleemann *et al.* 2008).

In the early 1990s, crowdfunding was mainly related to artistic, creative and cultural industries, as well as charitable projects. Artists who solicited their fans via websites to finance a tour, include the British rock band Marillion, which raised $60,000 in 1997, and independent filmmaker Mark Tapio Kines, who raised $125,000 that same year to complete an unfinished feature film (Maalaoui and Conreaux 2014). In 2000, the English website Justgiving provided online tools for collecting charitable donations. In the mid-2000s, the Kiva website was launched; this microcredit platform is still one of the most popular in the world today. By June 2015, the site had lent more than $727 million to microcredit institutions. The births of Indiegogo in 2008 and Kickstarter the following year, marked the advent of a new form of crowdfunding, and now the participants do not expect repayment, but receive a counterpart in the form of a reward: hence, reward-based crowdfunding was born.

The following decade saw the emergence of funding for entrepreneurial projects with platforms such as GrowVC in 2010, and Crowdcube in 2011, or Wiseed in 2008 for France. This stage marks politicians' awareness of the economic potential of this type of financing, which meets the so-called "equity[3] gap" needs of seed companies (Belleflamme *et al.* 2014). Regulatory frameworks will then adapt to this nascent industry in order to support its development, while protecting individual investors.

Looking to the future, the European Commission's report from May 3, 2016 lists the likely developments expected, which include:

– institutionalization of investors: this trend is evident in the trajectory of the last 3 years, with investor involvement at 45% in 2016, compared to 28% in 2013, for UK platforms;

– consolidation of the sector: the growth in the number of platforms in the European Union is declining, with 96 new platforms in 2014, compared to 133 in 2013;

– the internationalization of platforms is foreseeable, both through the implementation of legal provisions that favor the phenomenon (European passport), and because of the business model of crowdfunding. The latter requires economies of scale and an increase in the investor base and project pipeline;

– the development of segments refocused on niche markets, more traditional and more secure than the market of technological innovation, so real estate crowdfunding is currently in full development;

– the emergence of an organized secondary market;

– investors' awareness of the real opportunities and risks involved.

3 For Lefèvre and Popescu (2015), the equity gap, or capitalization hole, refers to companies having difficulties in obtaining financing for amounts between €500,000 (borne by the BA) and €1,000,000 (borne by the investment funds).

The foreseeable rapprochement, which is already at work between the banking sector and crowdfunding platforms in various forms (partnership, acquisition, etc.) can be added to the list.

1.1.1.3. *State of play of crowdfunding*

The growth of the crowdfunding industry around the world is strong, as shown by the figures in Table 1.2.

Indicator/year	2012	2013	2014	2015
Funds raised ($ billions)	2.7	6.1	16.2	34.4
Rate of growth		126%	166%	112%

Table 1.2. *Evolution of crowdfunding in the world (source: Massolution Crowdfunding Industry 2015 report[4])*

As Table 1.3 shows, the crowdfunding industry is not equally developed in the major regions of the world. North America, China and Europe account for 99.5% of the activity, with North America alone accounting for 50% of crowdfunding activity, and China in second place with the highest growth rate, with a tripling of funds raised over the period.

Region	Growth rate in 2015 (%)	Funds raised in 2015 (in billions of dollars)
Northern America	82	17.25
South America	50	0.08
Europe	98.6	6.48
Africa	101	0.024
Asia	210	10.54
Oceania	59	0.069

Table 1.3. *Distribution of funds raised by crowdfunding by region in 2015 (source: Massolution Crowdfunding Industry 2015 report)*

An analysis by business line reveals that crowdlending clearly dominates the other segments, accounting for three-quarters of total funds raised (see Table 1.4).

4 See: http://crowdexpert.com/crowdfunding-industry-statistics/.

Donation	2.85
Reward	2.68
Lending	25.10
Equity	2.56
Royalty	0.41
Hybrid	0.81

Table 1.4. *Breakdown by profession of funds raised by crowdfunding in the world in 2015 (in billions of dollars) (source: Massolution Crowdfunding Industry 2015 report)*

1.1.1.3.1. Crowdfunding figures for Europe

In the European Union, 4.2 billion euros were raised in 2015, compared to 1.6 billion in 2014. The contributions are mainly divided between reward-based crowdfunding (30%), equity crowdfunding (23%) and crowdlending (21%). The United Kingdom accounts for a significant proportion of the funds raised, the number of projects financed and the number of platforms (143). In this metric, France is in second place with 77 platforms and Germany is in third place with 65 platforms[5].

1.1.1.3.2. Crowdfunding figures for France

The latest 2017 crowdfunding barometer, conducted by the association Financement participatif France, in association with KPMG, shows a steady and constant increase in funds raised over the last 3 years, with a total of 1,655,603 funders in 2017 alone, compared with the total number of 3,892,044 funders, since the launch of the platforms.

Year	2015	2016	2017
Funds raised (in € million)	167	234	336
Rate of growth		40%	44%

Table 1.5. *Evolution of crowdfunding in France (source: Crowdfunding barometer in France, 2017[6])*

The evolution by business (see Table 1.6) shows a clear difference between the donation and crowdlending businesses, which saw their

5 See: https://ec.europa.eu/info/system/files/crowdfunding-report-03052016_en.pdf.

6 See: http://financeparticipative.org/wp-content/uploads/2018/01/Barometre-CrowdFunding-2017_KPMG-FPF_page-à-page.pdf.

collected funds double, and the reward-based business line, which saw a moderate increase, while the crowd-investing business line saw a decline. For the latter segment, a communicating vessel effect with crowdlending is one possible explanation. More specifically, this effect is potentially due to the emergence of real estate loans (in the form of loans rather than securities), whose attractive interest rates, low default rates and short investment maturities are likely to overshadow equity crowdfunding, which has a low positive exit rate for a much longer period of immobilization.

Funds raised by business (in million €)/year	2016	2017	Rate of growth (%)
Donation	7.2	14.7	104
Reward based	61.4	68.1	11
Crowdlending	96.6	195.4	102
Crowdinvesting	68.6	58	–15

Table 1.6. *Evolution of funds collected by business over the last 2 years (source: Crowdfunding barometer in France, 2017)*

1.1.2. *Equity crowdfunding within the crowdfunding family*

1.1.2.1. *Presentation of equity crowdfunding*

The main objective of equity crowdfunding is financing young companies by strengthening their equity capital (Poissonnier 2016). It is a kind of counterpart to Initial Public Offering (IPO) for unlisted companies.

As Hervé *et al.* (2016) note, this form of crowdfunding is truly within the scope of finance insofar, as it concerns investment decisions and not philanthropic donations or forward purchase contracts (prepurchase). Therefore, as these authors suggest, caution should be exercised before transposing the results obtained in other segments of crowdfunding, to equity crowdfunding, because the incentives and motivations are not strictly identical.

Equity crowdfunding started and developed more slowly than other crowdfunding businesses due to the regulatory constraints applied to public offerings in most countries of the world.

For the investor, this innovation is a new diversification tool. Until now, while it was possible to contribute to the startup of young unlisted companies by purchasing units of certain mutual funds (venture capital (VC) mutual funds, community investment funds, etc.), the choice of companies to be financed was left to the manager of the management company. Conversely, equity crowdfunding gave control to the individual investor through the reappropriation of his investment choices (Maalaoui and Conreaux 2014), at a time when confidence in intermediaries and stock markets was undermined by the 2008 financial crisis. Moreover, equity crowdfunding is democratic: the system is open and is aimed at everyone, regardless of their wealth (entry tickets are sometimes just a few euros). As Iizuka (2014) notes, it is no longer necessary to join an investors' club or a business angels' association (now called BA).

For the entrepreneur, equity crowdfunding responds to a very specific financing need, for amounts between €500,000 (high limit of amounts financed by BA) and €1,000,000 (low limit of amounts financed by investment funds), that the traditional players in the financing chain do not provide (Lefèvre and Popescu 2015).

As noted by Bessière and Stéphany (2017), equity crowdfunding is a credible response to this financing hole, called the valley of death (or equity gap), but not only that: this mode of financing can also address the needs of entrepreneurial projects that do not meet the high expectations of return on investment of professional investors (Hornuf and Schwienbacher 2015a).

Thus, equity crowdfunding is a new link in the historical financing chain (Poissonnier 2016), which naturally follows love money, public aid, bank loans and BA, but is before VC. This situation in the financing chain is not strict; in fact, BA financing can occur after equity crowdfunding, or be concomitantly syndicated. These financing methods are complementary and interdependent in that each success promotes the confidence of subsequent investors. Also, for Lefèvre and Popescu (2015), the success of an equity crowdfunding campaign acts as a signal to other categories of investors (BA or VC).

Equity crowdfunding has similarities with BA financing. The first common feature is that it is an intervention at the same stage of development, that of seed capital. Secondly, both BA and crowdfunding bring cognitive resources to the company. Finally, their motivations are not exclusively financial (Mason and Stark 2004; Hemer 2011).

Nevertheless, the differences between BA and equity crowdfunding investors are significant. As Poissonnier (2016) notes, BAs are often wealthy, successful former entrepreneurs or senior executives, who are actively involved in management by bringing experience, network and strategic advice for substantial entry tickets worth tens of thousands of euros. Crowdfunding equity investors do not necessarily have a sophisticated investor profile, their stakes are more modest and although they bring cognitive resources, their involvement remains limited. For the BA, the relationship with management is direct and the contractual terms are negotiated, unlike equity crowdfunding, which operates in a "take it or leave it" mode with conditions negotiated with the platform acting as intermediary (Schwienbacher 2015).

1.1.2.2. *Operation and business model of the platforms*

1.1.2.2.1. Operation

In order to be entitled to offer a financial securities underwriting service, the legislation requires platforms to register with the French Organization for the Single Register of Insurance, Banking and Financial Intermediaries (*organisme pour le registre unique des intermédiaires en assurance, banque et finance* (ORIAS)[7]), as either a participatory investment adviser (*conseiller en investissements participatifs* (CIP)), or an investment services provider (*prestataire en services d'investissement* (PSI)[8]); section 1.1.3.2 provides information on these two statuses.

There are several steps in structuring a crowdfunding equity fund raising:

– a selection committee preselects the projects according to a discretionary criteria grid; this is the screening phase. Beyond elementary points (legally constituted company, sufficient share capital for the platform's investors to take a minority stake, etc.), the committee decides on the suitability of the project with the platform's positioning. Iizuka (2014)

7 The *registre unique des intermédiaires en assurance, banque et finance* (Single Register of Insurance, Banking and Finance Intermediaries) has been responsible for the registration of participatory finance platforms since 1 October 2014.

8 See: http://www.amf-france.org/Publications/Guides/Professionnels?docId=workspace%3A%2F %2 FSpaces Store%2Fa784a82d-295c-4371-8d04-f9b51895d370.

specifies that once these prerequisites have been validated, the following points are studied:

- the seriousness and commitment of the leaders,

- the existence of a market,

- the quality of the business plan,

- the ability of the management team to popularize and communicate,

- the consistency of the fundraising objective with the financing requirements;

– the crowd of investors may be invited to vote on the quality of the projects. Only projects that have re-collected sufficient subscription intentions (reservations) are selected; this is called precollection. A blog most often allows an exchange between the crowd and the managers. Physical or virtual meetings can complete the system.

Generally speaking, the project presentation file includes a presentation of the company, an operational summary, a business plan and the curriculum vitae of the managers.

However, as Bessière and Stéphany (2017) note, the evaluation documents communicated to the public contain little information on the financial strategy, financing needs, investment plan or financial outlook. Priority is given to marketing documents presenting the product or service, its positioning, the competition in the sector, etc.

The assessment, therefore, depends more on the perception of the business outlook, than on financial data, so the approach is more consumer than financial:

– the selected projects are audited by experts in accordance with a due diligence procedure, that concludes with the drafting of a shareholder agreement, the evaluation of the company's value and the setting of the price of shares. The valuation is the result of a mix between the application of traditional methods (discounted cash flows, multiples, etc.) and negotiations with management;

– the investment phase can start according to a preestablished schedule;

– when the investment objective is reached, the holdings can be managed in two ways: a holding company or a "club". For "all-or-nothing" operations, when the threshold is not reached, the investors are reimbursed and the project is not financed. In the "club" model, each investor is a shareholder directly with the financed company, whereas for the holding model, an *ad hoc* legal entity (holding company) brings together the platform's shareholders in order to organize the capital outflow, but also to simplify the governance of the financed company;

– the platform prepares a periodic status report for shareholders.

Schwienbacher (2015) evokes more sophisticated operations with syndication schemes, BA co-investment with the crowd. Agrawal *et al.* (2016) show that, in this case, the BAs reduce information asymmetry through their expertise and reputation. They advise other investors on the best business opportunities and may receive a carry (a fraction of the profits made by the other syndication investors) in return.

1.1.2.2.2. Business model

The platforms' business model is based on volume. Lefèvre and Popescu (2015) identify the following remuneration methods:

– commission in the form of a percentage (5% on average) applied on the total sums raised and taken from the financed company. This commission alone accounts for more than half of the turnover;

– billing for services such as white label use of IT infrastructure;

– carrying charges on the capital gain earned by the investor at the time of exit;

– listing fees on the platform.

1.1.2.3. *Advantages/disadvantages of equity crowdfunding*

The following advantages and disadvantages combine the analyses of Bessière and Stéphany (2017), Schwienbacher (2015), Hendrickx (2014), Lefèvre and Popescu (2015), and Maalaoui and Conreaux (2014).

1.1.2.3.1. Benefits for entrepreneurs

The following are the benefits:

– access to a source of capital for needs that are not financed by banks (intangibles such as patents);

– the speed of the operation;

– receiving feedback from Internet users (market research and crowdsourcing);

– benefiting from the ambassadorial effect of these new shareholders;

– the success of a fundraising campaign is a signal that facilitates possible future fundraising with other investors (BA and VC);

– benefiting from media coverage.

1.1.2.3.2 Disadvantages for entrepreneurs

The following are the disadvantages:

– the cost (5–10% of the capital compared to 2% for a referral service by a BA association);

– heavy governance in the case of an investor club (monitoring and communication);

– sharing power with shareholders who have a say in strategic orientations;

– it is impossible to filter investors, who may have a different view of the company's strategy;

– possible hindrance to subsequent rounds of financing, if the capital structure is widely dispersed following equity crowdfunding;

– risk of counterfeiting as a result of disclosure of strategic information.

1.1.2.3.3. Advantages for investors

The following are the advantages for investors:

– investment opportunity in a selected company;

– involvement in a concrete project;

– participation in a community with shared interests and/or values;

– tax incentives.

1.1.2.3.4 Disadvantages for investors

The following is the advantage for investors:

– multiple risks (capital loss, illiquidity, managerial incompetence, fraud, etc.).

1.1.2.4. *Some figures for the French equity crowdfunding industry*

Based on the figures from the latest 2017 crowdfunding barometer mentioned above, and supplemented by the figures from the previous 4 years' barometers of the association Financement participatif France[9], we have reconstructed the evolution of the main equity crowdfunding indicators for France, in Table 1.7.

Indicator/year	2013	2014	2015	2016	2017
Funds raised (in € million)	10	25.4	50.1	68.2	57.5
Average number of funders per project	N/A	N/A	N/A	112	78*
Average contribution per project	N/A	4,470	4,342	6,343	7,745*
Average amount collected per project	N/A	376,733	448,460	411,341	417,780

* For these two indicators, the figures given for the year 2017 are calculated over a period that runs from the creation of the platforms.

Table 1.7. *Indicators of the equity crowdfunding industry in France between 2013 and 2017 (sources: Crowdfunding barometers of the association Financement participatif France)*

The funds collected form a curve whose initial strong growth decreases over the years; the year 2017 marks a decline.

The average contributions per project and per investor are increasing overall, to over €7,000. This increase can be explained by the growing participation of institutional investors, as mentioned by the European Commission in its report dated May 3, 2016.

The amounts collected are about €400,000, which corresponds to the lower end of the equity gap, i.e. the amount that the BAs can no longer finance on their own.

1.1.3. *The regulatory framework for equity crowdfunding*

The emergence of equity crowdfunding took place within a preexisting legal and regulatory framework that was not designed for this phenomenon, because it allows the issuance of financial securities, by bypassing traditional intermediaries. As a result, this framework was inappropriate due to

9 See: http://financeparticipative.org/barometres-crowdfunding/.

requirements that were too burdensome for new entrants (capital requirements, compliance, etc.).

Aware of the potential of equity crowdfunding to irrigate the economic fabric and fill a need in the financing chain (the equity gap), state governments have decided to legislate in order to provide an *ad hoc* legal framework that promotes and accompanies the development of this new industry, while protecting the investor.

As Schwienbacher (2015) points out, equity crowdfunding allows for the issuance of securities and calls for public savings, so this subject encompasses several regulations: that of the issue of securities, financial intermediaries and investment advisory activities.

The author also points out that the purpose of regulating the issuance of financial securities is to ensure investor protection and, by creating the conditions for confidence, to develop financial markets (La Porta *et al.* 1998). The implementation of these objectives is reflected in the reduction of informational asymmetry and the resulting risks (moral hazard, fraud, etc.) through the introduction of transparence. The latter takes the form of the requirement of standardized information documents (prospectuses), enabling investors to make informed decisions. This type of regulation exempts "qualified investors", VC professionals or BAs, who are deemed capable of acquiring and processing the necessary information; so, it should logically apply to equity crowdfunding, which uses the public savings of the crowd in all its diversity.

1.1.3.1. *The European regulatory framework*

The European Directive 2010/73/EU (Prospectus Directive) organizes a harmonized European framework, for the issuance of financial securities without a prospectus to the general public, under certain conditions called exemptions. As Schwienbacher (2015) points out, the majority of equity crowdfunding transactions take place under these exemptions.

The conditions for prospectus exemptions are non-cumulative and relate to the amount of the issue (which must not exceed €5 million), the number of non-qualified investors (of no more than 150), the nominal value of the securities (in excess of €100,000), the minimum holding required for each investor (in excess of €100,000) and the total offer, that must be less than €100,000 over a 12-month period. If one of these conditions is met, then the issuing company is exempted from having to issue an onerous prospectus to be approved by the country's financial authority (the AMF for France).

The Directive also allows Member States to raise the financial threshold for exemption, which is set at €100,000 by default with a ceiling of €5 million. This criterion significantly differentiates the legal frameworks of European countries, as shown in Table 1.8, which compares the regulations of several European countries.

Country	France	Germany	United Kingdom	Italy	Belgium
Date of the reform	2014/2016	2015	2014	2013	2014
Investor protection	Transparency requirement but no ceiling according to resources	Ceiling according to resources and heritage	Resource-based ceiling (in the absence of intervention by a certified advisor)	Transparency requirement but no means tested ceiling	Investment amount ceiling at €1,000 per bid for raising an amount of €100,000≥
Prospectus exemption threshold	€1,000,000 raised to € 2,500,000	€2,500,000	€5,000,000	€5,000,000	€300,000
Funding target	All sectors, all types of companies (including SAS)	All sectors	All sectors	Innovative startups or solidarity	All sectors

Table 1.8. *Comparison of regulations in European countries (source: adapted from Bessière and Stéphany 2017; supplemented by the 2016 report of the European Centre of Expertise for Alternative and Community Finance[10])*

It should be noted that for Belgium, the investment ceiling of €1,000 per bid does not seem likely to promote equity crowdfunding, due to a likely crowding-out effect of the BAs, as they invest much larger amounts on average (Schwienbacher 2015). Secondly, this ceiling obliges platforms to bring together a large number of investors per project, which constitutes a second brake on the development of this industry (Hendrickx 2014).

The table shows that there are significant regulatory differences in these countries, which may limit the development of transnational platforms. European institutions have taken up this issue with the ambition of

10 See: https://www.sbs.ox.ac.uk/sites/default/files/Entrepreneurship_Centre/Docs/OxEPR2/current-state-crowdfunding-europe-2016.pdf.

developing an appropriate uniform framework and a common European statute (Bessière and Stéphany 2017). In March 2018, the European Commission presented a draft regulation[11] aimed at creating a specific European passport for crowdfunding platforms wishing to raise funds in all EU countries. This passport will have to be accredited (European Crowdfunding Services Provider (ECSP)) and will allow up to €1 million to be raised over 12 months; the activity of the accredited platforms will be supervised by the European Securities and Markets Authority (ESMA).

1.1.3.2. *The French regulatory framework*

Before discussing the specific nature of the French regulatory framework, Bessière and Stéphany (2017) review the spirit and objectives of its reform. These objectives were mainly:

– to develop the Equity Crowdfunding (ECF) industry and to develop national champions who can compete internationally;

– to give credibility and legitimacy to this new method of financing by defining operating rules that ensure investor protection: providing clear and transparent information and limiting the risk taking of participants;

– directing the savings of the general public toward VSEs and SMEs, which generate employment, through short circuits, by relying on the capacity of individual investors to identify quality projects and also to support them beyond the strict capital contribution.

The device resulting from the ordinance of May 30, 2014, which came into force on October 1, 2014, has defined a first regulatory framework with a single prospectus exemption limit of 1 million euros, raised to 2.5 million euros (threshold subject to conditions) as of October 31 2016.

Equity crowdfunding platforms can opt for two statuses, Investment Service Provider (PSI) and Participating Investment Advisor (CIP), and register with the ORIAS. The PSI status is the majority status because it is less demanding and does not impose a minimum threshold for equity funds. On the other hand, this status limits the type of transactions offered to certain financial securities [12] and mini bonds, does not allow the holding of funds or

11 See: https://ec.europa.eu/info/law/better-regulation/initiatives/com-2018-113_en.

12 The Decree of October 28, 2016 extends the initial list of financial securities eligible for CIP equity financing, to the following securities: ordinary shares, preference shares, simple fixed-rate bonds, bonds convertible into shares and equity securities.

client securities, and limits the activity in France. Platforms that have opted for PSI status provide investment advisory services and must be capitalized to at least €50,000, if they do not receive funds or securities from clients; otherwise, the threshold is €125,000. This status allows the platform to operate outside France via a European passport, valid in member countries of the European Economic Area (EEA).

Equipped with CIP or PSI status, platforms must first and foremost provide an investment advisory service to investors and must act, in all circumstances, in their best interests, at all stages of the investment process: selecting offers, conducting due diligence, warning about risks, conducting suitability tests (see Box 1.1), providing the level of information needed for decision-making, etc. (see Box 1.2).

Only platforms with one of these two statuses can use an official label, whose purpose is to send a signal of confidence to investors (Lefèvre and Popescu 2015).

As a direct consequence of their loyalty and transparency towards their clients, platforms must inform investors of the risks incurred in a step-by-step approach and incorporate explicit warning messages on the risks of total or partial loss of capital and illiquidity.

Furthermore, in the absence of a prospectus, sufficient information must be provided on the preselected offers, so that the decision-maker can make an informed choice. Information on the issuer's accounts (past and forecast accounts), articles of association, specific risks and business activity must be set out in clear language and in a balanced manner between the prospects of return on investment and risks. It should be noted that it is the issuer (the startup) that is responsible for the completeness and accuracy of this information; the platform must simply check the consistency, clarity and balanced nature of these documents. Also, since the *issuer and the platform are judge and jury, it seems to us that this information package can only be presented in a favorable light.*

Box 1.1. *Investor information*

Participating investment advisory service is defined as "providing personalized recommendations to a third party, either at its request or at the request of the firm providing the advice, on one or more transactions involving financial instruments[13]". The AMF's policy states that the sending of bulk messages is the responsibility of the investment

13 Article D.321-1 of the Monetary and Financial Code.

adviser if it is accompanied by a request, recommendation, opinion, or value judgment on the advisability of carrying out a transaction involving financial instruments.

For the purpose of investor protection, platforms must provide investment advice that is consistent with the investor's profile through the suitability test.

In accordance with MiFID[14], the suitability test, carried out by means of a questionnaire, must provide information on the knowledge and investment experience of the client or prospect with regard to the type of product or service offered, the client's financial situation, capacity to incur losses, tolerance for losses and investment objectives.

As Stucki (2014) points out, the Internet channel makes this obligation difficult to implement for platforms that do not directly know their many customers and prospects. Moreover, as the author points out, the motivations of equity crowdfunding investors can be very diverse and their objectives are not always reduced to the traditional maximization of the risk/return ratio. Finally, the "affective and/or collective" dimensions may explain the "apparently lacking rationality" of investing in seed stage companies with a statistically very high risk of capital loss. *It also seems to us that the suitability test is incomplete as it stands; we will come back to this later.*

Box 1.2. *Investment advice and suitability testing*

1.1.3.3. *The US regulatory framework*

The JOBS Act of April 2012 initiates the legalization of crowdfunding in the United States with the primary objective of protecting the investor, but also to support innovation through simplified financing for startups (Bessière and Stéphany 2017). Entered into effect May 16, 2016, Title III of the Act now allows investors not accredited by the Security Exchange Commission (SEC) to invest in ECFs; startups can raise up to $1 million per rolling year.

The major difference between this law and the French regulatory framework concerns investor protection and the exposure limits imposed on investors, according to their level of resources or assets. More specifically, the Crowdfund Act (S.2190) stipulates that investors with an income or wealth in excess of $100,000 may not invest more than 10% of their annual income or wealth, up to a limit of $100,000 per fund raising. For other investors (whose annual income and assets are less than $100,000), the maximum amount invested per fund raising is 5% of their annual income or assets, up to a maximum of $2,000.

14 MiFID II Directive 2014/65/EU of May 15, 2014.

The control of these investment limits is the responsibility of the platforms, which are preliminarily registered with the SEC, and whose other obligations include educating investors in financial risk culture and reducing the risk of fraud.

Fundraising amounts may not exceed $1 million and companies must comply with stringent transparency requirements.

Another significant difference with French regulations is that the implementation of a trigger threshold mechanism is mandatory. The objective is to avoid a company from getting a partial financing that does not allow it to implement the project exposed to investors (Agrawal *et al.* 2014).

1.1.4. *The crowd of investors*

The crowd of investors is, along with platforms and entrepreneurs, the third major player in equity crowdfunding.

The crowd's first mission is to finance projects by providing capital, but its role does not stop there: it also brings knowledge. Investors are future consumers or prescribers of the products and services financed. As such, they can bring multiple cognitive resources to the entrepreneur: expert advice, experience feedback, networks and contacts, etc. This knowledge can constitute a competitive advantage, as much sought after by the entrepreneur as the financing itself (Charreaux 2002).

It is possible to first consider the crowd as an abstract entity, an aggregate of individual investors, and then look at the individual investor and more specifically, at his or her ability to judge the advisability of investing in a project.

As the crowd determines the success or failure of fundraising, it is then possible to question its ability, as an entity, to evaluate and judge projects.

The concept of crowd wisdom or collective intelligence reflects the ability to do at least as well as the average expert. In their research, Mollick and Nanda (2015) compare the choices of artistic projects (plays) supported by crowds with expert evaluations. For this category of projects, it was expected that the preferences would be very different, yet the result showed a convergence of judgments, qualitatively and quantitatively, between experts and the crowd, which reinforces the idea of crowd wisdom. However, this supposed wisdom of investors comes up against a limit: the herd bias, by mimicry.

The mimicry is explained by the attempt to deal with information asymmetry, as some investors put more trust in the judgment of other investors, who are supposed to be more of an expert, than in their own judgment. This decision-making mechanism is used by financial professionals. This phenomenon, which is well known and documented in financial markets (Mangot 2008), is also common in the VC universe. Dubocage (2006) explains that the non-competent venture capitalist uses a valuation method based on mimicry: by imitating the venture capitalist deemed competent to deal with uncertainty about the value of equity investments. Similarly, in equity crowdfunding, we can cite the work of Kim and Viswanathan (2016) that points to the influence of crowd experts on decision-making. In this study, depending on whether the expertise relates to the product (mobile applications) or to the market for the product, mimicry operates on projects at different stages of development (application at the concept stage or already operational application). Mimicry involves a diversity of individuals, some of whom have the leadership role conferred by their real or supposed expertise. We can conclude that the phenomenon of herd bias necessarily involves a heterogeneous crowd, consisting of experts followed by novices or individuals with an intermediate profile.

In order to better understand the composition of the crowd, it is possible to apprehend it from a community perspective, as Belleflamme *et al.* (2014) do. According to these authors, entrepreneurs considering equity crowdfunding must integrate the need to build a federated community through non-financial incentives, particularly via Internet social networks, into their communication strategy at a very early stage. The existence of this community is one of the key conditions for the success of equity crowdfunding campaigns. This community dimension of the crowd is also found in crowdsourcing.

As already mentioned, the latter is sometimes considered to be closely related to crowdfunding (Onnée and Renault 2014). Also, Bessière and Stéphany (2017) propose to consider equity crowdfunding investors in the light of the crowd typology proposed by Lebraty and Lobre-Lebraty (2013). Lobre-Lebraty (2013) describes a community population made up of three groups (see Table 1.9). The first is that of individuals guided by passion, sharing the same vision and desire to make the product evolve; the second is guided by interest, financial incentive being the reason for their rallying to the community; and finally, a third group presents mixed characteristics between passion and interest.

Type of community	Intrinsic motivation	Level of skills
Competent enthusiasts	Beauty of gesture, belonging to a community as an end in itself	Focused on a brand or product-related task Variable level but limited spectrum
Passionate skills	Remuneration, tax exemption	High level of skills Variable according to the proposed business model
Hybrids	Status, opportunities	Variable level

Table 1.9. *Typology of crowd communities (source: from Bessière and Stéphany 2017; adapted from Lebraty and Lobre-Lebraty 2013)*

This classification reveals investors of varying degrees of competence, and the diversity of the crowd is confirmed by this table.

For another classification of the investors making up the crowd, we can, like Onnée and Renault (2014), consider the dynamics of investor aggregation. This is done in three stages, which successively define three concentric community circles.

The first circle is the family, relatives and fans of the businessperson. The second circle consists of the relationships of the members of the first circle who are attracted by the project. The third circle is made up of unknown entities, attracted by the cumulative investment dynamics of the first two groups. The importance of the entrepreneur's social network, especially family and friends, is attested by several studies (Agrawal *et al.* 2011; Mollick 2013).

This classification has the merit of highlighting the randomness that prevails when determining the investors for a project. In fact, there is no *a priori* reason why the family, close relations or relationships of those close to the businessperson, should have any particular expertise.

Moreover, according to Andrieu and Groh (2018), this lack of expertise is one of the elements that differentiates individual investors from BA and VC, which partly explains their lesser commitment to the financed company. The authors define equity crowdfunding investors as passive – not actively involved in the development and control of the investee company – as opposed to active investors such as BA and VC.

Bessière and Stéphany (2014) take a more detailed look at the question of the expertise of equity crowdfunding investors, considering that while the latter are essentially non-experts on the financial dimension of valuation, they may be more or less competent (ranging from novices to experts) in the field of activity of the financed project.

In support of this proposal, the study by Skoglund and Stiernblad (2013) provides descriptive statistics for a sample of 390 equity crowdfunding investors from the Swedish platform FundedByMe. The results reveal that 72% of the investors have no expertise in the field of activity of the company in which they have invested and 77% have never invested in an unlisted company.

Nevertheless, *each investor, despite this lack of expertise – whether it concerns the financial evaluation dimension, or knowledge of the field of activity – makes a judgment on the overall quality of the project and decides whether or not to invest.* Little work is available to explain how individual investors make judgments about projects. Mollick and Nanda (2015) note that the crowd, which by nature has no admission criteria, is very diverse, making it difficult for non-expert investors to understand the conditions for identifying quality projects.

However, a factual element on the decision-making process can help in understanding the judgment of equity crowdfunding investors: this process is fast and necessarily not very thorough. In Skoglund and Stiernblad's study (2013), 72% of the 390 crowdfunding equity investors allocated less than 10 minutes to the analysis prior to their investment, which is comparable to the average time of 20 hours allocated to due diligence by US BAs (Dorff 2014).

This last point can be explained by Mollick and Nanda (2015) who, seeking to determine whether the crowd is wise in its investment choices, relative to the choice of experts, justify the low motivation of investors to collect information by the small amounts invested, sometimes limited to a few euros (Hornuf and Schwienbacher 2015b). For Mollick and Nanda, this low incentive may also explain the information cascade effects.

1.1.5. *The risks of equity crowdfunding for the individual investor*

As noted by Iizuka (2014), equity crowdfunding shifts the risk of corporate financing from a highly professionalized sector – the banking sector, to which VC must be added – to the average person, who is asked to mobilize part of one's savings. Moreover, equity crowdfunding is the business of crowdfunding, which admits the highest levels of risk borne by investors (Poissonnier 2016).

There are many risks associated with investing in equity crowdfunding, some of which are linked to the model of this type of financing, while other, more traditional risks are both upstream and downstream of the transaction.

As Bessière and Stéphany (2017) point out, there is a risk specific to the practice of equity crowdfunding and that of the platform's role as an intermediary. Firstly, the technical platform for the intermediation of transactions between investors and financing startups may be the target of cyberattacks or more traditional technical failures (computer bugs). Secondly, the company operating the platform may fail and be subject to compulsory liquidation. The probability of default is all the greater since, as Lefèvre and Popescu (2015) indicate, the business models of platforms struggle to prove their validity, as few platforms are in financial equilibrium.

Beyond the risks related to the platform and the company managing it, a distinction must be made between the economic risk, inherent in any financing operation for a company in the seed phase, and the more traditional risks, some of which are amplified by the operation of equity crowdfunding: the risks of valuation, liquidity and lack of control.

Economic risk can have several origins. The incompetence of inexperienced entrepreneurs is one cause. This could be favored by a lax selection (screening) by platforms whose business model is based on volumes. The "lame ducks" having been refused a bank loan, could then pass the filter of platform selection (Lefèvre and Popescu 2015). However, this assumption seems to be contradicted by the drastic selection rate (around

3%) practiced by equity crowdfunding platforms (Poissonnier 2016). The risk of fraud, another determinant of economic risk, is favored by the low amounts at stake, which induces a less intense due diligence process than in OTC VC (Agrawal *et al.* 2014). However, these same authors point out that the large number of potential investors reviewing the business plan increases the probability of detecting fraud, along the lines of the crowd control of community content sites such as Wikipedia. Furthermore, these authors point out that entrepreneurs may not be part of a long-term logic aimed at building trust and reputation. This lack of incentive for a long-term orientation can encourage fraud and one-shot deals. But without even considering the honesty and competence of entrepreneurs, equity crowdfunding is mainly aimed at companies in the seed phase (seed capital), which is the earliest stage in a company's development cycle (Schwienbacher 2015) and consists of making an idea viable. However, as Cumming (2007) points out, this stage is the riskiest because it has the highest probability of failure and default, in other words, of total capital loss.

Valuation risk, taken in its broadest sense, is upstream of the transaction; it concerns the selection, evaluation of the company's development potential and expected profitability, determining the value of the company from which the share price is derived. The valuation is based on the analysis of available information, which is carried out by two players: the platform and the individual investor. First of all, the platform has a legal obligation to advise investors[15]. It makes a selection according to its predetermined criteria in the absence of precise criteria indicated by the texts. It then mobilizes internal or external resources (independent consultant, chartered accountant, etc.) to carry out due diligence and set a share price. Finally, investors choose the project in which they wish to invest. The valuation risk results, in part, from the asymmetry of information, which is particularly strong at this stage of the company's development. Desbrières (2001) points to the importance of informational asymmetry in VC, in relation to the financing of listed companies by financial markets. The consequences of this asymmetry are the risk of adverse selection and moral hazard. Counterselection risk describes a situation in which the agent holding the information does not fully disclose

15 For France, whether the platform is a CIP or a PSI, it has an obligation to provide advice that takes the form of a suitability test between the investor's profile and the financial security (this test covers the level of knowledge, experience, financial situation, financing objectives and the investor's risk appetite).

it. For example, the entrepreneur may embellish and present favorably accounting projections with figures that he or she knows are exaggerated. For Agrawal *et al.* (2014), the inability to properly evaluate projects on information by default could deter the managers of high-quality startups from using equity crowdfunding, effectively leading to the risk of adverse selection, following the same mechanism described by Akerlof (1970), for the used car market. With regards to moral risk, this is the case of an agent who, working in his own interest, does not fulfill certain contractual obligations, taking advantage of their unobservable nature. While crowdfunding equity platforms must logically have sufficient resources and expertise to reduce valuation risk, the same cannot be said for the individual investor, as mentioned above. Aware of this fact, the platforms produce consumer information rather than financial information for investors (Bessière and Stéphany 2014). *The information analyzed by the individual investor is therefore oriented and truncated, or at least simplified.* It should also be noted that given the stage of development of companies in financing (Hornuf and Schwienbacher (2015b) report a median age of 1 year for 181 observations in their study), *accounting history is practically non-existent.*

Liquidity and control risks concern downstream, posttransaction risks.

Liquidity risk, i.e. the inability to sell an asset at its price, is primarily due to the absence of a secondary market. Also, the impossibility of unwinding the transaction over a period of several years exposes the investor, who becomes a shareholder, to the risk of partial or total capital loss. Moreover, this constraint is all the more penalizing for this type of investment, since seed companies are rarely in a position to pay dividends, which would mechanically reduce their self-financing capacity. As a result, the return on an equity crowdfunding investment is usually zero until an eventual exit (Stucki 2014).

The risk of lack of control corresponds to the weakness of the disciplinary governance mechanisms available to the equity crowdfunding investor. For example, the various levers for triggering liquidity or, more broadly, for disciplining the management team are most often lacking. These may be financial instruments (bonds convertible into shares and preference shares) or clauses included in the shareholder agreement, and traditionally negotiated by the BA or the venture capitalist: automatic exit clause, promise to purchase, sequential financing, etc. It should be noted, however, that for

France, as of October 31, 2016, the type of transactions proposed are extended to bonds convertible into shares and preference shares[16], which represent an advance for the investor.

Finally, as Bessière and Stéphany (2015) point out, few holding companies are represented on boards of directors, whose role is to control the management team, so the investor does not have a hands-on role.

1.1.6. *In conclusion*

The purpose of section 1.1 was to provide the context for this research. Starting from the general to the specific, we successively presented crowdfunding, equity crowdfunding and its regulatory framework, the crowd of investors and the risks to which they are exposed in this segment.

In addition to the growing success of the emerging crowdfunding industry and specifically, equity crowdfunding around the world, we would like to highlight three points:

– individual investors in equity crowdfunding are not sophisticated investors, they do not have the expertise to judge the opportunity to invest in a project;

– the financial information available for the evaluation of each project is necessarily a summary because of the stage of development of the company: seed;

– the information available for project evaluation is potentially biased and skewed because it is provided by the managers of the company applying for funding and is controlled by the platform. However, both are interested in the success of the operation.

1.2. A success that raises questions about the rationality of investors

Section 1.2.1 sets out to explain the surprising success of equity crowdfunding by two reasons that are abundantly documented in the equity crowdfunding literature (investor motivations and the social dimension of

16 Joint AMF and ACPR information note "S'informer sur le nouveau cadre applicable au financement participatif (*crowdfunding*)", published on September 30, 2014 – updated on August 26, 2016 and May 9, 2017.

equity crowdfunding), while section 1.2.2 justifies the emphasis on a third reason, that has so far been little explored: emotional reactions.

1.2.1. *Elements of explanation for a surprising success*

1.2.1.1. *Surprising success*

As we saw in section 1.1 of this chapter, the figures for crowdfunding and more specifically, equity crowdfunding, reflect the success of this emerging industry. An increasing number of individual investors are taking the risk of subscribing to the capital of young companies.

As we have observed, individual investors in equity crowdfunding are not sophisticated investors. While they may have expertise in the field of activity of the company seeking financing, they do not have the knowledge and experience necessary for in-depth due diligence or financial evaluation.

In addition, the risks to which the equity crowdfunding investor is exposed are multifold and are increased by the early stage of the projects financed. In particular, the lack of accounting and financial information, which is logically limited, reduces the scope of financial analysis and makes evaluation more complex. In addition, while information is scarce, it is also asymmetrical. In this regard, Agrawal *et al.* (2014) point to the surprising nature of investors who are potentially geographically distant from the financed company and who operate via the Internet, whereas in the VC sphere, geographical proximity is necessary to establish personal and due diligence relationships that can reduce uncertainty and information asymmetry.

The investor's analysis, prior to his choice of investment, is based on the information available, which is provided by the platform. The platform has a legal obligation to inform investors and must provide them with sufficient information to enable them to make an informed assessment of the investment opportunity. At the same time, this information is provided by the managers of the company applying for financing, before it is controlled by the platform and thus, it runs the risk of being biased, as both players are interested in the success of the fund-raising operation.

Focusing on the profitability of equity crowdfunding investments, Dorff (2014), who is very critical of this new financing method, believes that in the absence of data on the profitability of equity crowdfunding investments, the best way to approximate these results is to proceed by analogy with BA activity. In contrast to crowdfunding investors, BAs are sophisticated investors. Nevertheless, despite their extensive experience in the field of activity of the companies financed, the time spent on due diligence (20 hours on average) and their ability to advise management, only 10% (approximately) of the companies financed generate significant returns. The two studies (one conducted in the United States and the other in the United Kingdom) on which the author bases his analysis report similar results: slightly more than half of the companies financed (52% and 56%, respectively) generated a financial loss, or even a total loss, of invested capital. The BAs reduce this economic risk through diversified management; they are also able to negotiate clauses limiting the dilution effect of subsequent rounds of financing. The *ex post* results of Signori and Vismara (2016) on returns on equity crowdfunding investments support Dorff's warnings: the distribution of returns for the financed firms in their sample is highly skewed, the average of the returns is above the median, the probability of high gains is low and the probability of losing all the invested capital is 10% in a relatively short period of time[17].

Finally, equity crowdfunding investors have neither the knowledge nor the experience to discriminate between business opportunities on crowdfunding platforms. Even if they had these assets, as is the case with BA, the information available on crowdfunding equity platforms to judge and evaluate projects is limited and presents a risk of bias. At the same time, the risks associated with investments in young companies are multifold and particularly high. Also, the growing success of equity crowdfunding and the increasing number of individual investors is surprising. It raises questions about the motivations of the crowd (or *why* savers choose to invest) and about the means mobilized by the individual investor to make his choices (or *how* savers cope with uncertainty without being sophisticated investors).

1.2.1.2. *Psychological explanations: the motivations of equity crowdfunding investors*

Due to the chronology of the emergence of platforms, the study of crowd motivations first concerned non-financial crowdfunding platforms, and mainly donation and reward-based platforms. Let us first note with Mollick (2013) that the goals and motivations of crowdfunders are very

17 The study covers 212 projects financed by equity crowdfunding between 2011 and 2015 on the Crowdcube platform. Twenty-two projects in this sample went bankrupt in March 2016.

heterogeneous; they can support a serious and important cause as well as an extravagant project. This diversity is verified in the exploratory work of Lin *et al.* (2014), who, on the basis of 2,000 projects supported by 180,000 crowdfunders on the Kickstarter platform, identify a typology of sponsors revealing four groups: the "active backers", the "trend followers", the "altruistic" and the "crowd".

Note that motivations are frequently classified according to the typology of the self-determination theory of Deci and Ryan (1985), in which a distinction is made between intrinsic motivations, for which behavior is driven by interest and pleasure in the task itself, and extrinsic motivations, for which behavior is motivated by an outcome outside of the task.

Schwienbacher and Larralde (2010) note that a large number of projects do not offer rewards but rely on donations, indicating that non-financial motivations are involved.

Among these, two intrinsic motivations – philanthropy and community – are mentioned in all studies and research.

We have already mentioned the community dimension of crowdsourcing (Lebraty and Lobre-Lebraty 2013). Bessière and Stéphany (2017) believe that this notion plays a role in all aspects of crowdfunding, whether they are philanthropic, commercial or financial in nature, as is the case with equity crowdfunding.

Agrawal *et al.* (2014) also describe crowdfunding investment as an intrinsically social activity whereby the crowdfunder wishes to communicate directly with the entrepreneur, to be part of the entrepreneurial adventure and to be part of a community of early adopters. More surprisingly for the authors, a philanthropic motivation plays a significant and observable role on platforms such as Indiegogo and Kickstarter. Altruistic crowdfunders sometimes support commercial projects without expecting a reward and without participating in the community activities of the platforms.

A study conducted in 2013 by the marketing research platform AdoctA, reveals that the two main motivations of crowdfunders are as follows: "helping a project" (philanthropic dimension) and "participating in a project" (community dimension) with a cumulative 39% of responses, far ahead of return on investment (12%) and tax exemption (9%). The willingness to help a project and its entrepreneur can be found in another statistic: 74% of crowdfunders want "aggressive promotion" of the project against only 3% who do not envisage an active role.

In their research, based on 83 interviews on three American reward-based platforms, Gerber and Hui (2013) also mention philanthropy as a motivation, the desire to help entrepreneurs in whom they have confidence and whose objectives are close to their own, or to projects related to a cause that is important to them. Community motivation also appears in this study. Through their contribution, crowdfunders wish to join a community of like-minded individuals. Another example is the work of Ryu and Kim (2014) who tested the effects of philanthropy and social relations (community) on investor behavior. Philanthropy has a negative effect on timing, i.e. pushing to invest at the beginning of the fundraising campaign, while social relations have a positive effect on the amount invested, i.e. lead to a larger amount being invested. Finally, let us mention the research of Lin *et al.* (2014), who also introduce the motivations of altruism (philanthropy) and social benefits (community).

In addition to these two intrinsic, people-oriented motivations, there are the extrinsic motivations of reward and reputation, which are also important in determining crowdfunder participation. For Ryu and Kim (2014), reward is the main determinant because its effects on the amount and timing of investment are the most significant effects in their econometric model. However, they believe that this alone cannot explain the behavior. Recognition is a motivation linked to image; it is the desire to be recognized by others and is very close to the extrinsic motivation of reputation. In their model, recognition has a positive effect on the amount invested. Note that the exploratory research on crowdfunder profiles by Lin *et al.* (2014) also integrates these two motivations.

Other motivations are mentioned in the literature. Gerber and Hui (2013) evoke an intrinsic motivation that derives from the perception of control and choice that sponsors have to freely select projects on the platforms. In the theory of self-determination, autonomy corresponds to one of the three basic needs of individuals, self-determined behaviors are motivated by an expression of the self; they are directly linked to interest in the activity or to the values of the individual (Fenouillet 2016). This motivation is interesting because it brings the behaviors of the crowdfunder and the consumer closer together.

Agrawal *et al.* (2014) state a specific motivation for the donation-reward form of crowdfunding: the possibility of being among the early adopters of new products through prepurchasing. They also evoke a motivation to formalize contracts that are usually informal for family and friends, who are the first supporters of entrepreneurs.

It should be remembered that the motivations listed above have been identified mainly on donation and reward-based platforms. Therefore, as Hornuf and Schwienbacher (2015b) note, caution should be exercised before transposing these results to equity crowdfunding.

The first motivation specific to equity crowdfunding is simply the possibility offered to the crowd to access a new form of investment (Agrawal *et al.* 2014) traditionally reserved for professionals, qualified investors or wealthy people. Equity crowdfunding democratizes access to startup capital for everyone.

Secondly, the question of the primacy of an intrinsic or extrinsic motivation is not settled.

According to Hemer (2011), crowdfunding equity investors most often engage in crowdfunding without careful examination or audit; their motivations are mixed but are first of all driven by intrinsic motivations such as:

– identification of project goals to personal projects;

– contribution to an important social cause;

– the satisfaction of being part of a community with shared priorities;

– the satisfaction of being able to track the achievements and success of a project that has been funded;

– the joy of interacting with the entrepreneurial team;

– the joy of contributing to the emergence of innovations;

– the chance to expand their personal network;

– hoping to attract investors for their own project.

It should be noted that these motivations can all (with the exception of the first) be divided into the two main drivers of donation and reward-based crowdfunding: philanthropy and community. In line with Hemer (2011), Collins and Pierrakis (2012) consider that the motivations of the ECF investor combine social (notably being part of the entrepreneurial adventure) and financial motivations.

In contrast to Hemer (2011), Cholakova and Clarysse (2015) conclude their experimental quantitative study of 155 genuine investors, registered on the Dutch Symbid platform, by the almost exclusive superiority (except for the necessary trust in management) of the extrinsic motivation of "reward", over other intrinsic motivations (altruism, community, etc.). The limitations section reveals, however, that in the design of the experiment, the choice was made for a collection campaign for a product, rather than for a project with a social, creative or community dimension. Further, the measurement scale created specifically for the study does not include potentially important motivations, such as the simple pleasure of the activity itself.

In addition, while it has been established that familiarity with the founders is a reason to help them financially, none of the participants in the experiment knew the entrepreneurs of the proposed project.

Having seen the reasons why savers invest, let us now look at how they deal with uncertainty, without being sophisticated investors.

1.2.1.3. *Sociological explanations: the social dimension of successful fundraising campaigns*

The social component of individual behavior and, more specifically, of financial decisions is proven in the field of finance (Mangot 2008). In particular, social interactions and the herd effect are documented by crowdfunding research. The common thread between these two phenomena is that they reduce the asymmetry of information in a principal–agent relationship, which limits the risks of moral hazard and adverse selection. Decision-makers rely on the information of the other actors and not only on their own information. The theoretical framework is that of signal theory (Akerlof 1970; Spence 1973) or information theory (Tirole 2017).

In his work, Mollick (2013) highlights the importance of social network size for the success of crowdfunding campaigns, for donation and reward-based projects.

It shows that founders with 10 friends on the social network Facebook have a 9% chance of succeeding in fundraising, compared with 20% if they have 100 friends and 40% if they have 1000 friends.

Wechsler (2013) describes similar results, noting that the success of fundraising campaigns is dependent on number of Facebook friends and Twitter followers, the latter being a powerful information multiplier for breaking out of the circle of friends and family and reaching strangers.

Thus, the social network plays the role of friends and family, priming the financing pump and serving as a quality signal for investors who are not within the entrepreneur's inner circles (Agrawal *et al.* 2011).

Informal social interactions are studied by Freedman and Jin (2014). These authors show that on Prosper, a personal lending platform, this type of social interaction increases the probability of obtaining financing. Lin *et al.* (2013) add that this effect is moderated by the characteristics of the borrower's friends, since these add information on signal quality and trust in the borrower.

While crowdfunding savers invest more when they have social interactions with other investors, Hervé *et al.* (2016) show that for women[18], the density of social interactions of all kinds has an influence on their investment choices. The authors suggest that this effect, reported on Wiseed.com, an equity crowdfunding platform, could be explained by a reduction in uncertainty because of the information and ideas collected during conversations, with women listening to the opinions of others more than men to form their judgment.

The herd effect, well known in the financial markets, is explained by the mimicry of investors. Mimicry consists of following the behavior of others and reflects the importance given to the information they hold, considered superior to private information. Ultimately, this effect leads to informational cascades. These occur when investors no longer take into account their own

18 It should be noted that women are underrepresented in the population of equity crowdfunding investors and their proportion is only 7% on the Wiseed.com platform.

information but base their decisions exclusively on that of others. In this case, financial market prices are no longer representative of the fundamental value of securities but are an extension of the investors' judgment at the origin of the cascade (Mangot 2008). Note that mimicry is also documented in VC, Dubocage (2006) argues that VCs who do not have sufficient skills to judge the quality of a company base their judgment on that of more competent VCs.

In the case of crowdfunding, Agrawal *et al.* (2014) note that the propensity for investing is proportional to the capital already accumulated by the project. On the Sellaband music project funding platform, they find that the probability of supporting a project that had reached 80% of its target was twice as high as that of a project that had reached only 20%. In reward-based crowdfunding, Kuppuswamy and Bayus (2015) study the dynamics of fundraising campaigns and the key role of social interactions in the investment decision. They identify a U-shape for the amount collected during a campaign. If the strong initial activity of investors is explained by the intervention of the inner circles of entrepreneurs (their family, friends, and circles further away from their social network), the increase in activity observable at the end of the campaign would be due to two effects:

1) when the funding target is close, this means that a significant number of sponsors have confidence in the project, which in itself is a quality signal capable of triggering investment decisions through the herd effect;

2) family and loved ones are remobilizing in the final weeks to help bring the campaign to a successful close.

This move up in the U is echoed in Wash's 2013 study of crowdfunding as a gift, in which the author describes a completion bias when the project is close to its goal. This bias is characterized by donations that are twice as large and a very high probability of success compared to projects that are further from their fundraising goal, at the same stage of the campaign.

In equity crowdfunding, Hornuf and Schwienbacher (2015b) also identify a U-shape for the dynamics of investment activity in campaigns whose securities are allocated according to a second price auction mechanism; and an L-shape for campaigns whose mechanism is "first come, first served". They show that investors base their decisions on the information provided by entrepreneurs and campaign communications, as well as on the decisions and comments of other investors, i.e. by imitating them.

Mimicry is all the more rational as the imitated actor is credible. Kim and Viswanathan (2016) show that the choice of crowd experts has a strong influence on the decisions of other unsophisticated investors, in a study of the Appbackr platform for prepurchasing mobile applications. Thus, investors rely on the quality of the signal sent by the first investors when they are identified as experts.

These experts in the crowd are described as spontaneous by Bessière and Stéphany (2017) because they are not officially recognized by the platforms; they correspond to the "active backers" of the typology of Lin *et al.* (2014). They can also be clearly identified, for example, in the case of platforms organizing syndications.

Agrawal *et al.* (2016) are specifically interested in the AngelList platform that offers this possibility. Syndication requires a lead angel who, with their expertise and reputation, can advise other investors on the best business opportunities. In return, this lead investor receives a fee: the "carry". The role of the lead angel is to reduce the asymmetry of information for non-sophisticated investors who rely on the expertise to establish their judgment.

1.2.1.4. *The two levels of choice of these explanations*

We have just outlined the reasons for the successful development of equity crowdfunding. These motives help to understand the paradox of unsophisticated investors investing in an extremely risky asset on the basis of limited or even biased information. These reasons are linked, on the one hand, to motivations (a motive that borrows from cognitive psychology and answers the question of why) and, on the other hand, to information theory (a motive that borrows from social psychology and answers the question of how). Indeed, this apparent paradox can be explained by the combination of these two reasons, because when the motivations are intrinsic, then the financial dimension is secondary (Lin *et al.* 2014), which favors risk-taking; when they are mixed or only extrinsic, then social interactions and mimicry reassure the investor.

Let us now consider these two reasons in turn.

Social interactions and mimicry are unambiguous about their purpose; they reduce information asymmetry, allowing the investor to choose between several projects competing on one or more platforms. They are therefore linked to the *choice of projects* and answer the question of *how* savers choose their investment projects.

Motivations have a more ambiguous purpose in that they can both explain the crowdfunder's choice of project, as well as why the investor chose to invest in equity crowdfunding rather than in any other asset: government bonds, listed shares, derivatives, etc. Moreover, in the research previously mentioned, the question related to motivations is what a person's motivations are for participating in a crowdfunding campaign, as the following two quotes demonstrate:

1) in the study by Gerber and Hui (2013), the question asked is:

"What motivates and deters creators and supporters from participating in crowdfunding?"

2) for the AdoctA study, the question asked is:

"What were or would be the essential motivations for investing in 'Crowdfunding' for you?"

However, the question, "What are your motivations for participating in a crowdfunding campaign?", can be rephrased as: "What are your motivations for choosing to participate in a crowdfunding campaign?", it being understood that this choice could just as easily be made for other asset classes: equities, bonds, derivatives, etc.

Thus, if social interactions and mimicry relate to project choice, *the motivations* may relate both to the *choice of project* (equity crowdfunding investment) and *to the prior choice of asset class* (equity crowdfunding or other asset class). The motivations expressed answer the question of *why* investors invest in equity crowdfunding, but also *why* investors choose this or that project on an equity crowdfunding platform.

For this reason, we feel it is important to specify what level of choice is being considered:

– a choice that we will refer to as the "first order", which distinguishes between different asset classes (equity crowdfunding, equities, bonds, future contracts, etc.);

– a choice of the "second order", which distinguishes between projects, once the equity crowdfunding category has been chosen beforehand (the first-order choice).

As far as motivations are concerned, these two levels of choice are closely linked, since the motivations that led to the first-order choice are, logically, still active at the time of the second-order choice. An investor guided exclusively by the lure of gain, having chosen to invest in equity crowdfunding (the first-order choice) in the hope of betting on the next Google, will probably choose the project that seems most promising in terms of expected return (the second-order choice). In this case, the same motivation (here, the lure of gain) applies to both levels of choice. Conversely, the same investor, initially guided on an equity crowdfunding platform by financial motivation, may ultimately choose a project that interests him/her particularly among those that he/she considers potentially profitable. In this second case, the motivations of the first- and second-order choices are different and combined.

In their search for a general conceptual model for crowdfunding, Ryu and Kim (2014) link motivations and project choices by cross-referencing possible motivation types with project characteristics (Table 1.10). In other words, Ryu and Kim associate motivations and second-order choices, even though the motivations they have identified in the literature relate to a first-order choice; the distinction between the two levels is not made, which amounts to positing that the motivations are identical for the two levels of choice. We will come back to this point when discussing the issue later in the book.

Table 1.10 is read by column; for example, investors motivated by "interest in the project" are attracted to projects with the following characteristics: novelty, social contribution, rewards and sponsor commitment.

Characteristics/ motivation	Interest in the project	Game	Philanthropy	Award	Acknowledgement	Relation
Novelty	++	++		+		
Social contribution	+	++	++		++	+
Reliability						
Dynamism of the creator						–
Feasibility						
Awards	++	+		++		
Interactivity of the creator			+			++
Commitment of sponsors	+	++	+		++	++

Table 1.10. *Matrix of correspondence between investor motivations and project characteristics (source: Bessière and Stéphany (2017), based on Ryu and Kim (2014))*

1.2.2. *An emotional dimension not very present in the explanations of the investor's choice*

In section 1.2.1.4, we presented two reasons to better understand the apparent paradox of successful equity crowdfunding: unsophisticated savers choosing to invest in high-risk assets on the basis of limited and potentially biased information. We will now focus our attention on the choice of projects by an investor who has previously decided to invest in equity crowdfunding, which is tantamount to focusing on a second-order choice. We have seen that the investor may be guided by motivations, particularly those that led to the first-order choice and that are still active, as well as by the phenomena of social interaction and mimicry. In this section, we look at the treatment of the choice of equity crowdfunding projects in the literature on entrepreneurial finance; we then highlight a specific characteristic of this mode of investment (a context of persuasive advertising) before explaining the consequence (the need to take more account of the emotional dimension of the choice of equity crowdfunding projects).

1.2.2.1. *How choice is handled in the literature on equity crowdfunding in entrepreneurial finance*

In the literature on equity crowdfunding, it is possible to identify two distinct forms of treatment in the selection of equity crowdfunding projects. The first is explicit, as the authors explain the workings of the investor choice mechanism, the second is implicit, as it is based on the study of the success of equity crowdfunding campaigns.

Explicit studies on investor choice are part of signal theory, as we have already seen with research into the social dimension for the success of fundraising campaigns (for example, Kim and Viswanathan (2016) fit into this theoretical framework from the outset), and this manner of reading is once again used when researchers explore the mechanisms of individual investor choice, other than mimicry. The information that can reduce information asymmetry is then *the* determinant of choice.

Before the first empirical results are available, Agrawal *et al.* (2014) consider *a priori* that, in order to develop, the nascent equity crowdfunding industry should create the conditions of confidence by providing investors with quality signals on projects. By relying on the mechanisms of the platforms that are the precursors to crowdfunding (donation and reward-based), they believe that their transposition to equity crowdfunding would reduce the risks associated with asymmetric information. According to the authors, entrepreneurs must gain the confidence of investors through an ethos based on reputation (possibly that of the brand), as well as on disclosed quality signals. On this point, the literature on financing seed stage startups indicates that the most relevant information to reduce information asymmetry is guarantees, patents, previous entrepreneurial achievements of the managers and level of education (MBA, PhD, etc.).

Lin *et al.* (2014) are interested in the crowd heterogeneity reported by Mollick (2013), as it is said to be the source of inconsistent results on the objectives and motivations of crowdfunders. For this reason, they establish a typology of investors using a hierarchical, bottom-up statistical classification method. In a second step, they study the link between the four identified archetypes and financing choices. To do so, they develop two sets of hypotheses, based on the two theories put forward by previous research, to understand this phenomenon: signal theory and the herd effect. Their aim is to reconcile these two theoretical frameworks insofar as mimicry – at the origin of the herd effect – is based on the choice of other investors, which, in itself, is a signal on the quality of projects.

Ahlers *et al.* (2015) conduct one of the first empirical studies related to investor choice. They find that equity crowdfunding is primarily aimed at individual investors who lack the sophistication and experience of BA and VCs and, more often than not, lack the capacity, availability, cognitive and financial means, or sufficient incentive, to extensively evaluate competing startups. They therefore consider this clear difference between sophisticated and non-sophisticated investors to be the result of new research.

Having clearly noted this difference, they nevertheless invoke the traditional framework of signal theory, rightly justifying this choice by the problem of asymmetry encountered by individual investors, a problem similar to that encountered by BA and VC. Consequently, they rely on the results of previous research in the field of VC to develop their hypotheses, i.e. to identify the information likely to guide the choice of investors (characteristics of the board of directors and the management team, presence of VCs or BAs in the capital, involvement of the founders, etc.). Based on a sample of 104 projects, their results highlight the weight of the financial roadmap (IPO or planned buyout exit strategy), risk factors (amount of securities offered and financial forecasts) and management experience (number of managers and level of education).

Their conclusion aligns with that of Agrawal *et al.* (2014) that entrepreneurs need to signal the quality of their projects in order to attract individual investors, and to succeed in their equity crowdfunding campaigns.

Finally, for Hornuf and Schwienbacher (2016), investors base their decisions on the updates from investors throughout the campaign, as well as comments, from the crowd. Although this assumption is more general, since it is based on a dynamic approach (and a social psychology approach), it is again information that is the key to understanding decision-making.

Note that the signal theory approach to choice, which dominates financial literature, is a cognitive approach in which the investor seeks to rationally identify the startup sending the best quality signals, i.e. the one offering the best return prospects. This approach falls within the framework of instrumental rationality (or consequentialism), as well as utilitarianism.

The second form of choice treatment is implicit and is based on the study of the success of fundraising campaigns. Indeed, establishing that the campaign of startup S is successful because of factor F is tantamount to saying that investors chose S because of F. It is therefore a choice but at the aggregate level: that of the crowd. The choice of the crowd can be explained by the postulate of methodological individualism, which posits that social phenomena result from the combination (simple aggregation as far as we are concerned) of the actions of individuals (Boudon 2004). Thus, if the campaign of startup S is successful, it is because the number of investors sensitive to the effect of factor F is sufficient to achieve the desired objective. However, if research generalizes this result and states that the hypothesis, "F is a success factor for campaigns", is empirically validated, this tells us that F is a factor of choice at the individual level as well. Indeed, *reductio ad absurdum*, if F was not an individual choice factor, then it would not be at the aggregate level either.

So far, we have focused on the main determinant, widely used in crowdfunding literature, to explain the success of fundraising campaigns: social interactions and mimicry at the origin of the herd effect.

However, other factors are identified in the literature on crowdfunding:

– *the presence of pitch videos* on the campaign page and the *frequency of updates*: Mollick (2013) considers these two factors to be a good signal;

– *geographical location*: a difference in behavior between local and remote investors (a preference for local investment) is highlighted by Agrawal *et al.* (2015). However, the authors explain that for local investors, friends and family are over-represented, which means local distance is a proxy for social capital. Moreover, for Agrawal *et al.*, the difference in behavior observed between the local and the remote comes from the information gap, the locals, essentially, being relatives with privileged information on the seriousness of the entrepreneurs and the quality of their project;

– *cultural differences*: Burtch *et al.* (2014) show that, in microfinance, these are more important than geographical differences (although both have a significant effect) on the decision to lend to an individual borrower. The authors conclude on the likely role of cultural difference in the trust placed in the borrower.

Once again, we see that the implicit reasons (for the success of fundraising campaigns) for the choice are systematically apprehended through the prism of information asymmetry.

1.2.2.2. *A choice made in the context of persuasive advertising*

Before presenting advertising persuasion, it is worth mentioning the weight of images in decision-making. In this regard, Slovic *et al.* (2002) state that many studies have demonstrated a strong relationship between images, affects and decision-making. They add that stories and narrative processes are particularly effective in generating images charged with affects.

Equity crowdfunding campaign pages use video and photo materials and storytelling, a narrative process that involves telling stories.

The marketing field is interested in the influence of videos on consumer behavior. For example, let us mention the work of Graillot (1996), who studied the effects of images of vacation spots on consumers' emotional states and, ultimately, on their choice of destination. Graillot shows that when holiday locations are evoked by rich media, like videos, this increases the probability of choosing the destinations viewed by mediating favorable emotional states.

A marketing theory allows us to understand the effects of images and videos when they have a persuasive aim, as is the case with advertising: persuasive advertising. In short, this theory looks at the consequences of advertising screens on consumer attitudes toward the brand and the advertisement, both of which are determined by the emotional reactions triggered by the advert (Derbaix and Filser 2011).

Obviously, equity crowdfunding borrows the codes of advertising, a campaign page systematically includes a description, a possible storyboard and a video of the entrepreneur's pitch. As mentioned, Mollick (2013) identified campaign page videos as a determinant of fundraising success. He formulated this hypothesis by drawing inspiration from the recommendations of the Kickstarter platform, which strongly urges project owners to create a video to optimize their chances of success.

It should also be noted that equity crowdfunding seems to meet the conditions identified by marketing research and sets the preconditions for consumer behavior to be based on affective reactions. Cohen *et al.* (2008) list the following four conditions in a synthesis work:

a) *consumer motivation to process information is low*: for Hornuf and Schwienbacher (2015b), the low motivation of investors to collect information can be explained by the amounts invested, sometimes limited to a few euros;

b) *they are distracted, cognitively constrained or under time pressure*: investors are not professionals and have limited time to analyze entrepreneurial project files (Bessière and Stéphany 2014). As indicated above, 72% of the 390 equity crowdfunding investors in the Skoglund and Stiernblad study (2013) spent less than 10 minutes on pre-investment analysis;

c) the *basis for assessment is ambiguous*: the information available and controlled by the platforms is provided by companies waiting for funding; both actors have a stake in the success of the fundraising, meaning the information may have a presentation bias. In addition, given the stage of development of the company, generally in the seed phase, historical quantitative information is limited;

d) *they lack expertise in the field*: although the crowd is heterogeneous, equity crowdfunding investors are not, typically, sophisticated.

1.2.2.3. *The importance of emotional reactions*

We make the choice of focusing on the second-order choice, i.e. a decision, that of investing in a particular project on an equity crowdfunding platform, because as Lesourne (1965) states, "a decision is a choice between several possible acts".

The role of affective reactions in guiding judgments, decisions and behaviors is well established by cognitive psychology and, more broadly, by the social sciences (Zajonc 1980; Frijda 1986; Loewenstein *et al.* 2001; Slovic *et al.* 2002; Kahneman 2003).

Thus, the persuasive advertising context of equity crowdfunding campaigns would only reinforce the role of the emotional aspect in decision-making.

It should also be noted that the hypothesis of a choice that would not be exclusively cognitive, but a mixture of cognition and affect is supported:

– in the press, at the time the French government issued the ordinance regulating this emerging sector, the newspaper *Les Echos* had the headline, "*Crowdfunding, finance émotionnelle ou rationnelle?*" (Crowdfunding, emotional or rational finance?) and questioned the rationality of the investor by evoking faith, emotion and ethics as psychological underpinnings[19];

– in the assessment of the French regulatory authority (AMF) for which equity crowdfunding is an investment of conviction: "You invest your money in initiatives that make sense for you, are close to your heart, correspond to your aspirations and your values"[20];

– in the European Commission's report of May 3, 2016, in which the results of a study conducted by the University of Brighton are included. These results show that while peer-to-peer lending investors are attentive to return, equity crowdfunding investors are guided by interest in the project and emotions;

– in the literature on crowdfunding; Hendrickx (2014) reports that all the crowdfunding players he met in the course of writing his book stressed that the investor's first instinct is emotional; sponsors first fall in love with the idea, and then they think about it, especially for large sums of money;

– Stucki (2014) also points out, with regard to the suitability test and MiFID II Directive 2014/65/EU of May 15, 2014, that the investment firm must obtain a wide range of information enabling it to provide personalized advice on recommended transactions. This information includes investment

---

19 See: http://archives.lesechos.fr/archives/cercle/2014/05/29/cercle_98939.htm.

20 See: http://www.amf-france.org/Epargne-Info-Service/Produits-et-supports-d-investissements/Types-de-produits/Financement-participatif-crowdfunding.

objectives. The author notes that in the context of equity crowdfunding, investment objectives cannot be reduced to maximizing the risk/return ratio, particularly because of a choice guided by other factors: emotional and/or collective;

– in the academic work on equity crowdfunding, we can refer to Bessière and Stéphany (2014) who are explicit in stating, "affect then plays an essential role" and point out the marketing dimension of campaigns, as well as the behavior of investors: "for some members of the crowd, marketing logic prevails over financial logic";

– in their research on crowdfunder motivation, Gerber and Hui (2013) note the relevance of using the fields of psychology and marketing to better understand the role of objectives, information and affects in the decision-making process;

– finally, academic work is emerging to investigate this path, which is the subject of the following section.

1.2.2.4. *The absence of affective reactions in academic work on equity crowdfunding*

Before referring to recent work on the role of emotional reactions in crowdfunding investment choices, it is necessary to specify that the aforementioned work, on the effect of the size of an entrepreneur's social network on the success of fundraising campaigns (Mollick 2013; Wechsler 2013), can be interpreted as an emotional bias: the familiarity bias.

Indeed, if the authors link these results to signal theory by arguing that friends and family have private information that reduces information asymmetry, it is possible to adopt another reading grid by leaving the cognitive and instrumental dimension of choice to draw on social psychology, with the simple exposure effect of Zajonc (1968). In this case, the attitudes and behaviors of friends and family are guided by affect and their preferences and not by rational calculation.

Apart from this familiarity bias, which is implicit in the results of corporate finance, there does not seem to be any research to date in this field that focuses on the emotional dimension of individual investors' choice of equity crowdfunding.

Nevertheless, taking a step aside, in the field of entrepreneurship, research is emerging on the theme of the emotional reactions provoked by pitching, the narrative power of entrepreneurs and their ability to persuade investors through video messages.

For example, Milovac *et al.* (2015) examined the influence of the entrepreneur's affects (mood, passion and emotions) on the success of their pitch, i.e. the evaluation, financing and success of fundraising campaigns.

Davis *et al.* (2017) study the emotional reactions of investors to entrepreneurial pitches. They show that perceived innovation for a product is positively related to the performance of crowdfunding, both directly and indirectly through mediation of their own emotional reactions, with this indirect relationship being moderated by the perceived passion of the entrepreneur.

Wuillaume *et al.* (2016) highlight the effect of the expression of entrepreneurial emotions in the narrative on investors' attitudes toward the project and the decision to invest. In line with these results, they show that the emotional tone of the narrative determines the number of sponsors of donation and reward-based projects, as this effect is weaker for equity crowdfunding, in which the cognitive dimension is more prominent (Wuillaume *et al.* 2017).

Allison *et al.* (2017) propose a model of persuasion in reward-based crowdfunding.

In addition, pitches, narration and persuasion use videos as a medium. Josue and Bahm (2016) propose an original method to measure the emotions triggered in potential sponsors by pitch videos from crowdfunding platforms; this research falls within the field of human–machine interactions.

Before concluding this section, we summarize, in Table 1.11, explanations in management science literature relating to the choices of equity crowdfunding investors.

	Individual choice	Aggregate choice (the crowd)
First-order choice **(decision to invest in equity crowdfunding)**	(Explicit) psychological explanation by individual motivations	(Implicit) explanation by individual motivations and by the reasoning of methodological individualism (*)
Second-order choice **(choice of equity crowdfunding project)**	(Explicit) explanation by cognition and by signal theory *Emergence of (implicit/explicit) explanations by the affect in the field of entrepreneurship*	(Implicit) explanation by campaign success factors

*The crowd's first-order choice (aggregated) is a relative choice. For example, in 2017, for France, the total funds raised in equity crowdfunding was EUR 58 million[21], an amount to be compared to the EUR 336 million raised for all crowdfunding activities. The choice of equity crowdfunding therefore represents 58/336 ≈17.3% of the investment effort in crowdfunding, compared with 34.5% (≈115.8/336) for crowdfunding by bonds. The crowd chooses, or rather favors, crowdfunding by bonds over crowdfunding by capital subscriptions.

Table 1.11. *Explanations given by management science literature on investment choices in equity crowdfunding*

1.2.3. *In conclusion*

This section began with the seemingly paradoxical success of the equity crowdfunding industry, a paradox that, at the individual level, raises the questions of why investors invest in equity crowdfunding and how they make their project choices.

The question of why (a first-order choice) is answered in research on investor motivations.

The question of how (which concerns a second-order choice) is addressed by the literature in entrepreneurial finance from the perspective of signal theory, or a cognitivist approach, based on an implicit assumption of instrumental and utilitarian rationality.

21 See: http://financeparticipative.org/wp-content/uploads/2018/01/Barometre-CrowdFunding-2017_KPMG-FPF_page-à-page.pdf.

However, we have seen that the context of equity crowdfunding is specific and differs from that of traditional financial assets due, in particular, to a context of persuasive advertising.

It also seems necessary to take into account the affective dimension of the choice of projects. We believe that affective reactions are a mobilizable concept, already borrowed from the field of entrepreneurship, to improve our understanding of the choices of equity crowdfunding investors.

The field of marketing has long incorporated the emotional reactions of consumer behavior; as Filser (2015) indicates, the first formalizations of consumer choice incorporating the affect date back to Howard (1963).

We believe, like Pare and Rédis (2011), that the development of research programs, specific to entrepreneurial finance, and the borrowing of concepts from other disciplinary fields is all the more necessary for equity crowdfunding as it is a recent phenomenon where research literature remains in relatively short supply (Hornuf and Schwienbacher 2015a).

1.3. What role for values and the affect?

1.3.1. *Issue*

1.3.1.1. *Justification*

As we noted in section 1.2.2, academic work on crowdfunding, focusing on the determinants of individual investors' choice of projects, has so far been largely based, to our knowledge, on signal theory. The quality of a project's signal then results from a combination of information provided by the entrepreneurial team (description page, pitch video, business plan, etc.) and social interactions on the platform (information updates by the project team, exchanges between investors or between investors and the management team via a blog, collection rates, etc.).

This consequentialist and utilitarian approach (in the narrow sense given by economics) is cognitivist, underpinning a hypothesis of instrumental rationality by which the investor is driven by the objectives of reducing information asymmetry and maximizing the risk–return ratio. If this choice of rationality is adapted to an investment for which the motivation is exclusively extrinsic, in the case of equity crowdfunding, it seems that the motivations at play in the choice of investment are mixed (intrinsic and extrinsic). We do not reject the calculation and pursuit of financial self-interest as a determinant of choice, nor the instrumental rationality approach, but it seems insufficient to us to explain the observed behaviors in detail.

Moreover, the context of equity crowdfunding investment is singular in that the investor is subject to persuasion, which is similar to the phenomenon of advertising persuasion, studied in the field of marketing through the means implemented on the platforms. Thus, the investor would be influenced by the narration (the pitch), images and videos; however, these artifices have demonstrated their influence on decision-making via two complementary paths: cognition and affect.

It is indeed the emotional dimension of the choice that seems, to us, to be insufficiently explored in the context of equity crowdfunding investment and which we propose to study.

Beyond this theoretical motivation, we believe it is important to better understand the emotional dimension of equity crowdfunding choices in order to protect investors, who must be protected, including from their own judgmental biases, through preventive information, for which the AMF is responsible (in France), and which is a guarantee of a more informed choice.

1.3.1.2. *Presentation of the problem*

1.3.1.2.1. Research object (problem)

The state of the art in this first chapter has allowed us to identify the object chosen for this research:

> Explaining the project choices of equity crowdfunding investors by the emotional dimension of the choice.

The central (main) question is a theoretical one, aimed at filling a gap in the entrepreneurial finance literature regarding the emotional dimension of choice.

1.3.1.2.2. Central issue

To what extent do emotions and values guide the choice of the individual equity crowdfunding investor?

While the hypothesis of an affective effect on investment choices has been put forward and justified above, the role of "values" does not arise directly from the state of the art on crowdfunding, but from a combination of an abductive approach, inferences from a body of qualitative data and a review of complementary literature.

The methodology presented in section 1.3.1.4 of this chapter returns to this point.

The word "measurement" of the central question is related to the desire to quantify the effect of values and emotional reactions on choice, a quantitative study has made this measurement possible.

A second question, strongly connected to the central question, aims to study the comparative effects of the cognitive and affective dimensions.

1.3.1.2.3. Secondary issue

What are the respective weights of the cognitive and emotional dimensions in the choice of the individual investor in equity crowdfunding?

The thesis defended in this book is the following.

1.3.1.2.4. Defended thesis

In the context of equity crowdfunding, i.e. investment in a situation of uncertainty in which the tool of persuasive advertising is used, investors' choice is overdetermined by emotions and their values, as their deliberative judgment is only an antecedent to marginal causal power.

1.3.1.2.5. Remarks

This proposal is only valid within the constrained framework of this research, explained below, in which the determinants of social interactions and the herd effect, in particular, are excluded from the scope of the study.

In other words, we are not claiming that the affect dominates the cognitive in real-life situations when all the effects are present.

1.3.1.3. *Delimitation of the field of research*

In order to clarify the problem, we provide details on the subject of choice before defining the scope of this research.

1.3.1.3.1. A contextual choice

According to Mangot (2013), the first developments in the field of behavioral finance revealed the limits of the neoclassical economic assumptions that had prevailed in finance until then. The hypothesis of individual rationality was confronted with the empirical reality of behavior, giving rise to biases, heuristics, subjective preferences and context effects. The latter reflect the sensitivity of preferences to different effects: *presentation* or framing *effects*, social environment (social norms, herding behavior bias, etc.), internal states (moods, emotions, etc.), and so on.

Schmidt (2010) explains that the discrepancies between economic logic models and behavioral models arise from the invariance hypothesis, which posits that the solutions to a rational choice problem do not depend on how the choice is presented. As a result, the decision-maker and the decision-maker's observer need not be distinguished. However, if this is true for a situation of pure logic (choice between several options with a probability distribution or lottery), it is no longer true for a behavioral analysis. In this case, decision-makers are faced with a situation of choice that may contain a direct stake existing only for them and not for observers; this stake may be of an affective nature (hoped-for pleasure, feared sorrow, etc.) or cognitive and, depending on the *subjective representations induced by the context*, the latter may be defined in a somewhat vague way as "all that envelops the situation of choice".

The objective of this research makes the impact of the context on the decision the central element studied, which contrasts with the approach that prevails in economics, particularly in decision and game theories, where total decontextualization makes it possible to focus on a rational approach to decisions and, in addition, is the guarantee of greater external validity of the results (Petit 2013).

1.3.1.3.2. A second-order choice

We find ourselves in the context of a financial investment made by an individual investor.

We define the *first-order choice* as selecting one asset class over another (e.g. equity, bond, passbook and equity crowdfunding).

We define the *second-order choice* as the selection of a specific asset in the asset class previously chosen by the first-order choice. The second-order choice corresponds, for example, to the ISIN code of a financial instrument on the markets or to the company name on an equity crowdfunding platform.

In our case, we make the choice not to rely on psychoanalytic theory: the first-order choice is that of equity crowdfunding, so the "choice" referred to in the central and secondary questions is a second-order choice of choosing one project among others on an equity crowdfunding platform.

According to Shefrin and Statman's (2000) positive portfolio theory or behavioral portfolio theory, individual investors use mental accounting to construct a layered portfolio, forming a pyramid oriented from the least risky investments (the bottom) to the riskiest investments (the top). Each layer or compartment represents an asset class that is based on an investment objective (security objective, income objective, growth objective and wealth objective). However, according to Fenouillet (2016), an objective (or purpose) is the target to which an incentive is directed.

These elements allow us to specify that the first-order choice is linked to the investor's objectives, which are themselves associated with their motivations. The literature on equity crowdfunding tells us that the motivations of crowdfunding sponsors are multiple and mixed (intrinsic and extrinsic), so the associated objectives can be decoupled from the risk/return trade-off. We therefore do not limit ourselves to the four objectives of the Shefrin–Statman pyramid.

D2 is the set of the second-order choice determinants; these are of an affective and cognitive nature. They are also contextual, i.e. linked to the characteristics of the project being evaluated. These determinants cover certain motivations for the first-order choice, which persist during this second phase (intersection M1 and D2).

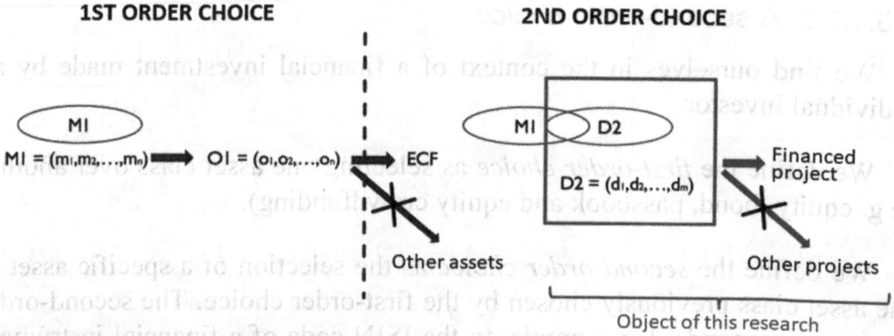

ECF = equity crowdfunding.
M1 is the tuple of the investors' motivations for 1st-order choice.
O1 is the tuple of objectives associated with M1 motivation.
Each component of O1 is associated with a component of the same rank (i) in M1: $_{mi}$ ~> oi.

Figure 1.1. *Graphical representation of the research object*

As already mentioned, the first-order motivations should persist at the time of the second-order choice, which is why M1 appears in the "second-order choice" field.

Finally, this research focuses on D2, the tuple of affective and cognitive contextual determinants[22] of an individual investor's choice between several crowdfunding equity projects available on a platform.

EXAMPLE.– Figure 1.1 could illustrate the case of an investor who initially chose to invest in equity crowdfunding mainly because of an intrinsic, altruistic motivation (m_1) and then because of an extrinsic financial motivation (m_2). Indeed, the investor, above all, wants to have a positive social impact (o_1), if possible by generating a return (o_2).

Or with the selected ratings:

M1 = (m_1, m_2) = (altruistic motivation, financial motivation)

O1 = (o_1, o_2) = (social impact objective, financial profitability objective relative to an aspiration level and a risk level)

22 The term "contextual determinants" should be understood to mean "context-related determinants".

In a second stage, investors in a position of choice on an equity crowdfunding platform could finally choose a social and solidarity economy startup, without worrying about their financial forecasts (i.e. m_2 is inoperative at this stage), because they know, through the media, the founders who expressed themselves in a radio program. In this case, D2 is the pair of determinants (d_1, d_2) = (altruistic motivation, familiarity), where d_2 is an affective determinant linked to the context of the project.

1.3.1.3.3. No sociological or psychoanalytical approach

As noted earlier, the sociological (and social psychology) dimension of choice, through social interactions and the herd effect, has received much attention from the management research community. This dimension is crucial for understanding investor choices. However, in order to explore new and complementary explanations, we will exclude these effects from our analysis.

As we shall later see, the empirical study testing the model proposed in this work is based on data from an experiment whose protocol was designed to isolate participants from any exchange. Since information on the project was limited to the pitch video and the business plan, the subjects also had no information on the collection rates and were not linked by a blog exchange between participants, or between participants and entrepreneurs.

This research falls within the field of behavioral finance, a field that first focused on the cognitive dimension of individuals' reasoning, judgments and decisions, by empirically identifying biases and heuristics. More recently, a subfield has emerged, that of emotional finance, which approaches this problem through the prism of emotions by trying to better define cognitive-emotional articulation. Taffler (2014) adds that this research trend is based on the psychoanalytical understanding of the human mind.

Although this work could logically fall within the subfield of emotional finance, we choose not to rely on psychoanalytic theory for the following reasons:

– are the reading grids from psychoanalytic theory robust? Popper (1968) argued that the discipline was not science because it did not meet the criteria for falsification. Conversely, Eric Kandel, psychiatrist and neuroscientist, Nobel Prize winner in 2000, praised psychoanalytic theories (Taffler 2014). This debate is still relevant today (Signol 2011);

– the use of psychoanalytical theory is not the only way; the psychology of emotions is a field of research at the crossroads of the fields of cognitive, social and clinical psychology that accounts for emotional phenomena (Sander and Scherer 2014).

1.3.1.4. *Methodology*

Let us begin by specifying that from an epistemological point of view, this research is part of a postpositivist perspective.

It is exploratory in nature; its purpose is to enrich the theory by proposing a set of hypotheses, as well as an original theory, able to account for the project choices of equity crowdfunding investors, by taking into account the emotional dimension of the choice.

Indeed, the purpose of this research was initially developed through an initial intuition on what, *a priori* and without extensive knowledge of the literature on the subject, could explain investors' choices. This naive conjecture of an emotionally driven investor was later confirmed by the data in our possession[23]. An extensive reading of the research on the subject then convinced us that we had identified a deficiency in the theory. This deficiency results from the comparison of the main theory used to explain the choice of projects of equity crowdfunding investors in entrepreneurial finance literature, the signal theory, with the data. The data were discordant because investors' discourse, justifying their choice of investment in a specific project, was not consistent with that expected from an agent driven by an instrumental rationality, as assumed by signal theory. For example, the testimonies cited reasons such as support for the project, interest in the idea, or the suitability of the project for the investor's values, and not only the soundness of the *business plan*, the founders' qualifications, the financial prospects, etc.

We then decided to focus our research on the question of project selection in equity crowdfunding and formulated an initial conjecture: the choice of investors is partly explained by the affective and not exclusively by cognition and reasoning. In doing so, we have precisely respected the definition of abduction: "abduction is a mode of inference highlighted by the

23 Data in the form of a qualitative corpus of 3,020 responses from investors justifying *ex post* their choice of equity crowdfunding investment through public testimonials collected on Wiseed.com, the main platform for equity crowdfunding in France by funds raised.

pragmatist philosopher C.S Peirce, which consists in making conjectures about the possible causes of a certain observed phenomenon" (Gavard-Perret *et al.* 2013).

Dumez (2012) adds, "it is about imagining a new hypothesis to explain the confusing fact that the *background theory does not explain*".

Beyond the useful contribution to the formulation of the research object, this corpus of qualitative data naturally led to a recursive loop research approach, presented in Figure 1.2.

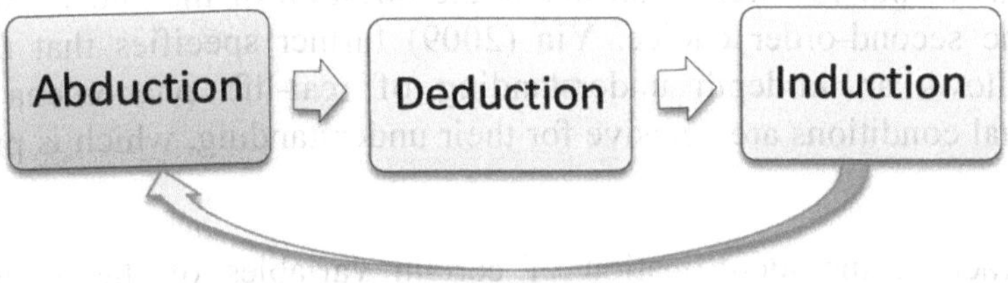

Figure 1.2. *Modes of inference and recursive loop of this research*

This *back-and-forth approach between the field and theory*, recommended by David (1999) for management sciences, makes it possible to achieve maximum objectivity, according to Peirce, whose thinking is summarized by Carontini (1990):

> All knowledge begins with hypotheses and ends with observations framed by hypotheses, these observations stimulate readjustments of the hypotheses, therefore new observations, and so on *ad infinitum*. It is in this sense that Peirce was able to conceive objectivity as the ideal end of a recursive type process.

The conjectures established by the abductive approach must be put "to the test through rigorous theoretical criticism and empirical testing" (Bhaskar 1998), which is why theoretical foundations have been identified, sometimes in fields far removed from entrepreneurial finance.

In addition, in order to achieve maximum objectivity, we have multiplied the methods to get as close as possible to reality. Thus, we have used both qualitative and quantitative methods.

The body of qualitative data was initially used as a case study. If we consider that the two questions asked at the end of the literature review on equity crowdfunding, namely, why investors choose equity crowdfunding rather than another active class, and how investors make their project choices in equity crowdfunding, are exploratory questions relative to "why" and "how", then the case study is the tool of choice according to Yin (2009). The focus of our research is on the single question of the "how", which is about the second-order choice. Yin (2009) further specifies that the case study allows an in-depth understanding of real-life phenomena whose contextual conditions are decisive for their understanding, which is precisely our case.

In practice, the identification of certain variables of the explanatory model was the result of an induction/abduction approach, following a skim-read associated with an analysis of the content of the qualitative corpus. These hypotheses later found theoretical support.

Yin (2009) adds that some case studies go beyond qualitative research and present a mix of qualitative and quantitative methods.

Specifically, the depth of our qualitative corpus of 3,020 testimonies authorized the use of quantitative lexicometric tools, this time to confirm the choice of variables in the proposed model. The lexicometric analysis of the corpus also played an important role in the operationalization of the variables and the choice of dimensions for several constructs imported from distant fields.

The development of the causal links in the explanatory model required a new abduction process, borrowing concepts or theories from other fields of social science. We have used what Carontini (1990) calls the third level of abduction, which can consist of "extending to a new field an explanatory principle belonging to a remote field".

Finally, to empirically test the hypotheses of the explanatory model, we used controlled experiment data collection and quantitative structural equation methods.

1.3.1.5. *Organization of research*

This research begins with a review of the literature that explores the role of the affective in decision-making and leads to the theoretical framework in which the hypotheses take root (Chapter 2). Modeling enshrines the abduction/deduction/induction phases through the contribution, among others, of analyses on the qualitative corpus; Chapter 1 of Volume 2 also includes the operationalization of concepts. The experimental protocol used for data collection is then presented (Chapter 2 of Volume 2). The last chapter (Chapter 3 of Volume 2) tests the hypotheses and discusses the results obtained.

1.3.2. *To summarize*

In section 1.3, we have justified the usefulness of this research, which is intended to fill a gap in entrepreneurial finance literature on the role of the affective dimension in the choice of projects by equity crowdfunding investors. This gap is revealed by the internal incoherence of the literature which, from a neoclassical persective, subjects this choice to an exclusively rational and cognitivist approach in which the investor seeks to reduce the asymmetry of information in order to maximize the risk–return ratio, while at the same time, several studies highlight the intrinsic motivations of the choice of investment in equity crowdfunding. This gap is also justified by the obvious dimension of a persuasive advertising context in which the choice is made, as well as by the emergence of research on the role of persuasion, narrative and affect in the field of entrepreneurship.

We then set out the problem and clarified its framework. The central and secondary issues are articulated around a "choice", described as the second order and operating in an idiosyncratic context. Furthermore, this research will not be based on psychoanalytical theory but rather on psychology. We choose to exclude the effects of social interactions and the herd effect, as they have already received a lot of attention by the community.

Finally, the epistemological posture adopted is postpositivist. The methodology is organized by recursive loops between abductive, deductive and inductive inference through a qualitative corpus. The quantitative and qualitative methods are mobilized in order to achieve maximum objectivity.

1.4. Conclusion

This first chapter began with a presentation of the crowdfunding industry, accompanied by a brief review of the current situation. The specificities of equity crowdfunding were then presented. In particular, the paradox of an average, unsophisticated investor basing his or her choices on simple, and potentially biased, information to invest in a high-risk asset was posed. A review of the literature on equity crowdfunding has revealed some explanations for this paradox: on the one hand, investors are driven by intrinsic and extrinsic motivations and, on the other, if they do not have the ability to assess the opportunity, they can rely on information from other individuals (friends and family, other investors, etc.) through face-to-face interactions or as a result of social interactions (online blog) and through mimicry (collection rates, opinions of other investors, sophisticated or not). We then confine the subject to the topic of project choice by equity crowdfunding investors; in current theory, this choice is based on an essentially cognitive, rational and utilitarian approach that relies on signal theory. This leads us to highlight what appears to be a gap in the literature on entrepreneurial finance: the role of the affective dimension of choice is poorly documented, even though it seems relevant in the context of equity crowdfunding, particularly because of the persuasive advertising context in which the choice is made. Finally, the resulting problematics are presented, along with the methodology adopted to address them.

2

Transdisciplinary Approach to the Issue of Investor Choice

This chapter first sets out its objective and the methodology adopted (section 2.1), followed by a review of the literature (section 2.2) and then a presentation of the theoretical framework chosen for this work (section 2.3).

2.1. Objective and methodology

2.1.1. *Objective*

The first chapter raised questions about an apparent paradox in equity crowdfunding investment. This paradox has to do with the growing number of unsophisticated investors taking high financial risks by becoming part of this industry. This first state of the art also allowed us to validate the existence of a gap between our naïve conjecture on the role of the emotions in investors' project choices and the explanations given on this subject in the field of entrepreneurial finance. Thus, the problem posed is the result of a first review of the literature. Moreover, according to Dumez (2011), it is an original question because it is situated at the limit of knowledge: "[...] it is the very purpose of a literature review to specify the sphere of the already-done and already-known, and to identify the frontiers of knowledge in order to determine an original research question".

It should be noted that while we are at the limit of knowledge, we are not beyond it, because, during this first stage, we discovered a few articles (though they were rare) adopting a reading prism that was close to ours, even if they are located in the field of entrepreneurship.

For this second phase of the literature review, our objective is to build a theoretical framework that specifies the concepts, theories and models on which we will base our research (Gavard-Perret *et al.* 2013).

2.1.2. *Methodology*

According to Dumez (2011), a literature review proceeds by two consecutive and inverse steps. The first one is exploratory, it is open to new disciplines, ideas and concepts and moves away from the initial point. The second step narrows the epistemic space to arrive at a relevant theoretical framework. Figure 2.1 represents this approach.

Figure 2.1. *The two consecutive and inverse steps of the literature review*

The literature review of this chapter crosses the social sciences; this transversality appeared, to us. As evidence for our subject: the choice that is "the decision", studied in many fields of knowledge. Also, like Dumez (2011), we think that "[…] many advances in a field are simply transpositions of what has been done in a neighboring field".

In addition, the theme of values is, alongside the affect, at the heart of our problem. On the subject of values, Tirole (2017) points out that decisions based on an axiological dimension are beyond the scope of traditional economics. The author cites the example of the abolition of the death penalty, because it is a decision that is based only marginally on an economic approach of the incentive or cost–benefit type, but much more on a framework linked to the social psychology of values. Tirole (2017) concludes this example on the necessary convergence of the social sciences:

> We are witnessing a gradual reunification of the social sciences. This reunification will be slow, but it is inevitable – in

> fact, as I said in the introduction to this chapter, anthropologists, economists, historians, legal scholars, philosophers, political scientists, psychologists, and sociologists are interested in the same individuals, the same groups, and the same societies. The convergence that existed until the end of the nineteenth century must be reestablished. This will require these scientific communities to open to the techniques and ideas of the other disciplines.

Finally, in this chapter, we take a cross-disciplinary approach to social science through two consecutive and inverse steps. The opening phase is the subject of section 2.2 and the contraction phase is the subject of section 2.3 "Towards a synthetic theoretical framework". The literature review section follows a spiral trajectory from its center and starting point (decision theory) to move away, by centrifugal force, toward other disciplines of management sciences (capital market literature, marketing and human resource management (HRM)) and finally to cognitive and social psychology. The second point in section 2.2 borrows from psychology, and sets out definitions of the various emotional experiences, which are useful for reading the following points. Section 2.3.1 presents the theoretical framework selected for this research, based on proposals established throughout the chapter to link the concepts and theories with one another. Finally, two graphical representations articulate the concepts and theories that make up the theoretical framework defined and facilitate the approach (Gavard-Perret *et al.* 2013).

2.2. Theories that can be used to explain the choice of investors

This literature review opens with the rational choice theory because it remains unavoidable; as soon as we approach decision problems, it constitutes a point of reference, including when we expose its limits, such as psychological biases, which are only biases in relation to this theory. Moreover, a return to the sources of its origins links it to our subject. This is followed by a presentation of affective experiences, a point necessary for the clarity of the rest of the chapter. The following sections will deal successively with decision models integrating affects (normative and psychological), affects in finance, affects in consumer marketing theory and the concept of organizational attractiveness; the section will conclude on value theory and the psychology of emotions.

2.2.1. *Choice as a rational decision: expected utility theory*

2.2.1.1. *A normative theory*

When looking at the decisions of economic agents, such as investors, it is difficult to ignore expected utility theory, also known as rational choice theory. The influence of this theory goes beyond the strict framework of the economic discipline whose field it delimits. As Lopes (2005) points out, explanations are considered to be economic in that they presuppose rational agents whose decisions are consistent with this theory. Rational choice theory is normative, it is part of an efficient framework by dictating the optimal choice made by a rational agent (Buttard and Gadreau 2008). This type of approach – normative – is generally opposed to empirical approaches that seek to identify the psychological mechanisms underlying the observed behaviors (Broihanne *et al.* 2004).

The postulates of rationality of this rational agent or *homo œconomicus* are that of a selfish individual, guided by their self-interest, expressed in terms of utility. The agent's cognitive capacities are infinite; the agent is omniscient, maximizing and behaves in the same way, regardless of the time horizon. A key point for us is that *the agent's rationality is instrumental and consequentialist*, because the agent is only interested in the results of their decisions (Buttard and Gadreau 2008).

If we go back to the origins of decision theory and the concept of utility, it is Bernoulli (1954) who, in 1738, formulated a criterion, independent of any axiom, explaining the behavior of decision-makers with regard to certain games of chance. This criterion has the merit of providing a solution to the St. Petersburg paradox, presented in Box 2.1.

The St. Petersburg paradox raises the following question: why are individuals not willing to bet all their wealth in exchange for a note whose mathematical expectation of winning is infinite?

The game considered is the following: the player bets in exchange for a win determined by a succession of draws of a coin. In the first draw, the payout is one monetary unit; in the second draw, the payout is 2 monetary units; in the *n*th draw, the payout is 2^{n-1} monetary units, and so on.

The winning expectation of the game (without considering the initial bet) is infinite:

$$E = \frac{1}{2}.1 + \frac{1}{4}.2 + \frac{1}{8}.4 + \cdots = \sum_{k=1}^{\infty} \frac{1}{2^k}.2^{k-1} = \sum_{k=1}^{\infty} \frac{1}{2} = \infty$$

Any player should "logically" agree to play this game, regardless of the initial bet, but, in reality, this is not the case, as players cannot stand the pressure of taking the risk of the bet because of an "aversion to risk". Indeed, the bet is a sure loss while the win is random. If the player agreed to bet a sum equal to the mathematical expectation of the win (which in this case is not possible), it would mean that he would be indifferent to the risk.

To resolve this paradox, Bernoulli introduces *the utility of the gain, i.e. its subjective perception*, a quantity that depends on the player's wealth. This function expresses that an increase of 1 monetary unit for wealth A is more "useful" than an increase of 1 monetary unit for wealth B if B > A, which translates into a concave utility function.

When we insert a utility function of the Napierian logarithm type in the calculation of the winning expectation of the heads or tails game presented above, we obtain:

$$EU = \sum_{k=1}^{\infty} p_k . u(2^{k-1}) = \sum_{k=1}^{\infty} \frac{\ln(2^{k-1})}{2^k} = \ln(2) \sum_{k=1}^{\infty} \frac{k-1}{2^k} = \ln(2) < \infty$$

This modification does offer an explanation for this paradox, since the certain equivalent of this game is a small monetary quantity: ln (2) monetary unit.

Box 2.1. *The St. Petersburg paradox behind the utility function*

The criterion of expected utility is developed in Neumann and Morgenstern (1944). It is based on an axiom of behavior, i.e. a set of conditions for the consistency of the model. This theory was initially developed to formulate the choices of individuals faced with a risky situation. Each choice is associated with a probability distribution of consequences (or lottery L). The utility function represents the individual's preferences and the expected utility E(U[L]) reflects their satisfaction with the choice considered. The rational individual chooses the choice with the highest expected utility:

$$E(U(L)) = \sum_{I=1}^{n} U(x_i).p_i$$

In this formula, x_i are the consequences and p_i are the associated probabilities.

As Kast (2002) explains, this theory will find applications in the analysis of decision-making problems in the context of uncertainty, i.e. without knowledge of the probabilities of consequences. Savage (1954) is credited with this major generalization, which makes it possible to move from objective probabilities to subjective probabilities, the latter representing the decision-maker's assessment of the likelihood of random events. In this extension, called subjective expected utility, choices are explained by the preferences (utility) and beliefs (subjective probabilities) of the decision-makers.

Thus, the individual's own subjectivity is taken into account as an initial datum in the decision-maker's preferences and beliefs, but the theory is not interested in its psychological origin. The only condition required is that the evaluation does not contradict the axiom of behavior postulated by the theory (Jean-Pascal Gayant 2017).

Lopes (2005) notes that the contemporary evolution of utility theory has strayed from the foundations of the early neoclassical economics marginalists, for whom utility was associated with a psychology of wants and needs. Today, the theory has discarded all psychological postulates and only the axioms remain, ensuring the logical coherence of a formal model. Utility now only measures the degree of satisfaction of the individual with regard to goals that are outside the scope of the theory. *Motivations are therefore outside the framework of economic science* or, as Sugden (1991) puts it: "the utility function is absolutely silent on the way in which preferences are formed, postulated exogenously."

Let us note, with Fenouillet (2016), that while rational choice theory rejects the psychology of the decision-maker outside its boundaries, expected utility theory, on the other hand, permeates and influences many motivational psychological models, such as expectation and value theory.

2.2.1.2. *The absence of the affective dimension of the original theories in the expected utility theory*

According to Bryan (2013), Jeremy Bentham is the founder of a moral philosophy that John Stuart Mill would later name "utilitarianism". Utilitarianism is the act of judging the usefulness or harmfulness of an action by its consequences. These are the source of pleasure or pain, so the conduct to be favored in any situation is that which maximizes pleasure and minimizes pain. According to Mill, this hedonic philosophy has the advantage of simplicity, with a single criterion for good; the right actions are those that tend to promote general happiness (Lopes 2005).

In the second half of the 19th Century, the psychophysiologist Fechner established a mathematical law, inspired by Bernouilli's work on risk measurement, linking the objective measurement of a physical stimulus to the subjective measurement of the sensation felt by the subject of the experiment. His work was taken up by several economists, including Jevon and Edgeworth. Edgeworth attempted to link pleasure and pain with the consumption of a certain quantity of a good, using a mathematical model derived from infinitesimal calculus. Thus, Edgeworth introduced the principle of hedonic calculation and therefore the economic utility of an action, calculated as the maximization of the pleasure felt by the agent (Schmidt 2010).

It is important to note that utility, the set of pleasures and punishments at stake in the utilitarian approach, is felt at the time of consequences and not at the time of choice, whereas in recent economic decision theory – or rational choice theory – utility is anticipated and experienced at the time of choice. In order to clarify this point on the temporality of utility, Kahneman and Thaler (2006) call the utility of rational choice theory "desirability" and the utility experienced at the moment of the choice's consequences "utility experienced". At the beginning of the 20th Century, utility as experienced disappeared from the discourse of economists in favor of anticipated utility, the "desirability". For the authors, this change in the meaning of utility is damaging for modern economic decision theory, because empirical results show that experienced utility is often different from anticipated utility, i.e. the choice resulting from *ex ante* maximization does not produce maximum *ex post* utility. The original version of the utility had a simple meaning: do people choose the option that really gives them the most pleasure?

Today, many researchers believe that the evolution of economic decision theory is leading it away from a positive view of behavior.

For Kahneman (2003), usefulness is inseparable from emotions, especially regret. The psychologist believes that a theory of choice that ignores emotions can neither pretend to describe reality nor lead to prescriptions that maximize experienced utility, such as that of Jeremy Bentham.

Slovic *et al.* (2002) see empirical work on the experiential system, anchored in the affective and complementary to analytical judgment, as an impish sign from the founding father of utilitarianism that emotions do participate in individuals' decision-making.

Bechara and Damasio (2005), two neuroscientists and psychologists behind the somatic marker theory, which supports the idea of the necessary role of emotions in judgment and decision-making, also believe that rational choice theory cannot ignore emotions because decision-making is physiologically linked to the emotional system.

Finally, Zeelenberg *et al.* (2008) consider that economists have wrongly abandoned emotions, which were central to the precursors of decision theory, probably because of their unpredictability, instability and objectively unstable nature.

2.2.1.3. *The explanatory weakness of expected utility theory in the face of choices based on complex rationality*

As Kast (2002) explains, decision theory evolves over time according to a logic of generalization, in order to respond to a succession of empirical challenges. These generalizations resolve the paradoxes posed by older theories. Some of these paradoxes characterizing the quasi-systematic violation of axioms are famous: the St. Petersburg paradox (presented in Box 2.1), the Allais paradox, the Ellsberg paradox, etc. In addition to these paradoxes, experiments carried out by psychologists and economists have been trying to identify the real behavior of decision-makers for 30 years. Also, although normative, decision theory tries to improve its explanatory power by adhering to the observed results. Developments take several forms. First of all, theorists are looking for axioms that are representative of the observed behaviors and applicable to the greatest number of people, so this axiom of behavior is regularly weakened. Secondly, in order to respond to the subjective appreciation of decision-makers, overestimating small probabilities, these are distorted and no longer linear. The treatment of problems under ambiguity, i.e. the case where the probabilities are partially known, is solved by replacing the probability measure by a non-additive measure, which indicates a further weakening of the assumptions as a means of extending the scope of the theory. Additionally, we have already mentioned the major advance in generalization that consists of substituting subjective probabilities, which are similar to beliefs, for objective probabilities, in order to respond to decision problems in uncertainty and no longer simply in risk and ambiguity.

As summarized by Jean-Pascal Gayant (2017), regardless of the refinements considered, the decision theory choice criterion is defined as a function of the consequences of this choice (called the preference function or value function and corresponding to the expected utility or the subjective expected utility), regardless of whether the probabilities associated with these consequences are known, partially known, or unknown. In other words, if the decision theory operates within the framework of risk, ambiguity and uncertainty, it applies only to rational agents who establish their choices on the exclusive basis of their consequences. This utilitarian theory therefore presupposes a purely instrumental rationality, i.e. rational in purpose (Cuin 2001), because the choice made is the one that maximizes, via the criterion, the utility of the consequences, which is its purpose (Lopes 2005). However, the rationality of the investor that we consider in this work, explained below, is more complex and if the agent is consequentialist, he is only partially consequentialist.

Moreover, as Orléan (2010) notes:

> It seems to us that a large part of the difficulties experienced by *neoclassical finance* is due very specifically to the fact that it *has rejected the idea of Keynesian uncertainty* in order to model the relationship of financial actors to the future in a strictly probabilistic form. However, the probabilistic model adopted by neoclassical finance does not correctly capture the real forecasting difficulties experienced by economic players, including those working in financial markets. *This model does not make it possible to understand how real investors think and make their decisions*.

Our approach is exploratory and its primary objective is explicative. This reason in itself is enough to make the framework of the normative theory of rational choice unsuitable for our research.

As we have seen, rational choice theory is not unrelated to pleasures and sorrows. Section 2.2.2 provides theoretical insights into the various concepts related to affects and useful for the following developments, which focus on affective responses.

2.2.2. *Emotions, affective reactions and other affective experiences*

Since the end of the 19th Century, psychological sciences have initiated research on the study of emotions ahead of other disciplines. Three streams structure this field of research.

The first is the biological stream, based on Charles Darwin's theory of evolution. His book on the expression of emotions in humans and animals (Darwin 1872) marks the beginning of scientific research on emotions. Darwin endeavored to show that emotions are limited in number, present themselves analogously in all cultures and have an adaptive function useful for survival through facial and postural manifestations. For example, opening one's eyes wide open and focused in surprise would make it easier to identify a danger (Rimé 2016). Later, Tomkins (1962) reformulated the theory by conceiving of emotion as an adaptive system whose function is to amplify signals to trigger action. He also believed, like Darwin, that the subjective experience of emotion is the result of feedback from the facial muscles to the cerebral cortex that leads to an individual's awareness. The work of Paul Ekman and Carroll Izard is an important extension of the theses of Tomkins, their professor, on the facial expression of emotions.

The second is the physiological stream, which focuses on the study of bodily changes in emotions. James (1884) followed by Lange (1885) are the pioneers of this stream: the peripheral or peripheralist theory of emotions. This theory runs counter to the prevailing view at the time, that if we face a wolf on a walk in the woods, fear grips us and, as a result, we start to tremble. James reversed the perspective by using Darwin to argue that, in this situation, our bodies shake first and then the perception of that shaking (at the periphery of the nervous system) triggers fear. More generally, we respond with reflex reactions; genetically programmed and prior to any consciousness, it is the physiological changes that are the origin of the emotion. Additionally, a particular physiological reaction corresponds to each type of emotion. Following them, William Cannon described the physiological responses of the body in an emergency, which established the adaptive role of emotions. During a dangerous situation, the ordinary functioning of the body, particularly the digestive system, is interrupted by a discharge from the sympathetic nervous system and a release of adrenaline, the pulse rate increases and blood pressure rises, which promotes muscular mobilization for fight or flight. On the other hand, Cannon (1927) contradicted James on the singularity of physiological reactions associated with emotions; his work shows that different emotions can induce similar physiological reactions. It should also be noted that this stream is at the origin of current developments in neuropsychological studies of the nervous system. In particular, we will present the work of Damasio (2006) already mentioned on the neural mechanisms underlying emotional responses in decision-making.

The third stream is the most recent, the cognitivist approach, which only started in 1960, the year of the "cognitive revolution". According to Schachter (1964), the physiological changes described by Cannon, which are similar in all situations, are not sufficient on their own to create the emotional state. The identification and differentiation of emotions is the result of an attribution process that removes this ambiguity. The attribution process is based on the detection of an element that may be responsible for the current physiological state given the context defined by the thoughts and the situation. This stream is of particular interest in the study of the role of cognitive processes in triggering emotions. Emotion does not result directly from the event or stimulus, but from the subjective interpretation of it. We will further discuss cognitive appraisal or "cognitive evaluation", the dominant theory explaining the triggering and differentiation of emotions by cognition. Other objects of research cross this field, such as the study of the links between emotions and perception, memory, decision, motivation, and so on.

It should also be pointed out that a fundamental debate between those advocating the primacy of emotion over cognition, led by Zajonc (1980, 2001), and those defending the opposite hypothesis, led by Lazarus (1982, 1984), has long persisted. Moreover, neuropsychological literature still holds an intermediate position in distinguishing between primary emotions and reflexes triggered by a stimulus without cognitive intervention and secondary emotions, the result of a cognitive assessment (Damasio 2006).

According to Zajonc and his supporters, it is not necessary to be aware of a physiological change to feel the emotion; it is triggered automatically without any prior cognitive process. Zajonc's thesis is based on a famous experimental result, known as the "mere-exposure" effect (Zajonc 1968). According to this hypothesis, the simple, repeated exposure of a neutral stimulus (even a subliminal one) generates a preference for it. Lazarus (1984), however, believes that a cognitive process may have occurred in all cases before the emotional response, with all ambiguity ultimately resting on the definition of cognition. According to him, cognitive activity is a necessary condition for emotion, because individuals must establish a relationship between their well-being and the environment in order for an emotion to be triggered. This debate is now outdated, as these two visions are reconcilable and compatible, once a broader acceptance of cognitive processes of appraisal, including unconscious mechanisms, is adopted (Sander and Scherer 2014).

Defining affective experiences is not easy because affect is a polysemic notion as well as a generic term referring to multiple experiential concepts such as moods, emotions, attitudes, evaluations and preferences (Zeelenberg *et al.* 2008).

Nevertheless, we will distinguish and define the concepts of affective reaction, emotion, mood and preferences that are referenced in this book.

2.2.2.1. *Affective reactions*

First of all, affective reactions constitute an encompassing class for emotions, moods, feelings, attitudes and preferences, although this list is not exhaustive. Zajonc (1980) listed 12 properties common to affective reactions, among which the following seem particularly salient: (1) their holistic and hedonic dimension (we may or may not like an object or the target of our attention); (2) their experience is inevitable, although it may be camouflaged; (3) they are irrevocable and always true (unlike knowledge); (4) they are often difficult to verbalize and (5) they are most often independent of cognition. The cardinal dimension of affective reactions, which is sufficient to define them, is valence, a term borrowed from physics and chemistry that refers to a positive or negative, pleasant or unpleasant experience. Valence is bipolar and distinguishes between pleasure and displeasure depending on whether the affective experience is attractive or repulsive. According to Zeelenberg *et al.* (2008), any experience that can be characterized as good or bad is affective. The PAD model (standing for pleasure, arousal and dominance) by Mehrabian and Russel (1974) defines a three-dimensional scale for measuring affective reactions. In addition to the valence (pleasure) already mentioned, this scale is based on two complementary dimensions: the level of activation (arousal), which measures intensity, and control (dominance), which measures the individual's ability to master the situation.

2.2.2.2. *Emotions*

Psychologists agree on the complex reality to which the term emotion refers, which involves processes of cognitive assessment of internal and external information of individuals, feelings of pleasure or displeasure, physiological changes and goal-oriented adaptive behavior (Piolat and Bannour 2008). Rimé (2009) sees emotion as a salient, intense and brief episode. The external observer notes abrupt changes (facial and postural expressions), while the individual internally experiences a specific motivational impulse. Emotion is not a stable state, but one of short duration. Scherer speaks of an emotional process in constant adjustment to changing circumstances in the environment. The author distinguishes between utilitarian emotions (anger, joy, fear, disgust, etc.), which are adaptive and necessary for well-being, and aesthetic emotions (such as those felt when listening to a Bach cantata, for example), which can also trigger obvious bodily reactions such as shivers or tears. The author notes that this second category of emotion is unrelated to the needs and goals of the individual, and therefore do not trigger a motivation to act for the realization of a goal (Frijda 1986). Emotion is object-centered, which is not the case with other emotional reactions, such as moods.

Biologists and neurologists are both only interested in objective physiological changes and observable behavioral changes that accompany emotion (Dantzer 2002). Neuropsychologists Bechara and Damasio (2005), who will be discussed later when we discuss the somatic marker hypothesis, define emotion as a collection of changes in the body and brain, triggered by a dedicated mental system in response to specific, perceptual or remembered stimuli related to an object or event. The consequences of emotion are externally observable (posture, facial expression, fight or flight behavior, etc.), but also unobservable to the outside observer (accelerated heart rate, secretions from endocrine glands, muscle contractions, etc.). These two authors prefer to use the term somatic (from the Greek "*soma*" for body) rather than emotion because of the multiple definitions of this word that prevail in the various disciplines.

Scherer's (2000) perspective is synthetic and integrative. Emotion is understood as a theoretical construct whose five components correspond to different functions (see Table 2.1). The cognitive and motivational components are of particular interest to us; they will be elaborated in section 2.2.7.3 for the cognitive dimension and section 2.2.7.5 for the motivational dimension.

Component	Function
Cognitive	Cognitive assessment of a stimulus or event that triggers the emotion.
Peripheral device	Neurophysiological regulatory reaction by the nervous system.
Motivational	Tendency to act, also known as adaptive behavior, allowing an individual to cope with their emotions.
Motor expression	Expression in the face, words, voice and gestures to communicate behavioral reactions and intentions.
Subjective feeling	Feeling corresponding to the subjective experience of emotion, often conscious and verbalizable with words.

Table 2.1. *Components of Scherer's emotional construct, adapted from Sander and Scherer (2014)*

2.2.2.3. *Moods*

Moods are emotional dispositions of low intensity, felt in a diffuse way and which form a positively or negatively toned backdrop. They are often unconscious and of indeterminate cause, although they may result from a sum of events of a pleasant or unpleasant nature. Finally, they are not characterized by specific facial expressions, as opposed to emotions (Derbaix and Filser 2011). According to Rimé (2009), "Mood refers to an emotional state whose duration can vary from a few moments to a few months without the person being aware of the triggering factors, it is not centered and difficult to verbalize other than by its bipolar dimension of good or bad mood".

2.2.2.4. *Preferences*

Preferences are also emotional judgments of relatively low intensity which, unlike moods, are stable over time. Preferences generate positive or negative feelings about an attractive or aversive stimulus, which may be an event you like or dislike or an object you like or dislike. The internal assessment producing these feelings is independent of the person's current needs and goals, and the impact on behavior is limited to a tendency to approach or avoid (Scherer 2005). Preferences are centered and allow for the classification of objects (e.g. brands). Finally, the preference for an object may result from the repetition of its "mere exposure" proposed by Zajonc (1968), already mentioned.

2.2.3. *Affect in the models of the judgment and decision-making field*

2.2.3.1. *Perspectives on decision-making models*

Interest in emotions and their role has varied throughout the history of science (Sander and Scherer 2014). Moreover, while in psychology, affects have long held an important place in many theories, they have rarely been recognized as an important component in individuals' judging and decision-making (Slovic *et al.* 2002). Modern historiography, another discipline, suffers from the same bias, underestimating the role of affectivity in historical causality, while the ancients recognized its importance. According to MacMullen (2004), modern history studies the motivations of human actions through the prism of purely materialistic, political and economic interest, whereas emotions are the deepest drivers.

To understand this enigmatic scientific omission, we must go back to antiquity, where the idea of mind–body separation was born and prolonged in Cartesian dualism and then in the emotion–cognition dichotomy. Moreover, in the West, philosophers, from Plato to Kant, portrayed emotion as a perversion of reason, or even a disease of the soul.

It was not until the 19th Century that, in science, Darwin (1872) restructured emotions by giving them an adaptive function appropriate to the demands of the environment. This biological and evolutionary perspective makes emotions the instrument for the survival of the species. As we have seen, other approaches followed: the physiological perspective, which relates emotions exclusively to somatic manifestations, or the cognitivist perspective, which assigns a role to cognitive processes in triggering emotions. In philosophy, Descartes and Hegel rehabilitated passions; they are no longer bad in and of themselves and even become the necessary springboard for people to achieve their goals. David Hume, a Scottish philosopher, gave passion, i.e. emotion, primacy over reason in the analysis of reasoned choices. The motivations for our behavior are rooted in our desires, emotions and passions, whereas reason has only the role of adapting the means to the achievement of our ends (Bryan 2013). Moreover, Schmidt (2010) connected Hume's thought, which apprehends emotions as triggers of choice processes, to the contemporary theory of somatic markers, which will be discussed in more detail below.

In economics, Smith (1822) gave prominence to the moral sense of sympathy that lies at the heart of complex social phenomena and to the happiness of individuals, making it a goal for institutions: "All constitutions of government, however, are valued only in proportion as they tend to promote the happiness of those who live under them. This is their sole use and end".

This utilitarian view of society will have a lasting influence on economic discipline and decision-making theories. Thus, Bentham (1789) is in line with the ideas of Hutcheson (1726), his contemporary, for whom "that Action is best, which procures the greatest Happiness for the greatest Numbers".

Bentham established a moral philosophy, utilitarianism, which, as we have seen, holds that the usefulness or harmfulness of an action should be judged only by its consequences, the pain or the pleasure, regardless of its motives:

> Nature has placed mankind under the governance of two sovereign masters, *pain* and *pleasure*. It is for them alone to point out what we ought to do, as well as to determine what we shall do. On the one hand the standard of right and wrong, on the other the chain of causes and effects, are fastened to their throne. They govern us in all we do, in all we say, in all we think: every effort we can make to throw off our subjection, will serve but to demonstrate and confirm it. In words a man may pretend to abjure their empire: but in reality he will remain

> subject to it all the while. The *principle of utility* recognises this subjection, and assumes it for the foundation of that system, the object of which is to rear the fabric of felicity by the hands of reason and of law.

In 1738, Bernoulli (1954) proposed a new theory of risk measurement and formalized a utility function describing the behavior of individuals in games of chance. In the 19th Century, Jevons (1871), Walrass (1874), Menger (1871) and Marshall (1890) set out mathematical theories based on the idea of measurable psychological utility.

However, the 20th Century saw a decline in interest in emotions, due to the cognitive revolution centered on the analogy between thought and computational models of information processing. Emotion was then seen as subjective, inaccessible and therefore useless for the understanding of cognition and behavior (Aïte 2013).

At the same time, in economics, affects were excluded from the economic calculation, which was centered on pure logic, because of a supposed kinship with irrationality. In psychology, as in economics, decision theories were apprehended through the prism of a calculation of expected value or utility. In economics, the consequentialist hedonism of the pioneers (Bentham, Jevon, Edgeworth etc. See section 2.2.1.2) was taken up again, but with a loss of substance, in the first normative models (Neumann and Morgenstern 1944; Savage 1954) in risk and uncertainty. These theories postulate a rational agent maximizing their profit and respecting a series of behavioral axioms (total preorder, monotony, continuity and independence of preferences for the expected utility).

These models were challenged by a succession of paradoxes arising from empirical observations revealing clear deviations from the underlying assumptions of rationality.

One explanation for these deviations would be the existence of a dual rationality, the first analytical and logical, and the second intuitive and emotional (Kahneman 2012).

A number of reasoning errors would be attributable to this competing dissonance between heuristics and algorithmic strategy.

This same second half of the 20th Century saw a renewal of interest in emotions, because of the work of Zajonc (1968) and his hypothesis of mere-exposure effect. The latter indicates that an object repeatedly presented to an individual induces a favorable attitude toward it. According to him, mere exposure explains a number of behaviors that are falsely related to an analytical evaluation:

> We sometimes delude ourselves that we proceed in a rational manner and weight all the pros and cons of the various alternatives. But this is probably seldom the actual case. Quite often "I decided in favor of X" is no more than "I liked x". [...] We buy the cars we "like", choose the jobs and houses we find "attractive", and then justify these choices by various reasons. (Zajonc 1980)

Research programs on the role of emotions in behaviors, particularly in decision-making, then developed in psychology, following the example of Zeelenberg *et al.* (2008), who believe that emotions allow individuals to overcome the cognitive limits of limited rationality by prioritizing certain goals and directing energy in a specific behavioral direction. Today, authors in the field of psychology agree that a decision theory that disregards emotional factors would not be relevant on a descriptive and explanatory level (Loewenstein *et al.* 2001).

Without claiming to be exhaustive in any way, several models, theories or hypotheses borrowed from the fields of psychology or neuroscience are presented below: the theory of perspectives, the choosing-by-liking hypothesis, the choice and the relative pleasure of consequences approach, the affect-as-information approach, the risk-as-feeling theory, the feeling-is-for-doing approach, the affect heuristic and the somatic marker hypothesis.

While the somatic marker hypothesis is based on a clinical approach and physiological measures, other theories, models or hypotheses are based on empirical observational data. Note that only the feeling-is-for-doing approach is interested in discrete emotions, which distinguishes by name between emotions of different natures (anger, joy, etc.). This approach is more sophisticated than those describing affective reactions by their bipolar valence (pleasure/unpleasure), but which lend themselves better to economic modeling of the decision (Zeelenberg *et al.* 2008). The latter approach simplifies modeling, however, to the detriment of predictive finesse because, as some works indicate, emotions with the same valence (fear and anger) can have opposite effects on the decision (Aïte 2013).

It should be noted that the detour through the neurosciences and the theory of somatic markers seems important to us because of its notoriety, and also because this theory marks a form of return to the origins of the theory of economic decision-making:

> Indeed, the development of what became known as the "Expected Utility" theory was really based on the idea that people established their values for wealth on the basis of the pain and pleasure that it would give them. So "Utility" was conceived as a balance of pleasure and pain. These notions of pleasure and pain were eliminated from notions of utility in subsequent economic models. The exclusion of current economic models of expected utility to the role of emotion in human decisions is therefore inconsistent with their foundations. (Bechara and Damasio 2005)

Finally, at the end of the 20th Century, in economics, the historical eclipse of the role of affects in decision-making theories is over, by virtue of the rapprochement between economics, cognitive psychology and neuroscience (Schmidt 2010). By way of illustration, we have chosen to present the normative model of Loomes and Sudgen (1982), which integrates the feeling of regret into the model of expected utility.

2.2.3.2. *The affect in a normative model: regret theory*

According to Bleichrodt and Wakker (2015), until the end of the 1970s, economists considered models derived from a *homo œconomicus* type of rationality hypothesis to be both normative and descriptive. Although many empirical biases were identified, theorists believed that these were too chaotic to be modeled and should be considered as mere noise.

In this context, Loomes and Sudgen (1982) proposed an original variation of the rational choice theory, which resolves certain paradoxes and empirical deviations (Allais's paradox, certainty and isolation effects, etc.) by formally introducing an affective reaction: regret.

Let us start by, first of all, clarifying the distinction to be made between two close emotions, regret and disillusionment or disappointment. First of all, these two emotions are reflected and triggered by the awareness of a difference in results. Regret concerns the actions, i.e. the choice itself – "I regret having chosen lottery A rather than lottery B" – while disappointment concerns the consequences of the choice, the results – "I am disappointed with the result obtained with lottery A because for this same lottery, the result could have been more favorable". Disappointment is therefore linked to the unfavorable difference between the expected and the obtained result, while regret is linked to the awareness of a wrong choice (Schmidt 2010). Disappointment also gave rise to formal theory and modeling (Bell 1985; Loomes and Sudgen 1987; Laciana and Weber 2008).

In addition, two types of regret can be defined.

The first is *ex post*, known as experienced regret, which is the one mentioned above. More precisely, experienced regret is related to counterfactual thoughts, i.e. the agent wonders what could have happened but did not. The agent has in the past chosen lottery A rather than B, then, on the consequence horizon, compares the result (gain or loss) of choosing A with the result they could have obtained with B.

The second type of regret is known as anticipated regret, which reflects a forecast of experienced regret, seen at the time of the choice (Magron 2014).

This anticipated regret is notably exploited by the Savage criterion (1951), one of the classic criteria for deciding in uncertainty. Also known as "minimax regret", it recommends choosing the decision that minimizes maximum regret. This criterion applies to the consequences of lotteries for which the subjective probabilities are not known.

This regret, or rather investor regret aversion, is, in fact, a generalization of loss aversion. In Kahneman and Tversky's (1979) prospect theory, the individual's value function is stronger below the reference point, e.g. 0 when considering stock market returns. The corresponding sentiment is then regret for having chosen a losing investment. Feelings of regret and pride are widely accepted as major determinants of investor behavior in the markets, and some performance criteria for funds, such as the Sortino ratio, incorporate a reference point (Mangot 2008).

The importance of regret in the understanding of individuals' behavior convinced Loomes and Sudgen to propose an original normative model, consisting of enriching the model of expected utility with the anticipated sense of regret. Bleichrodt and Wakker (2015) believe that this choice of modeling is ambitious enough, as it allows significant results to be obtained, whereas an integrative model of all known empirical results would be too complex, or even unusable.

Loomes and Sudgen's (1982) regret theory can be understood from the following formula:

$$A_1 \succcurlyeq A_2 \Leftrightarrow \sum_{j=1}^{n} pjQ\{C[A_1(s_j)] - C[A_2(s_j)]\} \geq 0$$

NOTATIONS.–

– A_k is the action k with $k = 1$ or 2;

– $A_k(s_j)$ is the monetary consequence of action k in the jth state of the world;

– Pj is the objective or subjective probability of occurrence of the jth state of the world;

– $Q\{.\}$ is the function of regret (or joy), monotonically increasing and symmetrical with respect to 0 (i.e. such that $Q[-x] = -Q[x]$);

– $C[.]$ is the subjective utility function.

This mathematical equivalence means that action A_1 is preferred to action A_2 if and only if the expectation of regret related to the utility gap generated by A_1 over A_2 is positive.

In other words, the usefulness of action A_1 is affected by the usefulness of action A_2, which the decision-maker could choose. This is why the decision-maker evaluates the anticipated gain in utility caused by the choice of action A_1 (i.e. the quantity $C[A_1(s_j)] - C[A_2(s_j)]$ if this is strictly positive) or the anticipated loss of usefulness (the quantity $C[A_1(s_j)] - C[A_2(s_j)]$ if this is strictly negative) for all the j states of the world on the consequence horizon. This utility gap gives rise to a feeling of regret or joy, which is a function of the sensitivity of the individual and formalized by the function $Q\{.\}$. Finally, the decision-maker evaluates the average probability (the expectation) of these feelings of regret or joy in all states of the world.

When the Q function is linear of the form αx (with α being a strictly positive real number), then, by removing α from the sum sign and multiplying inequality by the inverse quantity, the regret theory coincides with Neumann and Morgenstern's (1944) theory of expected utility, of which it is a generalization.

As noted above, normative models adopt a strictly consequentialist perspective, so we will not go any further in their presentation. However, it seems useful to mention that other normative models derive from the expected utility to incorporate, not affects, but moral motivations. For Lopes (2005), these developments arise from the same desire, that of economists wanting "[…] to model an economic agent more in the image of themselves than of *Homo œconomicus*".

For this author, this will, however, remain constrained by the requirement of the consequentialist hypothesis of the economic doctrine, which constitutes a real "[…] straitjacket for all those who wish to improve the explanatory and normative capacity of their discipline without condemning themselves to ostracism".

This constraint demands that actions be judged according to their consequences and not on the value of the actions themselves, which excludes any form of strictly axiological rationality. Indeed, these different models ultimately consider that any action, even if guided by an altruistic motivation, has value for the decision-maker only if it increases their personal well-being, i.e. its utility.

2.2.3.3. *Empirical explanatory models*

2.2.3.3.1. The prospect theory

Two psychologists, Kahneman and Tversky (1979), challenged the descriptive nature of Neumann and Morgenstern's (1944) expected utility theory through a series of empirical experiments. On this basis, they proposed a descriptive model of risk, the "prospect theory", which was to have a lasting influence on subsequent work in the field of decision theory and is, today, still the reference alternative to rational choice theory.

In this theory, decision-makers make their choice in two stages; the first is an editing phase that allows them to analyze the perspectives offered to prepare the second, more classic stage: the evaluation. The first editing phase is unusual in the field of economic decision-making, as it leads to the possibility of a context effect that is difficult to formalize and is, moreover, abandoned by risky choice models that are an extension of the prospect theory.

This descriptive theory also differs from expected utility theory by integrating two functions defining subjective utility: a value function and a probability distortion function associated with events.

While in expected utility theory, the utility function is applied to the final wealth state, the value function (equivalent to the utility function) in prospect theory depends on the variation between an initial wealth state and a final wealth state. The value therefore depends on a reference point, for example, the initial wealth state of the decision-maker, and the gains or losses are no longer absolute, but relative. This reference point separates two areas: relative losses and relative gains. It should also be noted that this value function is asymmetrical with respect to this reference point. In the gain zone, its shape is concave, as is the utility function of the rational choice theory, which reflects risk aversion, whereas in the loss zone it is convex and steeper than in the gain zone, which is interpreted as risk-lover behavior, associated with loss aversion.

Note that in finance, initial wealth capitalized at the risk-free rate is generally used as a reference point rather than the *status quo* (Broihanne *et al.* 2004).

The probabilities of events are distorted by a weighting function representing the decision-maker's subjective assessment of the probabilities. This function overweights low-probability events and underweights high-probability events.

Finally, prospect theory can be summarized in two points: a payoff-framing effect accompanied by a subjective distortion of the events' probabilities. We specify that a second version of this theory, called "cumulative prospect theory", has been created by Tversky and Kahneman (1992) in order to integrate the work of Quiggin (1982); this second version transforms the cumulative probabilities and no longer simply the probabilities.

This theory marks a break in the risk decision theory, as it offers a descriptive alternative that provides explanations that are considered as satisfactory to phenomena considered as puzzles by the expected utility theory (such as the equity premium puzzle or the volatility puzzle). Moreover, according to Martinez (2012), it spreads the idea that recourse to the psychology of economic agents helps to better understand and explain their behavior, even if this dimension is rejected outside the scope of the dominant economic doctrine. Finally, it introduces laboratory experimentation as a central tool for understanding the decisions of economic agents.

2.2.3.3.2. The choosing-by-liking hypothesis

As Frederick (2002) explains, although the prototype choice heuristics use the deliberative process more extensively than the prototype judgment heuristics, there are situations in which the choice is guided by simple intuitive impressions. Daniel Kahnemann's choosing-by-liking heuristic is based on intuitive affective impressions; it is global and non-analytical. Its immediacy makes it an easy and inexpensive basis for choice. Bargh (1997) believes that all stimuli are evaluated as good or bad in a fraction of a second.

Kahneman and Frederick (2002) illustrate this shortcut with an experiment in which subjects were asked to immerse their hands in a bucket of water at a temperature of 15°C for 60 s and then, after a pause, the subjects repeated the operation but kept their hands in the water for an additional 30 s during which time the water was warmed by 1°C. Subjects were then asked to indicate the intensity of discomfort experienced during the two trials. Later, when asked to choose which trial they wished to repeat, a large majority of subjects chose the longer sequence. The authors attribute this surprising result to the use of the choosing-by-liking heuristic. Subjects simply followed the following choice strategy: "When choosing between two familiar options, consult your retrospective evaluations and choose the one you like most (or dislike least)".

Liking or disliking is a product of system 1, the intuitive, experience-based, affective decision-making system (Kahneman 2012). In the case of this experiment, system 2 (deliberative, analytical) did not play its role of *a posteriori* control, which testifies to its "casual" nature. We will come back to this dual decision-making system later.

Frederick notes that this heuristic may be quite appropriate if the characteristics that cause emotional impression are also those that determine satisfaction. Empirical experiments show that this heuristic is effective and often more accurate than analytical judgment. However, the choosing-by-liking heuristic can be flawed and misleading for the following reasons, among others:

– it is not sensitive to the quantitative dimension of detail;

– it may be unduly influenced by irrelevant transient contextual signals;

– it is excessively influenced by familiarity, whereas familiarity is not necessarily linked to pleasure.

As we have mentioned, the choosing-by-liking heuristic precedes the analytical evaluation; let us add that it can also dominate it, especially if the thinking time is short. Secondly, this decision base is an easy answer that avoids a cognitive cost. Thirdly, the result of this heuristic can act as a binding anchor for the analytical judgment. Finally, it constitutes a default result that the individual clings to if no other choice stands out significantly.

Shane also notes that this heuristic does not work in all circumstances. When the choice situation is too "dry", i.e. has no salient emotional element, such as when choosing an insurance policy, motor oil or, more generally, options with abstract attributes, then deliberation can operate independently.

2.2.3.3.3. The choice and the relative pleasure of consequences approach

Mellers (2000) argues that rational choice theory is not suited to accounting for common situations such as participation in gambling or the purchase of insurance policies. Indeed, a rational agent whose choices are based solely on maximizing expected utility should not choose either of these two options. The reasons for these behaviors should be sought elsewhere: enjoyment of gambling and peace of mind.

The author believes that it is necessary to return to the utility of early decision theorists like Bentham (1789) for whom this concept represented a balance between pleasure and pain. Thus, she defined an empirical criterion that integrates the anticipated pleasure of a choice as a function of three factors: gain, anticipated regret and surprise.

While prospect theory (Kahneman and Tversky 1979) is the first descriptive theory to introduce asymmetry in the perception of gains and losses around a *status quo* reference point, Loomes and Sudgen (1982) introduced another reference point: the consequence that would have occurred with another choice for a given state of the world. In the case where this consequence is more favorable with the alternative choice, the decision-maker anticipates a feeling of regret, whereas they anticipate a feeling of joy in the opposite case. Thus, the utility function is modified in such a way that it incorporates the anticipated feeling of regret or joy regarding the consequences of this second choice.

Inspired by this work, Mellers proposed a utility function integrating the anticipated feelings of regret or joy in relation to the two-by-two comparison of the consequences of choice A (within-option comparison), coupled with the anticipated feelings of regret or joy associated with the comparison of the consequences of choice A with those of choice B (across-option comparison). Contrary to the hypotheses posed *a priori* on the form of the regret function by the theorists of normative models, the author relies on experimentation data. Box 2.2 details a textbook case of the theory.

Let us consider a decision-maker facing two options (lotteries); the first allows for two consequences A and B (with the subjective probabilities, or beliefs, of realization S_A and S_B) and the second allows for two consequences C and D (with the beliefs of realization S_C and S_D).

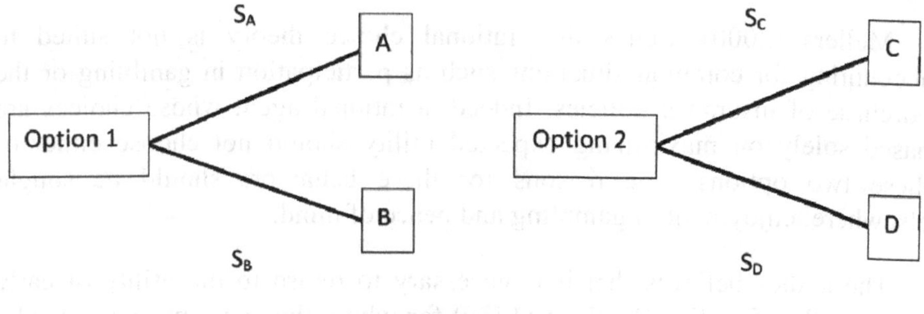

Figure 2.2. *Decision-maker's choice between two lotteries*

The following quantity expresses the pleasure anticipated by decision-makers imagining themselves choosing option 1 and anticipating that A would come true while, simultaneously, C would come true for option 2 in the same state of the future world:

$$R_{A(C)} = J[UA + d(UA, UB)(1 - S_A) + r(UA, UC)(1 - S_A)(1 - S_C)]$$

In this expression:

– *J* (for joy) is the anticipated pleasure function, it is linear;

– *UA*, *UB* and *UC* are the respective utilities of consequences A, B and C;

– *d*(*UA*, *UB*) is the within-option comparison function between the utilities of the two outcomes A and B. It is named d for "disappointment function";

– *r*(*UA*, *UC*) is the across-option comparison function;

– $(1 - S_A)$ is the surprise that A has come true; S_A is the belief (subjective probability) of the decision-maker that A has come true; it weights the disappointment *d*(*UA*, *UB*). Similarly, the joint surprise that A and C have come true (quantity $[1 - S_A]$ $[1 - S_C]$) weighs the regret *r*(*UA*, *UC*).

With this expression, it becomes possible to determine the expected pleasure for both options by a weighted average (by subjective probabilities) of the two-by-two comparisons of their consequences:

$$J(Option\ 1) = S_A S_D R_{A(D)} + S_A S_C R_{A(C)} + S_B S_D R_{B(D)} + S_B S_C R_{B(C)}$$

$$J(Option\ 2) = S_C S_A R_{C(A)} + S_C S_B R_{C(B)} + S_D S_A R_{D(A)} + S_D S_B R_{D(B)}$$

Ultimately, decision-makers choose the option (1 or 2) that maximizes their subjectively expected pleasure, i.e. that achieves max [*J*(*Option* 1), *J*(*Option* 2)].

Box 2.2. *Illustration of anticipated pleasure theory*

Mellers noted that this theory is a generalization of subjective expected utility theory. They are consistent when the comparison functions (disappointment and regret) are symmetric with respect to 0, but this is not consistent with the empirical evidence.

It should also be noted that the accuracy of the decision-maker's prediction of anticipated emotions becomes as important as their belief in the actualization of consequences.

Finally, according to Mellers, the strength of this theory lies in its power to explain surprising situations:

> Subjective expected pleasure theory can describe the fact that surprising smaller wins can be more pleasurable than expected larger ones, that a loss can feel like a win if an even larger loss was expected, and that a regrettable action can feel worse than a regrettable inaction if perceived control increases the subjective probability of the act.

2.2.3.3.4. The affect-as-information approach

For Clore *et al.* (2001), when, in the 1970s, the first research on the link between emotions, moods and judgment began, it was inspired by the traditional approach of the "judgment and decision" field, which advocates a multiattribute cognitive assessment. At the same time, early research on interpersonal attraction showed that it depended not only on the attributes of the person being judged but also on the physiological and emotional reactions of the evaluator to those attributes. Thus, contrary to the traditional perspective of decision theorists, Clore *et al.* proposed the affect-as-information approach, in which people make their judgments by asking themselves the following question: "What do I feel?"

It is an approach more than a theory, the principles of which are set out as follows:

– *the principle of experience*: subjective experience mediates between affective reactions and the cognitive consequences of affective reactions;

– *the information principle*: emotional feelings provide conscious information from unconscious assessments of situations. This principle is important because it means that emotional reactions are not only the results (output) but antecedents (input) in the chains of psychological processes. This is because affective reactions are the result of the cognitive assessment of the meaning of the situation (in accordance with the appraisal theory, presented below), so they convey the meaning of the situation both publicly, via facial expressions, but also privately, via feedback. This information (feedback), which is of an experiential nature, is then used to make judgments or decisions;

– *the principle of attribution*: the value of information and its cognitive consequences depend on the attribution or non-attribution of the affective experience to the object judged. As a corollary, emotional feelings influence concepts independently. Clore *et al.* noted that a misattribution toward an object, for example, an easily cognitively accessible object, is possible for moods;

– *the principle of immediacy*: affective feelings are reactions to the mental content of the moment. Furthermore, the influence of affect on the processing of information depends on the cognitive context in which the affective reaction is experienced. The effects may differ, for example, depending on whether one focuses on (1) objects in order to evaluate them, (2) tasks in order to perform them correctly or (3) the feelings themselves, in order to achieve satisfaction;

– *the principle of episodic constraint*: when their origin is not determined, affective reactions (moods) and brief cognitive perceptions have a similar effect and are governed by a similar process;

– *the principle of judgment* indicates that when one focuses on objects for the purpose of evaluating them, the positive or negative emotional response experienced, such as feelings of liking or disliking, can influence judgments and decisions;

– *the processing principle* states that when one is task-oriented, emotional reactions can generate a sense of confidence or doubt about cognitively accessible information, leading to a greater or lesser degree of trust in one's own beliefs, expectations and inclinations;

– *the principle of concentration levels*, also called cognitive tuning (Schwartz and Clore 2003), suggests that emotional feedback on goal-oriented efforts should also influence the overall and local focus of treatment, so that positive moods draw attention to overall aspects while negative aspects draw attention to local aspects of stimuli;

– *according to the principle of satisfaction*, positive or negative emotional reactions can be experienced as satisfaction or dissatisfaction, leading to greater or lesser persistence in an activity or task.

These different principles are found summarized in the affective judgment principle: "when one is object-focused, affective reactions may be experienced as liking or disliking, leading to higher or lower evaluation of that object of judgment."

Finally, it should be noted that the originality of the affect-as-information approach lies in the direct link that is made between affect and cognition, compared to the traditional approach that describes affect as influencing cognition through attention and memory.

2.2.3.3.5. The risk-as-feeling theory

For Loewenstein *et al.* (2001), most psychologists and economists interested in the question of choice in risky situations agree on the consequentialist hypothesis. This hypothesis postulates a choice based on the evaluation of the consequences of the alternatives involved. Rational choice theory (expected utility models and derived models) implements this hypothesis (see Figure 2.3). This is also the case for the models in the "judgment and decision-making" field, which incorporate anticipated emotions such as regret and disappointment (Loomes and Sudgen 1982; Mellers 2000).

In these models, which are also consequentialist, expected emotions are a component of the expected consequences of decisions as well as expected earnings (see Figure 2.4). These emotions are anticipated (anticipate emotions), or, in other words, they result from an assumed projection of emotions felt at the time of the consequences. They are therefore not emotions felt at the time of the choice.

In contrast, the risk-as-feeling theory introduces a new determinant for the choice of decision-makers: the emotions felt at the time of the choice (anticipatory emotions), immediate and visceral reactions such as fear, anxiety, dread, and so on. Figure 2.5 describes this model.

This theory differs from other emotional theories, also based on anticipatory emotions such as the affect-as-information hypothesis (Clore *et al.* 2001), the affect heuristic (Slovic *et al.* 2002) or the somatic marker hypothesis (Bechara and Damasio 2005), in the sense that contrary to the latter, emotional intuitions can diverge from cognitive calculation and are not necessarily an aid to decision-making. According to the authors, this last point is attested by a stream of literature in clinical psychology studying phobias and anxiety. However, one does not necessarily have to have a phobia for, for example, a fear of flying to impair judgment about the objectively infinitesimal risks of a crash. Risk-as-feeling theory therefore has the particularity of focusing on the divergence between emotional reactions and cognitive assessment. In other words, systems 1 (instinctive and emotional) and 2 (reflective and logical) of Kahneman (2012) are not necessarily complementary.

Also, this theory integrates two fields of literature. The first one describes the anticipatory emotion as information that assists decision-making. The second one describes the divergence between anticipatory emotion and cognitive assessment.

The importance of emotional reactions is also clarified, depending primarily on the vividness of the imagination (especially mental images), personal exposure or experience with the results, the conditioning of the decision-maker and situational factors such as the time horizon for realizing the consequences (Loewenstein 1987).

In support of their theory, Loewenstein *et al.* (2001) referred to the gender difference in risk-taking, which may be explained by the superior capacity of women, in comparison to men, to activate their mental imagery, but also to experience, on average, stronger emotions.

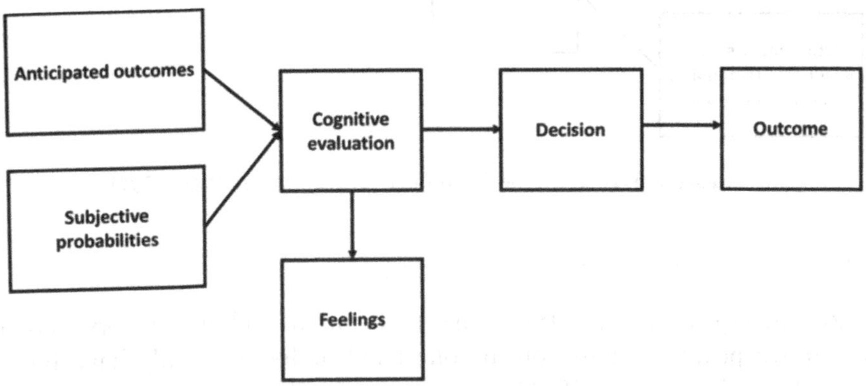

Figure 2.3. *Consequential models (Loewenstein* et al. *2001)*

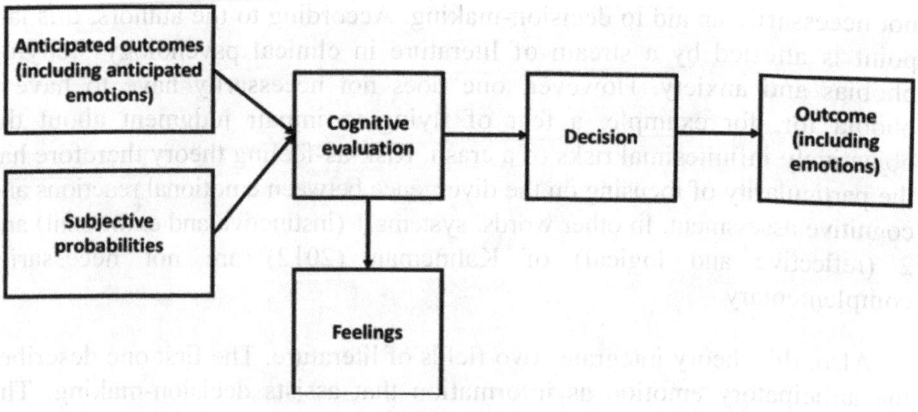

Figure 2.4. *Consequentialist models with anticipated emotions (Loewenstein* et al. *2001)*

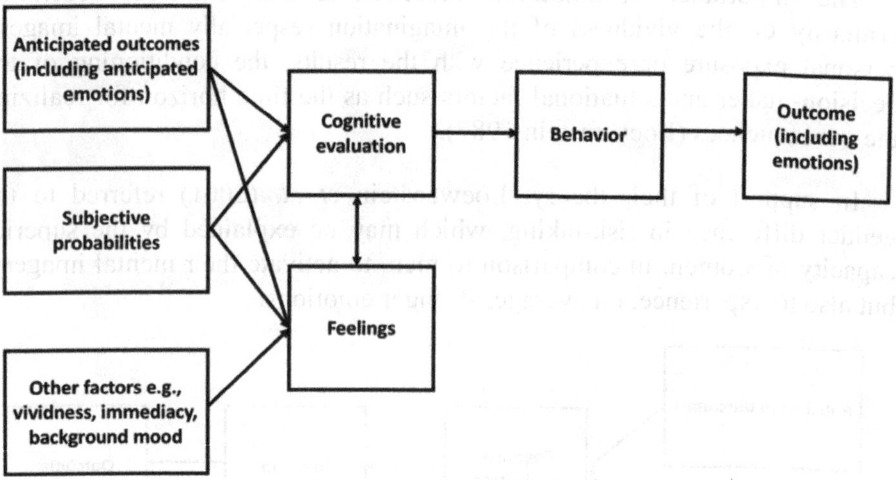

Figure 2.5. *Risk-as-feeling theory (Loewenstein* et al. *2001)*

2.2.3.3.6. Feeling-is-for-doing approach

Zeelenberg *et al.* (2008) argue that rational choice theory has no descriptive power because, on the one hand, individuals only have limited rationality (Simon 1955, 1956) and, on the other hand, studies show that the individual in a choice situation uses judgment heuristics that are less costly than an extensive comparative analysis. Moreover, limited rationality is assisted by emotions, whose function of focusing the decision-maker's attention on certain relevant options helps restrict the scope of the analysis. Beyond this focusing function, emotions are part of the decision-making process whether it is at the time of an important choice, when engaging in a meticulous analysis of weights, a source of negative emotions, or by anticipating the future outcome, a source of regret, disappointment, joy and surprise (Mellers 2000).

For the authors, the approach of emotions by simple valence, the "bipolar" dimension of pleasure/unpleasure, generally used by decision theorists, is not precise enough to account for the diversity of emotions and their consequences.

To consider, for example, that emotions of regret and disappointment are equivalent on the basis of a simple equal negative valence is a crude approach at odds with the empirical evidence. Indeed, research shows that these two distinct emotions lead to differentiated behaviors (Zeelenberg and Pieters 1999).

Also, the authors rely on Lazarus's (2001) theory of cognitive assessment (appraisal), a dominant theory in the field of emotion psychology that describes the specific emotions aroused by situational stimuli. These specific emotions are related to the singularity of problems that also require specific behaviors/responses; this first point is central to this approach.

The second key point is the feeling-is-for-doing approach, which focuses on the future and the motivational dimension of emotions. It explains how emotions are the instrument for achieving the goals that the subject has set. It provides the decision-maker with clear guidelines on how to achieve his or her goals (e.g. in case of danger: "I better climb this tree!"). Thus, this theory differs from informational, past-oriented approaches that report the feedback sent by emotions on the progress of a goal (with the same example: "I am not safe yet!"). Emotions are generated when an event or outcome is relevant to an individual's preferences; they prioritize behaviors and actions. Emotions act as a program for an intuitive decision that directs the decision-maker toward the most appropriate actions in a given situation to achieve his or her goals.

In synthesis, the feeling-is-for-doing approach, inspired by pragmatist philosophy, can be summed up in five points:

1) the emotional system is the primary motivational system for goal-oriented behavior;

2) each specific emotion serves as a distinct motivational function in the pursuit of objectives;

3) these motivational functions cannot be reduced to the overall valence of specific emotions;

4) the distinct motivational functions are rooted in the experiential quality of specific emotions;

5) emotions can be either endogenous or exogenous in relation to the process of achieving the objective, their effect on behavior is contingent on their perceived relevance to the objective.

2.2.3.3.7. Affect heuristics

Originally, affect heuristics arose from work done for the nuclear industry in the United States. The industry had commissioned a series of research studies to understand the gap in risk perception related to this activity between the general public and experts. While the general public considered the risk to be high, the experts assessed it as objectively low. These studies revealed a relationship between the perception of a high level of risk and any danger evoking fear. A second surprising result indicated that judgments about risks and benefits were negatively correlated (Lichtenstein *et al.* 1978). For example, the nuclear industry evokes nuclear weapons, which leads to fear and reduces the perception of the benefit of civilian nuclear power. Conversely, activities related to technologies deemed useful such as X-rays see their risk being undervalued.

The affect heuristic is first of all a heuristic, a quick mental operation that is essentially unconscious, intuitive and independent of any cognitive assessment, which serves as a shortcut for judgments. When certain conditions are met, as described below, individuals use their emotional feelings to judge the benefits and risks of an object without relying on cognitive reasoning. Thus, this heuristic can be used for judgments aimed at establishing a benefit/risk balance.

We make a first proposal (proposal 2.1) for our theoretical framework.

PROPOSAL 2.1.– The affect heuristic is the result of an emotional feeling, i.e. an affective reaction.

The main effect of the affect heuristic is to condition preferences without the causes of the affective reaction necessarily being determined or conscious.

According to Slovic *et al.* (2002), this heuristic can be explained by a system of representations of lived events. Mental images are labeled by the affective valence of the events; the sum of these life experiences constitutes a data bank that can be used by the individual facing a judgment or decision situation. The retrieval of the emotional label associated with the situation-related representation then serves as an informational signal and gives immediate guidance to the judgment or decision. Let us note with the author that this explanation is very close to the hypothesis of the somatic markers of Bechara and Damasio (2005) mentioned in section 2.2.3.3.8.

The affect heuristic is sensitive to the following conditions:

1) *the context of the decision is risky*: the affect heuristic is relevant to account for choice situations that can be analyzed from a benefit/risk perspective;

2) *the decision-making context integrates images or videos*: Slovic *et al.* (1991) identified several studies establishing a correlation between images, affect and decision-making;

3) *the time horizon of the consequences of the decision is long*: according to Slovic (2001), the longer the consequences are distant, the lower the perceived level of risk;

4) *the consequences are emotionally charged*: Loewenstein *et al.* (2001) showed that events with strong emotional significance (winning the lottery, being warned of a serious illness, etc.) alter judgment; individuals reason more in terms of possibilities and overestimate the subjective probabilities of events with minimal real probabilities.

It should be noted at the outset that equity crowdfunding investment meets these conditions. Indeed, it is a risky investment since the capital is not guaranteed, the collection campaign pages include images and a video pitch of the entrepreneurs, the horizon of the consequences is distant (the exit delays are in the interval of five to eight years) and the consequences are emotionally charged because, in a way analogous to lottery games, the gains are potentially very high.

As mentioned, studies have shown a strong relationship between images, emotional responses and decision-making. For example, Slovic *et al.* (1991) showed that the affective evaluation of spontaneous images associated with several cities is a good predictor of the preference of the test subjects. More broadly, certain methods of presenting information favor affective reactions and, consequently, the affect heuristic. Hendrickx *et al.* (1989) showed experimentally that warnings in the form of scenarios or anecdotes loaded with affect are more impactful than cold information like relative frequency of damage. Crowdfunding equity platforms systematically insert photos and narrative videos into campaign pages; in doing so, they elicit emotional reactions from the investor.

Another effect of the affect heuristic can be transposed to equity crowdfunding investment. When, in a situation of uncertainty, the consequences of a choice carry a significant affective load, then the associated probabilities are no longer decisive for decision-making. For example, Loewenstein *et al.* (2001) show that lottery players are indifferent to a winning probability of one chance in 10,000 thousand or one chance in 10 million. In a situation of uncertainty, players seem to reason in terms of binary possibility rather than probability. With equity crowdfunding, it is also possible to make big winnings if one bets on the next "unicorn". An investor who would have subscribed for 10,000 dollars in the Uber startup in 2010 would have seen his or her shares valued at 127,000,000 dollars in October 2015[1].

Finally, let us note with Slovic that this heuristic leads to two risks:

– A danger of manipulation of attitudes: the work of Finucane *et al.* (2000) shows that cigarette companies' advertisements improve the image and emotional appreciation associated with smoking and decrease the perception of the associated risk. These advertisements have an insidious persuasive effect that exceeds rational warnings from physicians. It is interesting to note that the marketing field proposes a related behavioral heuristic called affect-referral heuristic, whose mechanism is as follows: the

1 See: http://www.crowdfundinsider.com/2015/10/76123-how-much-money-would-you-be-worth-if-you-had-invested-in-uber-on-angellist/.

emotional memories associated with a product influence subsequent choices related to it (Wright 1975; Pham 1998).

– A second danger lies in the error inherent in the affect itself: the experiential system is subject to natural biases outside of manipulation. This is the case, for example, when the consequences of the assessment are remote or visceral in nature, as the irrational behavior of smokers provides a clear example (Slovic 2001).

2.2.3.3.8. The somatic marker hypothesis

Damasio (2006), a neurobiologist who studies the neural bases of cognition and behavior, argues that the somatic marker hypothesis challenges modern economic theory because it ignores the role of emotions in decision-making and judgment. The results of Damasio, Bechara and others are used in numerous works, particularly in psychology, as a basis for the link between emotions and behavior.

Somatic markers are synonymous with emotions, and are defined as physiological reactions, a collection of changes in body and brain states, triggered by a dedicated system in the brain that responds to the contents of perceptions, real or remembered, about a particular object or event (Bechara and Damasio 2005). Thus, memory and imagination generate somatic markers when associated events have a strong emotional value, such as a past encounter with a snake or a significant financial loss.

According to this hypothesis, in situations of uncertainty, people often base their judgments on intuition, visceral feelings and subjective assessments of the consequences that engage the neural circuit.

Moreover, knowledge and reasoning alone are generally not sufficient to make advantageous choices, emotion is beneficial to decision-making when it is part of the task, but can be harmful when it is not related to the task.

The somatic marker hypothesis thus demonstrates the complementarity of emotions to assist the cognitive reasoning process.

This theory comes from the observation of patients who have suffered damage to the ventromedial cortex region of the frontal lobe, leaving their intelligence, memory and logical capacity intact, but altering their ability to associate emotions and emotional feelings with the anticipated consequences of their actions. Observation of these patients led Damasio *et al.* (1990) to associate these brain lesions with a form of sociopathy which, in addition to “abnormal social behavior”, prevents patients from making rational decisions, i.e. to their advantage. The somatic marker hypothesis is then put forward; it attributes this inability to make advantageous choices in daily life to the dysfunction of the emotional mechanism whose role is to send immediate signals about the anticipated consequences of actions and to assist in the selection of advantageous options. Without this mechanism, patients rely on a cost–benefit analysis of options, which slows the speed of deliberation but also degrades the accuracy of the choices made.

To support these observations, Bechara *et al.* (1994, 1999) conducted several experimental studies of the “casino game” kind (which has since been called the Iowa gambling task) consisting of testing the results of two groups of subjects (normal control patients and patients with disabilities in the amygdala or the ventromedial cortex) who had to select a series of cards from several heaps with variable probabilities of gains and losses, with these gains and losses also being of variable amounts. The skin conductance (physiological measure) recorded during the game showed that, at the beginning of the experiment, the responses of patients in both groups were similar in terms of gains (reward) and losses (punishment). Thereafter, the results diverge. After a few trials, the control patients developed an electrodermal anticipatory reaction even before the selection of cards from the different packs. This reaction is of a greater amplitude for risky piles than for safer piles. However, it is not perceptible in patients with disabilities who have become myopic about the future and unable to learn from experience. In short, the cortex helps to make rational decisions, knowledge alone is not enough and unconscious emotional anticipatory signals activated and derived from previous experiences of reward and punishment deter the average subject from making disadvantageous choices.

In line with this hypothesis, Camerer *et al.* (2005) argue that, following the contributions of psychology to economics and the resulting emergence of behavioral finance, neuroscience can help the discipline take a new step forward through the observational possibilities of the “black box” that the human brain used to be viewed as. These contributions should help to understand the gaps between the prediction of rational choice theory and actual observed behavior. They propose a reading grid common to behavioral economics and neuroscience. This grid has two entries: function (cognitive or emotional) and processes (controlled or automatic). Figure 2.6

shows a quadrant, the first of which (quadrant I) corresponds to the scope of rational economic choice theory, which is concerned only with consciously controlled cognitive decisions. However, the work in neuroscience, and thus that of Damasio and his collaborators, highlights the interplay between conscious and automatic neuro-renal systems for reasoned choices inseparable from the affective content that accompanies the expectations of the outcome associated with the choice. Thus, a fine understanding of the mechanisms of decision-making requires the study of the entire quadrant by interdisciplinary research programs mixing economists and neuroscientists.

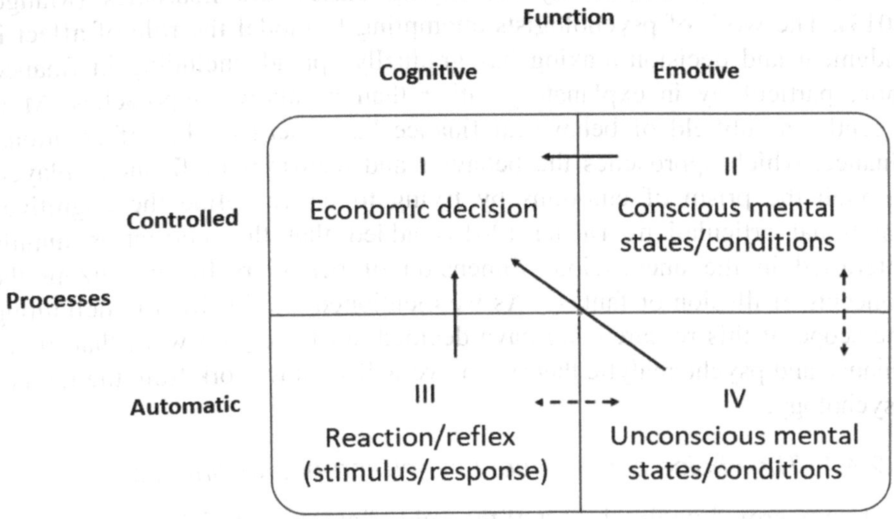

Figure 2.6. *The two dimensions of neuronal functioning (Schmidt 2010) based on Camerer* et al. *(2005)*

2.2.4. *Affects in finance*

Bessière and Stéphany (2015) estimated that in equity crowdfunding: "given the information mobilized, the evaluation of the project carried out by the crowd is of a rather intuitive, even affective nature, possibly reinforced by certain knowledge or beliefs about the sector of activity."

Attributing an effect to the affect during the financial decision-making process of economic agents was still unthinkable a few decades ago. In finance, especially in capital market literature, the instrumental rationality of *homo œconomicus*, the cold and omniscient calculator of neoclassical economics, was, until the end of the last century, the unsurpassable credo of all modeling. The exclusion of affects from this theoretical framework can be explained in part by a concern for the simplification necessary for formalization, but even more so because these are financial and not sentimental issues. However, the empirical results of researchers from the field of psychology will undermine the certainties about the explanatory power of the expected utility theory, but will also open a new path, that of behavioral finance. Historically, this field of research first focused on better understanding the cognitive dimension of individuals' reasoning, judgments and decisions by empirically identifying biases and heuristics (Mangot 2013). The work of psychologists attempting to model the role of affect in judgment and decision-making has gradually spread, including in finance, more particularly in explanatory rather than normative approaches. More recently, a subfield of behavioral finance has emerged, that of emotional finance, which approaches the behavior and decisions of financial players through the prism of emotions by trying to better define the cognitive–emotional articulation. Taffler (2014) added that this current is mainly interested in the unconscious dimension of behaviors by mobilizing the concepts of illusion or fantasy. As we mentioned and justified in delimiting the scope of this research, we have decided not to rely on work that mixes finance and psychoanalytic theory; so, we will stick to work from the field of psychology.

2.2.4.1. *The choice of investment in entrepreneurial finance*

Equity crowdfunding is part of the field of entrepreneurial finance, one of the themes of which concerns the choice of investors and, more specifically, the selection criteria of business angels and venture capitalists. In this context, a concept, "intuitive decision-making" (IDM) is of particular interest to us because it is based on affects. We then discuss two other concepts, emotional contagion and persuasion, recently proposed in the context of crowdfunding, to explain investor behavior.

2.2.4.1.1. IDM in BA and VC

The traditional seed capital players (BA, venture capitalists and seed funds) are intended to finance seed stage companies that have not found their financial equilibrium. Startups raising funds are by definition young and innovative; they have a common feature for the investor: the extent of uncertainty about their future profitability or even their survival.

Let us note with Bessière and Stéphany (2015) that equity crowdfunding, a newcomer in the seed capital universe, faces the same problem: the limited information available does not allow one to analyze the profitability-risk ratio on the basis of objective probabilities.

Seed capital players are therefore committed to reducing uncertainty, but cannot rely solely on statistical risk analysis tools. The study of the business plan offers an idealized vision of the future, but few quantifiable elements on the history of the trajectory allow for extrapolation and even so, the future is not strictly definable from the past because the world marches forwards – it is not stationary. The analogical method thus finds its limits with startups proposing breakthrough innovations for which there is no benchmark.

Mason and Stark (2004) looked at the selection criteria for seed capital. They distinguished between venture capitalists and business angels whose objectives do not fully overlap. Venture capitalists are exclusively oriented toward a financial profit objective, while business angels also expect a psychological return in the form of pleasure. Moreover, their approach to risk is different, with venture capitalists being more sensitive to market risk while business angels fear agency risk.

These differences are reflected in their respective selection criteria. In particular, business angels place less emphasis on financial projections and value the affinity they can build with executives.

Despite these differences, one common point remains: the financial information available for startup companies is not a significant criterion for discrimination in the initial screening phase. However, it will become important at later stages of the decision-making process. Also, studies (Wright and Robbie 1996; Mason and Stark 2004; Murnieks *et al.* 2015) show the importance of the subjective nature of selection (degree of involvement of entrepreneurs, potential, personality, etc.).

In venture capital, Manigart *et al.* (1997) and Dubocage (2006) found that the use of real options by professionals remains limited. In practice, valuation is subjective, relying on the experience of investors if they are competent, or on mimetic behavior if they lack expertise. The subjective opinion is based on an interpretative logic of signals (patents, alliances, etc.)

that testify to the quality of the company. Note that BAs are less interested in profitability and financial data than VCs and seem to base their decisions more on subjective opinion and intuition (Mason and Stark 2004). Also, Ola (2016) shows that the investment decision is the result of intuitive judgment. Intuition is said to be the key determinant of judgment in situations of uncertainty.

Dane and Pratt (2007) define intuition as "affectively charged judgments that arise through rapid, nonconscious, and holistic associations". It is distinct from reasoning, which is the alternative way of solving problems (Kahneman 2003).

This opposition between analytical and intuitive approaches to decision-making is the subject of a contradictory debate between Henry Mintzberg and Herbert Simon. The former defends the idea of an intuition whose nature does not allow for programming, while for the latter, the very essence of this concept rests on the organization of knowledge for rapid identification (Coget *et al.* 2009).

It should be noted that the precise concept we are interested in is IDM rather than intuition as such. Although the debates around IDM have not yet led to a unified theory, it is possible to extract the cardinal characteristics that are agreed upon: IDM (1) is the result of a quasi-conscious immediate activity; (2) is based on a holistic process and proceeds via associations; (3) provides the feeling of knowing without knowing why; and (4) is based on the past experience and emotional data of the subject.

Past experience as a determinant of IDM is a consensus among researchers (Burke and Miller 1999; Hogarth 2001). In equity crowdfunding, it is not uncommon for the investor to have experience in the industry of the company being supported. This knowledge can provide insights that can guide judgment and decision-making.

Moreover, when through long training, experience leads to expertise (a virtuoso musician, a chess champion, etc.), IDM can become a powerful and accurate tool (Simon 1987; Shapiro and Spence 1997).

Kahneman (2003) provided an explanation for IDMs with the concept of accessibility, which can be defined as the ease of retrieving stored information and would result from several mechanisms involving associative memory. Stereotypes and prototypes are good examples of the use of associative memory because their attributes are naturally accessible. One can imagine that a BA solicited by a Fintech working in the field of artificial intelligence will immediately have in mind characteristics such as high potential, patent, research and development, and so on, associated with the prototype of this category of startup.

The emotional dimension of IDM is also supported by the scientific community (Kahneman 2003; Sadler-Smith and Shefy 2004; Sinclair and Ashkanasy 2005; Dane and Pratt 2007). Thus, the ECF investor may feel concerned by a project whose product is linked to the memory of emotionally charged events.

2.2.4.1.2. Emotional contagion and persuasion through crowdfunding

Hatfield *et al.* (1993) defined emotional contagion as an automatic tendency to imitate and synchronize one's expressions, vocalizations, postures and movements with those of others. When synchronization is effective, individuals are able to feel each other's emotions.

The article by Li *et al.* (2017) uses this concept and associates it with the elaboration likelihood model (ELM) by Petty and Cacioppo (1984, 1986) to explain the choice of investors in crowdfunding.

The ELM postulates that when an individual is subjected to persuasive action, then if he or she has little motivation or ability to evaluate the arguments of persuasive speech, he or she will be influenced by irrelevant signals such as positive or negative affects, appearance, tone, and voice of the speaker. Conversely, if the individual is motivated, competent and can evaluate the argument, then he or she will focus on the relevant information to make a judgment.

By articulating ELM and emotional contagion, Li and his team showed that the passion of entrepreneurs, perceptible in pitch videos, arouses the enthusiasm of potential investors. They also established a causal link between the intensity of the passion emanating from the videos and the amounts collected.

Thus, while Mollick (2013) had already noted the importance of videos to the success of campaigns, Li *et al.* (2017) offer more refined insights into this causal link.

The study by Allison *et al.* (2017) also uses the ELM persuasion model. Their results suggest that relevant information like entrepreneur education matters more when investors have a good evaluation capacity and motivation for careful selection. However, irrelevant signals such as the influence of a group identity have a stronger influence among the most inexperienced investors and for small fundraising efforts.

Finally, emotional contagion through narrative and emotional tone was studied by Wuillaume *et al.* (2017) in the context of crowdfunding by donation, reward-based, loan and equity investment. Their research indicates greater participation for campaigns with emotionally charged narratives. However, this phenomenon is less noticeable for crowdlending and equity crowdfunding.

2.2.4.2. *Affective states in capital market literature*

Entrepreneurial finance is part of the capital family investment; however, this form of investment differs in many aspects from traditional finance (Desbrières 2001): limited accounting information, illiquidity, interventionism, profitability objectives, etc. (Desbrières 2001). Despite these specificities, the seed capital investor faces the same fundamental problems as the market investor: information asymmetry and agency problems. They are also confronted with them more acutely (Pare and Rédis 2011). Moreover, the situation of the equity crowdfunding investor presents similarities with that of individual investors in financial markets: they operate via a digital platform that offers them, at a given moment, a choice of selection between several securities and can generally follow the behavior of other investors. For this reason, we believe it is relevant to focus on the interaction of affects with the choices of investors in financial markets, as these results are potentially transposable to the issue of our research.

We choose to present emotions as a determinant of choice rather than moods, although the effect of moods has been proven in financial markets (Mangot 2008), as moods are not specific to a given firm (see Box 2.3). While we have already discussed the affect heuristic in the general framework of judgment and decision-making, we return here to a few studies that have tested this hypothesis in the context of capital market literature.

Moods are emotional dispositions of low intensity, felt in a diffuse way and which form a backdrop of positive or negative tonality. Unlike emotions, they are not object oriented (Derbaix and Filser 2011). A good mood (GM) makes one optimistic, biases the evaluation of past events, seen in a more positive light, and encourages risk-taking. A series of empirical studies has thus shown the role of weather and timing when it comes to the returns observed on financial markets (Broihanne *et al.* 2004).

The mood of the investor preparing to select a company on a crowdfunding equity platform is not, by nature, object oriented, but pre-exists and persists throughout the evaluation period of the various competing projects.

Let us take the case of investors in a GM; they will maintain their GM during the valuation period of companies A and B. Conversely, emotions are directed toward and triggered by an object. Thus, company A can trigger the emotion EMO(A) and company B EMO(B). Therefore, these investors will successively feel the affective states GM + EMO(A) when valuing company A and then GM + EMO(B) when valuing company B. Since GMs' GM is not specific to the object of attention, it is common to both valuations; in this sense, it does not have a discriminating role in the choice between companies A and B.

However, GM can influence investors' behavior whether they choose A or B, since they may invest more that day in A or B than if they had been in a bad mood (BM), in which case their experience of emotional states associated with the valuation of the two companies would have been BM + EMO(A) and then BM + EMO(B).

Our research focus is on understanding the investment choice, i.e. the selection and not the decision to invest, regardless of the project chosen, which is why we do not use moods as a determinant of choice.

Box 2.3. *Separate consideration of moods and emotions in understanding investment choice*

2.2.4.2.1. Investor emotions

According to Dantzer (2010), emotions, which are fleeting and vivid emotional reactions to an external or internal event, are accompanied by physiological and somatic changes. Considered useful for survival since

Darwin (1972), they influence our perceptions and partly determine our behaviors.

In his bestseller, *Irrational Exuberance*, on the eve of the stock market crash of 2001, Shiller (2000) warned against the American stock market, which he believed had been transformed into a veritable stock market bubble. To justify the overvaluation of this market, Shiller then cited the combined effect of the indifference of millions of people who were not interested in the long-term values of firms, but were more driven by their emotions, their arbitrary attention and their belief in a certain popular wisdom.

Emotions affect not only individual investors, but also professionals. The work of Lo and Repin (2002) demonstrated the role of emotions in the decision-making process of professional traders. In their study, they set up a protocol for measuring physiological data (electrodermal activity, blood volume, heart rate, etc.) of active traders while collecting price data in real time to detect market events. Their results showed that emotional responses are a significant factor in the financial risks evaluated in real time, as the captured physiological variables change significantly with market events.

Drawing on the work of Weiner and Graham (1989), Mangot (2008) developed a matrix of correspondences between events, consequences, emotions aroused and reactions triggered in stock markets. For example, the pride felt following the positive outcome of an investment strategy will lead to a response of the "return" translated by "risk-taking" action on the stock markets.

Regret and pride are used in capital market literature by Shefrin and Statman (1985) to explain the disposition effect, i.e. the tendency of investors to sell securities that have risen in value too early and to hold on to securities that have fallen in value for too long. The work of Khaneman, Tversky and Thaler demonstrates an asymmetry between pride and regret (regret is stronger) which explains the tendency for investors to take no action.

Another emotion, pleasure, was the subject of work by Kumar (2009). In the context of gambling, the researcher established correlations between the decisions of individual investors and their propensity to gamble, thus reinforcing Statman's (2002) comparison between traders and lottery players.

This dimension of pleasure felt during the investment selection phase can be related to the subject of "experiential marketing", which can be defined as the study of the consumer's experience prior to the act of purchase. Indeed, marketing distinguishes the benefits that the individual derives from the objective attributes of a good or service from the benefits attributable to the purchasing experience itself (Filser 2015). It should be noted that while we integrate certain marketing concepts into our research, we have chosen not to discuss the concept of experiential marketing in greater detail for the same reason that we do not retain information on the subject of moods in finance: while experiential marketing can improve the understanding of the phenomenon of time spent on equity crowdfunding platforms, or even the domination of this or that platform on the market by virtue of its ergonomics, it does not shed light on the selection of projects. Nevertheless, we will come back to the affective experience, more precisely the affective reaction felt when choosing a given project.

2.2.4.2.2. The affect heuristic

While we have already presented the affect heuristic in the general context of judgment and decision-making, we believe it is useful to look at the results of research specific to the field of finance. Indeed, the affect heuristic is easily transposable to finance because, as we have already mentioned, one of its consequences is expressed almost in financial terms. This is the inversion of the correlation between risk and perceived benefits (Lichtenstein *et al.* 1978): the risk is considered low and the benefits high for a favorably appreciated object, whereas the relationship is reversed for an object that is not appreciated. This result contradicts normative financial theory, which positively correlates risk and profits.

Moreover, according to Bessière and Stéphany (2014, 2015), this concept is clearly suitable for understanding equity crowdfunding behavior because the necessary conditions are met for an intuitive and affective evaluation: the majority of investors are not experts. They evaluate the project on the basis of little detailed and market-oriented information rather than financial data; their decision is made under time pressure, which favors judgment and affective evaluation (Finucane *et al.* 2000).

In terms of empirical results, two studies demonstrate the importance of familiarity that one has with a title, i.e. the level of knowledge one has of it, for its evaluation.

For example, Wang *et al.* (2011) showed that an individual's perception of the risk of a financial asset depends heavily on knowledge of that asset and weakly on objective measures of risk. This result is also found among professionals.

Ganzach's (2000) study shows that financial analysts' familiarity with assets distorts their perception of the profitability–risk ratio. When securities are familiar to them, risk is perceived as low and expected profitability is high; conversely, securities of unknown companies see their risk overvalued and their profitability undervalued. These effects can be explained by the affect heuristic and the mediation of the close link between familiarity and affects, already mentioned and attributable to Zajonc's (1968) hypothesis of mere exposure.

Second, several studies focusing on the image that investors have of certain assets or certain industries show that this image can influence their judgment and ultimately their choice of asset allocation. Let us recall that Slovic *et al.* (2002) closely linked images and affect heuristics: "several empirical studies have demonstrated a strong relationship between imagery, affect and decision-making."

Ackert and Church (2006) conducted three experiments with individual investors to assess the influence of information that has a positive or negative effect on the image of several companies without this information being relevant to their valuation. The findings indicate that participants invested significantly larger amounts in companies with a better image.

In similar work, MacGregor *et al.* (2000) conducted an experiment with students enrolled in a bank finance program and subjected to a protocol in which they had to associate images or ideas with several industry sectors to be evaluated emotionally afterwards. In a second step, subjects were asked to quantify the likelihood of their choice of investments in different companies belonging to these industries in the context of an IPO. The results show a correlation between the valence of the images, the affective evaluation of industrial sectors and the likelihood of investing in companies belonging to these industrial sectors.

Fehle *et al.* (2005) provided indirect support for the relevance of the use of the affect heuristic in finance by linking advertisements and returns on listed securities. Specifically, they uncovered abnormal positive returns for companies that promoted their image (and not that of their products) in at least two commercials during 19 Super Bowl appearances, with this result measured in the days following the advertisements. The influence of advertising screens on the purchase of securities was more relevant to individual investors, who were more sensitive to this phenomenon.

The study by Barber *et al.* (2003) also supports this work, showing that individual investors concentrate 56% of their share purchases in the top 30% of the most admired companies.

Finally, more recently, Aspara and Tikkanen (2011) conducted a study on the effect of the emotional attitude of 400 real investors on their motivation to invest. Their conclusion reveals that most of these investors have a propensity to invest beyond the indication of the risk/return trade-off, i.e. consciously accepting a lower return or a higher risk than those incurred with other, more efficient securities that can be explained by an affect. The more positive an individual's attitude toward the company, the stronger his or her motivation to invest, over and above traditional financial considerations.

2.2.5. *Emotional aspects of consumer purchasing behavior*

One of the most prolific fields of marketing research is concerned with consumer buying behavior. The grid for analyzing consumer behavior has been considerably enriched since Zajonc's seminal book (1980) with the integration of affective states, in particular emotions, as explanatory factors, alongside the cognitive processes of information processing that previously prevailed. While a cognitivist approach – positioning the cognitive dimension as the antecedent of the affective dimension – initially dominated modeling, a trend, initiated by the work of Derbaix, on the mechanisms of action of advertising messages on purchasing behavior, made it possible to free the affective from the cognitive to make it the autonomous inducer of intentions and behavior (Filser 2015).

In terms of equity crowdfunding, it should be noted from the outset that several studies have already highlighted the marketing dimension of investor behavior. In their work, Gerber and Hui (2013) refer to consumer theory as an appropriate benchmark for analyzing the motivations of crowdfunding actors. For the authors, investor motivations are the result of affective processing of perceived information, well described by psychological and marketing research.

In support of this, Bessière and Stéphany (2014) concluded that the behavior of some investors is no more driven by a financial deliberation. The latter would be driven by a marketing logic oriented toward consumers rather than shareholders, due to a limited public information base and a lack of financial expertise.

Equity crowdfunding seems to meet the conditions identified by marketing research, defining the necessary prerequisites for consumer behavior to be based on affective reactions.

Cohen *et al.* (2008), in a synthesis work, listed the following four conditions:

1) consumers' motivation to process information is low: the amounts invested are sometimes modest, even limited to a few euros (Hornuf and Schwienbacher 2015b);

2) they are distracted, cognitively constrained, or under time pressure: the crowd is generally made up of non-professional investors who have limited time to analyze entrepreneurial project files (Bessière and Stéphany 2014). In their study of real investors from the Swedish platform, FundedByMe, Skoglund and Stiernblad (2013) revealed that 72% of the 390 equity crowdfunding investors spent less than 10 minutes on pre-investment analysis;

3) other evaluation bases are ambiguous: the information available on the platform is most often fragmented and limited to descriptive documents of the business model (Bessière and Stéphany 2015);

4) they lack expertise in the field: it is essentially a non-expert crowd (Bessière and Stéphany 2014).

Below, we introduce three marketing concepts that have been selected to inform the choices of equity crowdfunding investors: persuasive advertising, the halo effect and the means-end chain model.

2.2.5.1. *Persuasive advertising: a push effect*

Participating in an equity crowdfunding campaign requires a significant amount of preparation work, prior to fundraising. Various elements need to be designed in order to optimize the chances of success of the project's communication plan. A campaign page includes a description, a possible storyboard and a video of the entrepreneurs' pitch.

For project leaders and platforms alike, the use of these marketing and communication tools is the main lever for attracting investors. Professionals in the sector are perfectly aware of this, since the platforms most often offer a support service aimed at perfecting company campaigns. In addition, many marketing and communication consultancies have diversified or even dedicated their activity to the realization or support of startups considering the use of crowdfunding.

O'Keefe (2002) defined persuasion as "[...] a successful intentional effort at influencing another's mental state through communication in a circumstance in which the persuadee has some measure of freedom."

In light of this definition, it is clear that the crowdfunding industry is engaged in the business of active crowd persuasion, which is why we call this voluntary approach a push effect – the prospect is "pushed" to invest through persuasive digital communication.

As mentioned above, several recent crowdfunding studies have used Petty and Cacioppo's (1984, 1986) "elaboration likelihood model" of persuasion to explain the choices made by investors. Although adapted to the purpose of our research, we choose instead to focus on the "persuasive advertising" model from the field of affective consumer purchasing behavior. Indeed, as Mollick (2013) noted, videos are a key determinant of the success of fundraising campaigns. However, the pitch videos of entrepreneurs are actually, in and of themselves, advertisements with persuasive arguments. Moreover, the model of persuasive advertising corresponds perfectly to our problem, since it distinguishes two causal paths of persuasion: one cognitive and the other affective. Moreover, Li *et al.* (2017) combined the ELM with the concept of emotional contagion to study the persuasive effect of video pitches, because the affective dimension is not central to the ELM; conversely, it is in the models of "persuasive advertising". For these reasons, we believe that the "persuasive advertising" model is an excellent framework for understanding the behavior of equity crowdfunding investors.

Beyond the specific context of pitch videos of crowdfunding campaign pages, video sequences are known to be powerful emotional drivers

(Gil 2009). Their influence on affective reactions has been demonstrated through work in marketing, notably that of Graillot (1996), which highlights consumers' favorable attitude towards travel destinations for which they had previously viewed a promotional video.

Persuasive advertising is the field of marketing concerned with the consequences of advertising screens on consumer attitudes, toward the brand and the advertisement.

Historically, models of persuasive advertising were derived from a strictly cognitive model in which exposure to the adverts triggered a chain reaction on indicators of belief and then attitude toward the brand. This model evolved due to the addition of a new construct, the attitude towards the advertisement itself, which becomes an antecedent of the attitude toward the brand. Researchers then integrated the affective reactions elicited by commercials (AREC) and agreed on their explanatory effect, both of the attitude toward the advertisement, but also of the attitude toward the brand (Derbaix and Filser 2011). Although many developments have taken place since then, adding constructs and causal links, we choose to remain with the original model of persuasive advertising (see Figure 2.7), which seems suitable to us for transposition to equity crowdfunding.

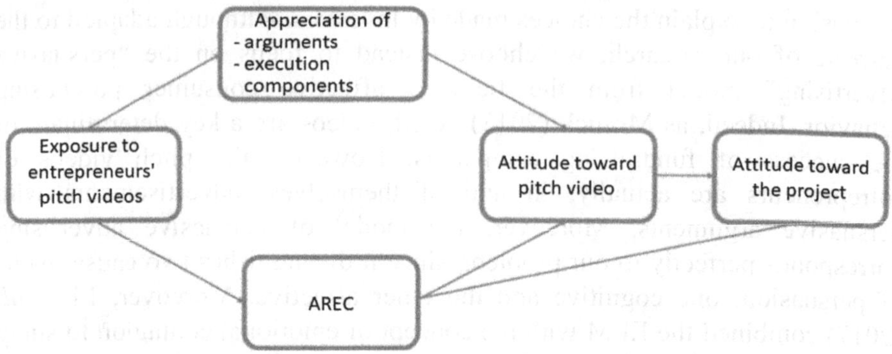

Figure 2.7. *Adaptation of the persuasive advertising model to the context of crowdfunding. Source: Adapted from Derbaix and Filser (2011)*

Funded companies are mostly in the seed phase, their brand name is rarely known to the general public. For this reason, we have replaced the brand attitude construct with the project attitude construct.

In his book on psychosociology, Mucchielli (2005) considered that models of persuasive advertising rightly attribute an important role to emotions in understanding consumers' purchasing behavior, but without going into the mechanisms that trigger these emotions. According to the author, the purpose of the communicated message is to solicit and activate the values of the receiving individual in order to arouse emotion. Advertising must speak the language of the cultural norms of the time in order to be understood; it is based on the social norms and values of the environment. It should be noted that the earlier work of Holbrook and O'Shaughnessy (1984) does not say otherwise and links the values and emotions aroused by advertisements. The authors emphasize the role of values as a trigger for the emotions induced by advertising messages.

Mucchielli, like Holbrook and O'Shaughnessy, therefore made the activation of values through argument an antecedent of emotion.

This idea can be found in the work of linguists, specialists in the argumentation of emotions. Since Aristotle, classical rhetoric has considered that one of the three pillars of persuasive discourse is pathos or emotion. The other two pillars are ethos, i.e. integrity, coupled with the power of eloquence, and logos, i.e. logical and rational argumentation. According to Sukiennik (2013), the separate works of Christian Plantin and Raphaël Micheli on the argumentation of emotions in linguistics come together on the cognitive anchoring of emotions in beliefs and judgments, making them accessible to argumentation. Moreover, both linguists rely on the work of Raymon Boudon to assert that an argument of emotions is not separable from an axiology, the reference point of the speaker to enhance or devalue it.

Boudon (1999) established this close link between values and emotions well when he described a traditional Israeli kibbutz as an egalitarian society in which all differences between individuals must be eliminated because they are perceived as incompatible with the value system and felt as an injustice. He took the example of a workshop in which an employee would have a minor advantage: an office with more sunlight than that of their colleagues. This situation would inevitably give rise to a sense of injustice that would be unacceptable to their colleagues, not because of a real interest, but because of a transgression of the rules of the value system. In this case, reason is not instrumental, but axiological. Boudon added that these affective reactions (here, the feeling of injustice) are based on a system of reasons, "the 'affective' reaction is all the stronger, as the reasons appear to the social subject as more solid".

Schwartz (2006), a value theorist to whom we will return later, agreed with this view when considering the first of the six main characteristics of values:

> Values are beliefs inseparably associated with affects. When values are "activated", they combine with feelings. People for whom independence is an important value are alert when their independence is threatened, desperate when they cannot preserve it, and happy when they can exercise it.

This digression on the activation of values as an antecedent to emotions in persuasive advertising is echoed in a recent doctoral thesis. Lajante (2013) used the theoretical framework of cognitive assessment (presented below) and, more specifically, the more general model of the component processes of emotion (Sander and Scherer 2014) to understand the events relevant to the individual subjected to persuasive advertising. One of these evaluation criteria is the relevance of the event to personal beliefs, social norms and values.

These developments lead us to make a second proposal (proposal 2.2).

PROPOSAL 2.2.– The emotions aroused in persuasive advertising are based on the activation of the values of the target individual.

2.2.5.2. *The affective halo*

The literature on equity crowdfunding discusses the likely role of the halo effect (Bessière and Stéphany 2014) in project assessment. The halo effect is a contagious effect in which the judgment of one characteristic of an object or individual affects the perceptions of all other characteristics. Thus, the positive perception of a characteristic will form a favorable overall impression. This effect is well summarized by the aphorism: "love is blind".

Thorndike (1920) is credited with the birth of this concept. This professor of psychology noted systematic errors in the scoring of individual characteristics within organizations, with assessors tending to judge a person superior or inferior overall, a general feeling that contaminated all the qualities of the person being assessed. Thorndike was convinced that no person, no matter how competent they may be – foreman, employer, teacher or department head – can extricate themselves from the influence of this overall emotional judgment to objectively assess the different qualities of the same person.

Nisbett and Wilson (1977) conducted an experiment to verify whether the halo effect occurs even when the characteristics of the individual being evaluated are unambiguous, and are documented with sufficient and distinct information. In this experiment, the same person, an English-speaking instructor with a strong European accent, behaved differently with two groups of students. He was friendly and warm with the first group, cold and distant with the second. After the exposure phase, students who were in contact with the warm instructor found his appearance, mannerisms and accent pleasant, while those who saw the distant instructor described these attributes as irritating. The result of this study therefore shows that the separate assessment of attributes is contaminated by the overall emotional assessment, even when sufficient information is available.

In the field of management, Rosenzweig (2007) drew on the analysis of real examples, like the iconic Dell computer case, to conclude that the halo effect is prevalent in the business and financial world, leading to misleading judgments and analyses. For the author, when a company achieves good results, with high profits, sales growth and share price growth, then observers (journalists, analysts, etc.) infer that its strategy is smart, its leadership visionary, its employees motivated, its corporate culture attractive, etc. On the other hand, if the same company sees its financial results decline, then the same observers will quickly conclude that the strategy is aberrant, its leadership uninspired, its corporate culture an obstacle to overcome, etc.

In support of Rosenzweig's proposal, Brown and Perry's 1994 article took, as its starting point, the list of most admired companies, published annually by *Fortune* magazine. These large companies are ranked according to eight qualitative attributes (quality of management, quality of products or services, long-term investment value, innovation, attractiveness, etc.). Although this study is based on a large sample of 8,000 professionals, directors, and market analysts, each of whom is an expert in the sector of activity to be evaluated, the results of the study are very strongly influenced by past financial performance. Past financial performance explains between 42% and 53% of the variance, and the eight attributes are highly correlated, with factor analysis indicating that a single factor explains 84% of the variance. These results show that the eight attributes make up an underlying reputational construct and result from the overall evaluative judgment of companies, i.e. a halo effect.

If, as we have just seen, the contaminating characteristic of the halo effect is not necessarily of an emotional nature, we believe that the same cannot be said for equity crowdfunding investment. Indeed, we have seen that the conditions under which consumer behavior can be dictated by emotional reactions are likely to be satisfied in equity crowdfunding. Therefore, the concept of "affective halo", i.e. the special case of a halo effect induced by an affective reaction, at the source of the contagion effect (Aurifeille 1991), seems appropriate to us to account for investor behavior.

In marketing, this effect occurs when a consumer likes a product and then overvalues all of its characteristics (Wilkie 1990).

Derbaix and Pham (1989) gave a telling example:

> "What a sensational car!" (first overall affective reaction) and after this pseudo love at first sight the evaluation of the different dimensions will take place (the comfort is remarkable, the price is just right, the handling is extraordinary, the consumption for such a car is not excessive…).

...of which this is a possible transposition to equity crowdfunding:

> "What a sensational project!" (first overall affective reaction) and after this pseudo love at first sight the evaluation of the different dimensions will take place (the management team is remarkable, the market positioning is just right, the financial forecasts are extraordinary, the risks are not excessive…).

We put forward proposal 2.3 that follows directly from the definition of this concept.

PROPOSAL 2.3.– The affective halo is the consequence of emotional reactions.

2.2.5.3. *Means-end chain model and the role of values*

In their conceptual research model – the crowdfunding participation model (CPM) – Ryu and Kim (2014) related investor motivations to project characteristics. For example, an attractive financial reward increases an individual's extrinsic motivation. This model builds on the work of Millette and Gagné (2008) and Rousseau (1977) to postulate that project attributes are a key element in the formation of motivations that directly influence funding intent.

If we consider values as a motivational model (Fenouillet 2016), the CPM finds a natural transposition to the field of marketing with the means-end chain model. This model, initially developed in the United States following the work of Gutman (1982), makes it possible to make the link between product knowledge and self-knowledge by moving up a logical chain, from the concrete characteristics of the product to the subject's terminal values (Valette-Florence 1994). Thus, it is possible to understand the cognitive structures associated with the purchase of a product or brand. This conceptual tool is based on social psychology research, highlighting the importance of values in the conduct of human behavior (Rokeach 1973), to which we shall return in the remainder of this chapter.

In the means-end chain model, the means (product characteristics) are an instrument for moving toward an end (the consumer's terminal values).

According to Salem Khalifa (2004), one of the merits of this model for marketing is to provide an explanation of the reasons the consumer has for atrributing different weight to the comparative benefits between alternative products (or services).

The means-end chain model is based on three levels: attributes, consequences and values, according to the central causal structure in Figure 2.8.

Figure 2.8. *Causality in the means-end chain model*

Olson and Reynold (1983) made a finer distinction between these levels, and duplicate them: attributes are concrete or abstract, consequences are functional or psychosocial and values are instrumental or terminal. However, this subdivision is not necessarily complete in the chains referred to by consumers.

Attributes are the entry point for the model and correspond to the characteristics of the product (concrete attributes, such as price, place of purchase, etc.), or to a subjective appreciation (abstract attributes, such as the smell of a perfume considered woody or flowery).

The second level of the model concerns the consequences or benefits. They can be positive or negative depending on the perception of the individual. Functional consequences are related to concrete attributes and derive directly from the use of the product, while psychosocial consequences depend on the functional consequences. Psychosocial consequences respond to psychological needs – "how do I feel?" – and social needs – "what do other people feel?" – in connection with the use of the product (Hadouni *et al.* 2009). The second way of reading consequences groups them into three sets: (1) utilitarian consequences are linked to the product's attributes of functionality, (2) hedonic consequences are based on the emotional rewards derived from the use or consumption of products and (3) symbolic consequences concern the recognition and membership of a social group.

At the end of the chain, values are central to the conduct of an individual's behavior. Rokeach (1973) defined personal values as "enduring beliefs that a specific mode of conduct or end state of existence is personally or socially preferable to an opposite mode of conduct or end state of existence". Gutman (1982) posits that values drive consumer choice. Moreover, instrumental values are modes of behavior or action, while terminal values are individual or social existential goals.

The means-end chain model is therefore based on a central question – "what is important for you?" – that allows chaining to be traced back to terminal values. However, it should not be forgotten that the real causality is the reverse; the values determine the desired consequences, which in turn allow the individual (consumer, investor, etc.) to discriminate between alternative products according to their respective attributes (Valette-Florence 1994).

Once again, it should be noted that the use of this model in the context of equity crowdfunding seems legitimate to us, since the recurring justification for investment[2] is that the project's values are in line with those of the investor.

---

2 The lexicometric analysis of the qualitative corpus (see section 1.2.2.1 of Volume 2) attests to the importance of a subject related to "values".

2.2.6. *Organizational attractiveness and PO-fit: a pull effect*

2.2.6.1. *Organizational attractiveness*

Organizational attractiveness can be defined as a positive emotional attitude towards an organization that is considered particularly desirable, combined with the motivation to establish a contractual relationship with it (Aiman-Smith *et al.* 2001; Read 2012).

Let us first note that the affective dimension of desire, inherent in the concept of organizational attractiveness, is also present in the relationship between crowdfunding equity investors and startups (Bessière and Stéphany 2015). Secondly, we logically qualify the "pull" effect as opposed to the "push" effect already mentioned for persuasive advertising.

The concept of organizational attractiveness is mobilized in the field of human resources to measure the attractiveness of an organization to job applicants. We consider that an equity crowdfunding investor considering providing equity financing to an entrepreneurial project is in a similar position to the candidate to be hired. The analogy between job applicants and potential investors was also put forward by Aiman-Smith *et al.* (2001), who believed that their respective apprehension of the coveted organization is similar. Indeed, in both cases, the individual is faced with the choice of entering into a contractual relationship with an organization and judges the appropriateness of this commitment, based on a subjective evaluation. The approach is also comparable: the individual seeking employment wishes to reduce uncertainty by collecting as much data as possible on the target company (Wanous 1992), in the same way as the equity crowdfunding investor, who is facing a strong information asymmetry (Agrawal *et al.* 2014). Also, just as the job seeker collects and analyzes the organizational attributes (such as remuneration policy, work/life balance, etc.) that contribute to the attractiveness of the company they plan to join (Turban *et al.* 1998), the crowdfunding equity investor uses the same cognitive process by evaluating the characteristics of the startup in search of financing: quality of product/market positioning, existence of patents, experience of the founders, financial forecasts, exit from the planned investment, etc. (Agrawal *et al.* 2014). However, this desire for analysis and rational evaluation comes up against the limited amount of information available to job applicants. In the end, they rely on a general impression of the attractiveness of the organization (Rynes and Barber 1990; Turban *et al.* 1998). The equity crowdfunding investor also has to make do with limited information and, due to lack of time, proceeds by means of a holistic assessment (Bessière and Stéphany 2014).

2.2.6.2. *The P-O fit as a basis for organizational attractiveness*

According to Capelli *et al.* (2015), several theoretical frameworks can be used to explain organizational attractiveness: social identity theory (Ashforth and Mael 1989), signal theory (Spence 1973) and the "Person-Organization Fit" theory (or P-O fit).

The theory of social identity links organizational membership and social identity; it seems irrelevant in our context, as a simple financial investment alone cannot influence an individual's self-esteem as is the case with an employment contract linking him/her to an admired society.

Signal theory describes a situation in which one agent provides information (the signal) to help another economic agent (the principal) make a decision in a situation of information asymmetry. This theory is not only transposable to equity crowdfunding investment, but is widely used, as we show in the first chapter. Despite the relevance of the signal theory, we deliberately choose not to make it the basis of organizational attractiveness, our objective precisely being to identify alternative and complementary theories.

The theory of P-O fit catches our attention. Chatman (1989) gave the following definition: "Person-organization fit is defined here as the congruence between the norms and values of organizations and the values of persons".

We formulate our fourth proposal (proposal 2.4) linking organizational attractiveness and P-O fit.

PROPOSAL 2.4.– Organizational attractiveness is explained by the P-O fit theory.

The P-O fit theory is part of the interactionist current for which individuals build themselves in relation to their environment; the social world is then seen as dependent on the interactions of its components. While most behaviorists accept the separate influence of the characteristics of the individual and the situation on behavior and interactionism, Chatman (1989) considers that only the conjunction of the individual and the situation makes it possible to predict behavior. Models linking person and situation are common in organizational research, such as the model linking personality traits and occupation (Holland 1985), or personality traits and job characteristics (Hackman and Oldham 1980).

Schneider's (1987) attraction–selection–attrition (ASA) model is part of the interactionist current, and is considered the precursor of the P-O fit theory. This model postulates that attractiveness derives from a correspondence of attributes between the individual and the organization.

Attraction is studied in the psychology of work and organizations, and it refers to the fact that people have varying degrees of attraction to different careers, depending on their interests and personalities. The dominant explanatory theory for this attraction phenomenon is proposed by Holland (1985), who showed that the people who make up the career environment that people join, resemble them. The literature on organizational choice provides evidence of the match between a person and a social environment. Tom (1971) showed that individuals' preferred environments are those that have the same "personality" profile as they do. Furthermore, the attraction, selection and retention of certain types of people creates a homogeneous social environment in which individuals resemble and are attracted to one another (Festinger 1954).

With the ASA model, Schneider (1987) introduced the idea that individuals are attracted by the achievement of the organization's objectives, on the condition that they correspond to their own objectives, which brings this model even closer to the P-O fit. However, the P-O fit model is more specific than the ASA model because the characteristics that the correspondence are related to are specified; the P-O fit describes individuals as being attracted to organizations whose values and norms are congruent with their values and behavioral norms (Chatman 1989; Kristof 1996; Chapman *et al.* 2005). Moreover, the strength of attraction is proportional to the intensity of the perceived fit between the values of the individual and those of the organization.

As previously mentioned, the privileged field for the application of the theories of organizational attractiveness and P-O fit is that of human resources management, where work has established the positive effect of institutional communication about CSR (corporate social responsibility) commitment on the attractiveness of organizations (Gond *et al.* 2010). In addition, Gully *et al.* (2013) established that a recruitment campaign that broadcasts advertising messages centered on values related to an organization's CSR commitment, significantly enhances its attractiveness (Gully *et al.* 2013). Also, Sharma *et al.* (2009) explained the effectiveness of this type of communication, by establishing a lasting emotional relationship with stakeholders through the sharing of values.

Once again, the analogy between a company communicating its CSR values to attract candidates with a good fit, and a startup in financing communicating its values to attract investors, seems reasonable to us.

2.2.6.3. *The values and theories of cognitive consistency as a basis for P-O fit*

The definition of the P-O fit theory and its application to the human resource management problem of recruitment (Kristof 1996; Judge and Cable 1997) makes values its cardinal underlying determinant: candidates are attracted to organizations whose characteristics fit in with their own values best.

This point is interesting for our research because (1) some works recognize that values have a motivational function in the choice of equity crowdfunding investors (Gerber and Hui 2013), we will present the importance of the concept of values for behavior in section 2.2.7, and (2) the affective dimension of organizational attractiveness can be understood as a result of the evaluation of values, if we invoke the cognitive assessment theory that we will present in section 2.2.7.

People's attraction to organizations made up of individuals who resemble them can be explained by a desire for coherence and a search for cognitive comfort. Therefore, it seems natural to us to connect the P-O fit theory with the cognitive consistency theory.

This theory revolves around the central idea that individuals try to reduce discomfort induced by dissonances, incongruities or inconsistencies, arising from situations in which two cognitions (attitude, idea, belief, etc.) are incompatible. Discomfort thus acts as a homeostatic motivational force that regulates and restores a satisfactory cognitive state.

The origins of cognitive consistency theory can be traced back to the seminal work of Kurt Lewin (Sharma *et al.* 2009).

The three main formulations of this theory are as follows: cognitive equilibrium theory (Heider 1958), congruence theory (Osgood and Tannenbaum 1955) and cognitive dissonance theory (Festinger 1957).

Heider's (1958) theory of cognitive equilibrium applies to relationships between individuals. In the theory, three entities (the subject P, the other O and the object X) are linked together by affective (attitude toward the other person or object), or union (similarity, proximity, causality, association and belonging) relationships. Affective and union relationships can be of positive (+) or negative (–) valence. The triad is balanced if the three relationships are positive or negative; otherwise, the imbalance creates a motivation (drive) to restore harmony through behavior, or a change in representations.

Osgood and Tannenbaum's (1955) theory of congruence applies to an identifiable source, like an organization, that has made a favorable or unfavorable assertion about an object or concept. For example, an organization may make a claim in favor of ethical values (concept). At the same time, consider an individual who has a favorable or unfavorable attitude toward the same object or concept, as well as toward the source. If the individual has a favorable attitude towards the organization (the source) and the ethical values (the concept), then there is no incongruity. With the same assumptions, if the organization engages in activities that are perceived by the individual as unethical, then a state of incongruence sets in. This situation generates a cognitive discomfort felt as pressure by the employee, leading to a change in attitude towards the organization or unethical behavior. This change in attitude re-establishes a state of congruence.

Finally, Festinger‘s (1957) theory of cognitive dissonance starts from the premise that the individual is in search of harmony and internal balance, i.e. cognitive consonance. Although the state of consistency predominates in the behavior of individuals, this theory focuses on the rarer cases of imbalance called "cognitive dissonance". This is why Vaidis and Halimi-Falkowicz (2007) considered that this theory was not a theory of consistency, but "an inconsistent avoidance theory that presents a motivational process of return to cognitive equilibrium".

Cognitive dissonance is a feeling of psychological discomfort (negative affect) caused by two discordant cognitive elements, plunging the individual into a state that motivates him or her to reduce this uncomfortable feeling. The motivational force produced by the state of discomfort is analogue to that of a drive, as described by Hull (1943); it is of the same order as hunger or thirst, and pushes individuals to reduce this dissonance. In order to do so, they adjust their beliefs, opinions and ideologies to the behavior they actualize; the relationship (belief implies behavior) is paradoxically reversed.

Let us specify that one condition is necessary for the awakening of dissonance: the individual must have a sense of freedom. In addition, Festinger stated several contexts that are conducive to the emergence of dissonance:

– an important or difficult choice, which is a function of multiple alternative evaluations;

– engaging in behavior contrary to one's opinions, beliefs, attitudes or convictions;

– exposure to information incompatible with pre-existing cognition(s);

– disagreement with others;

– the factual invalidation of a belief.

We note that the conditions of a "difficult choice and multiple valuation function alternatives" may characterize the situation of the equity crowdfunding investor.

On this basis, we formulate proposal 2.5 linking P-O fit theory, values and cognitive consistency.

PROPOSAL 2.5.– The P-O fit theory is based on the activation of the individual's values, induced by the consistency linking them to those of the target organization.

2.2.7. *Psychology, emotions and values*

2.2.7.1. *System 1/system 2*

Equity crowdfunding investment platforms simplify the investment process, a choice can be made in a very short time and with just a few clicks. Also, this investment modality probably favors the direct perception of information, relying on informal and even emotional associations. The choice of investment would be more intuitive than analytical, in other words, system 1 would prevail over system 2 (Bessière and Stéphany 2014).

Before defining these two cognitive systems, let us recall that this dual model is related to the field of finance. Indeed, the first work in behavioral finance, carried out in the 1980s and 1990s, focused on investor rationality (behavioral biases, judgment heuristics, etc.) and market inefficiency; however, the numerous results highlighting the gap between the forecasts of normative models of economic rationality and descriptive models, proved to be consistent with the approach of dual decision-making models (Mangot 2013).

Dual models of decision-making assume that individuals have two cognitive systems, called system 1 and system 2 by Stanovich and West (2000). While system 1 operations are typically fast, automatic, effortless, associative, unconscious, and often emotionally charged, system 2 operations are slower, effortful, conscious, analytical, and rule-based (Kahneman 2003). Prior to being labeled systems 1 and 2, literature referred to these two systems in a wide variety of terms (Stanovich and West 2000):

– *system 1: associative system, heuristic processing, tacit thought processes, implicit cognition, interactional intelligence, experiential system, quick and inflexible, intuitive cognition, recognition-primed decisions, implicit inferences, automatic processing and automatic activation*;

– *system 2: rule-based system, analytic processing, explicit thought processes, explicit learning, analytic intelligence, rational system, modules intellection, analytical cognition, rational choice strategy, explicit inferences, controlled processing, and conscious processing system.*

In most of these models, one of the functions of system 2 is the *a posteriori* control of the output results of system 1, which precedes it. However, Kahneman and Frederick (2002) found that this control was generally quite lax and allowed many intuitive judgments to be made, even if they were wrong.

More precisely, the corrective task of system 2 is disturbed by certain circumstances: time pressure, "multitask" activities, GM, performing an activity in the evening for "people who are morning people" and in the morning for "those who are night owls". On the other hand, certain factors are positively correlated with a better performing system: intelligence, interest in knowledge, and exposure to mathematical statistics.

Note that the label "intuition" applies to a judgment that directly reflects impressions, that have not been modified by system 2 (Kahneman 2003).

The reading prism of this dual cognitive system allowed Kahneman to establish an algorithm that describes the dynamic process of judgments and choices:

1) an intuitive judgment or choice is initiated; it is:

a) approved by the system 2,

b) adjusted (insufficiently) with other relevant characteristics,

c) corrected (sometimes excessively) when a bias is explicitly recognized,

d) identified and blocked as violating a valid subjective rule;

2) no intuition comes to mind; the judgment is calculated by system 2.

Empirical results suggest that cases 1a and 1b are the most frequent, while case 1d is very rare.

This sequential algorithm reflects two major assumptions about intuition and judgments or choices:

– most behaviors are intuitive, non-problematic, and successful;

– behavior is preceded by intuition, which serves as an anchor, but does not completely determine it.

In their review of the literature on affectivity heuristics, Slovic *et al.* (2002) referred to system 1 as an "experiential system", as it has an affective basis, so affect heuristics would be a form of expression of this system, in line with the approach taken by Epstein (1994):

> The experiential system is assumed to be intimately associated with the experience of affect, […] which refer to subtle feelings of which people are often unaware. When a person responds to an emotionally significant event, […] the experiential system automatically searches its memory banks for related events, including their emotional accompaniments.

> [...] If the activated feelings are pleasant, they motivate actions and thoughts anticipated to reproduce the feelings. If the feelings are unpleasant, they motivate anticipatory actions and thoughts anticipated to avoid the feelings.

In their 2010 paper, Glöckner and Witteman refine the theory and propose a categorization of the different modalities of operation of the intuitive system (or system 1), by grouping together the different current theoretical models. This classification distinguishes between:

a) associative intuition based on a simple process of learning and recovery;

b) intuition by correspondence and comparison with prototypes and examples;

c) intuition by automatic accumulation of evidence;

d) intuition built on mental representations.

In agreement with Kahneman and Frederick (2002) for whom the intuitive process relies on affective stimuli, both authors recognize a role for affect (as input and output of intuition) for these four categories of intuition.

We are particularly interested in associative intuition based on a learning-recovery mechanism (category a). Indeed, the authors state two forms of expression of this type of intuition in relation to the concepts seen previously:

a-1) intuition as a simple feeling of liking or disliking, influencing choices. This modality corresponds exactly to the heuristic of affectivity;

a-2) the intuition of emotional awakening, influencing choices. This second modality corresponds exactly to the hypothesis of somatic markers.

2.2.7.2. *The anchoring phenomenon*

Anchoring-and-adjustment is a heuristic based on salient (accessible) information that comes immediately to mind (intuitive) and which constitutes as an anchor, i.e. a starting point for later adjustments (Tversky and Kahneman 1974). The starting point may be implicit in the context, but it may also be explicitly provided, it may result from a partial calculation, it may be relevant (an economic growth rate or an inflation rate, etc.), or it may be irrelevant, and come from a random figure which the decision-maker is unaware of. This heuristic, which is studied in numerical evaluations, is very common and affects individuals' everyday decisions, especially when the decisions are unique (Baker and Nofsinger 2010). In the system 1/system 2 perspective, system 2 plays the role of control and adjustment, but the correction is usually not sufficient, resulting in a final outcome that depends on the starting point (Kahneman 2003). This inadequacy of correction could be explained by the procedure being halted as soon as an assessment which is deemed possible is reached (Mangot 2008).

Tested in various fields, the anchoring heuristic has been proven among real estate professionals: an experiment conducted with students and real estate agents, who were asked to estimate the price of a property, showed that subjects who received information (given anchor) including a higher selling price – asked by the owner – estimated a higher selling price as well (Northcraft and Neale 1987).

In finance, multiple numbers can act as an anchor in the case of mergers and acquisitions. The study by Baker *et al.* (2009) showed that bid prices are strongly influenced by the highest target price over the past 52 weeks. This easily accessible and salient price seems to serve as a psychological anchor and reference point, regardless of the current value of the target. Moreover, the probability of a successful transaction increases significantly when the offer to the target is above this threshold (Baker *et al.* 2009).

2.2.7.3. *The determinants of emotions: the cognitive evaluation theory*

Cognitive assessment or appraisal theories postulate that emotions experienced by individuals are the result of a cognitive evaluative process applied to an event or stimulus. Also, this cognitive process triggers a differentiated emotion based on the specific meaning that the individual attributes to the event or stimulus.

The idea of a subjective emotion produced by cognition is at the heart of appraisal theory: "[…] the evaluation of the event is a function of the motivations and values of a given individual at a given time" (Sander and Scherer 2014).

Bernard Rimé, quoted by Piolat and Bannour (2008), also expressed the idea of the subjectivity of emotion, by affirming that emotions always arise from the confrontation of the universe encountered (for example, a situation, an object, etc.), with the universe represented by the individual (his or her needs, desires, aspirations, values, etc.).

On this point, Pfister and Böhm (2008) are explicit: "Emotional construals are idiosyncratic, representing the event from a subjective point of view. Yet, there is one invariant feature: All emotional construals focus on the fundamental relationship between the self and the event, that is, on the relevance a particular event has on a person's vital concerns and interests."

In neuropsychological literature, the triggering of emotions is subject to several sub-processes. A distinction is generally made between cognitive processes that generate emotion and non-cognitive processes. These two subprocesses correspond to the categories of primary or reflex emotions and secondary or cognitive emotions (Damasio 2006). Primary emotions allow individuals to respond quickly to a stimulus without prior processing of the information; in the second stage, cognitive processing can trigger a secondary emotion (Ledoux 1998). Secondary emotions are based on emotional memory. If a person has been bitten by a dog in the past, then later on, that person will feel fear every time he or she encounters a dog again. Damasio's Somatic Marker Theory (2006) presented above, explains this phenomenon as follows: the trigger stimulus is associated with the emotional sensation named the "somatic marker" (memory of the past bite); when the individual is confronted with a similar stimulus (new encounter of a dog in the present), the somatic marker is then activated. This reactivation allows the evaluation of the desirable or undesirable character of a decision, and the choice of an appropriate escape behavior in the case of this example (negative emotions), or an approach behavior for other situations (positive emotions).

Nevertheless, this conceptualization of emotion triggering, separating purely affective emotions from those preceded by a cognitive assessment, is not unanimously accepted by emotion theorists. As mentioned above, the question of the primacy of the cognitive, over the affective, is a long-standing controversy that is difficult to resolve because of the different meanings of cognition. According to Sander and Scherer (2014), it is reasonable to consider the emotional system as a cognitive system in its own right on the same level as the memory and attention systems. To do so, it is sufficient to accept that the appraisal process takes place on several levels of processing, including automatic processes that are not conscious and are qualified as cognitive.

Lazarus (1966) laid the foundation for the theory of cognitive assessment. In this essential contribution, he stated the existence of a process of evaluation or appraisal of the triggering of emotions, but also of re-evaluation or reappraisal of possible changes in the initial impression, as well as in the emotion generated.

The first version of this theory distinguishes between primary and secondary evaluations. Primary assessment is a function of the enjoyment (pleasant/unpleasant) of the event, as well as its relevance to the achievement of the individual's goals. Secondary assessment is a function of the individual's ability to cope with the consequences of an event, in relation to his or her goals and resources. It is the interaction of these two types of assessments that differentiates the emotion triggered.

Subsequently, the theory was refined to identify the so-called assessment variables that trigger and determine the type and intensity of emotions felt (Scherer 2000).

While there is no consensus in the psychological literature on a specific list of assessment variables, some are shared by most theories (Ochs 2007).

Beyond the variables, it is the "individual evaluation structure" that determines the type of emotion evoked. This individual evaluation structure represents the subjectivity of the individual, because, as we have already pointed out, it is the evaluation of the event by the individual, and not the event itself, that triggers the emotion (Roseman 2001). For example, the OCC[3] model of Ortony *et al.* (1988) defines an individual evaluation structure based on the individual's goals, standards (i.e. the social and personal norms he or she respects) and tastes or preferences. The model associates an emotion group with each of these three criteria. Thus, emotions based on goals, standards and preferences are triggered by the criteria related to the goals, standards and preferences of the evaluation structure, respectively. Note that Poggi and Germani (2003) added a group of emotions triggered by the evaluation of events related to the individual's beliefs, such as interest, curiosity and confusion.

3 OCC is an acronym concatenating the initials of the three authors of the theory: Ortony, Clore and Collins.

This leads us to formulate proposal 2.6.

PROPOSAL 2.6.– Cognitive assessment is a process that has various assessment variables including goals (or values) as input.

The triggering of goal-based emotions is paramount in these models. For Lazarus, an event has an emotion-generating effect only if it affects one of the individual's goals. It is the relationship between the event and the goal, i.e. the consequence of the event on the goal, that determines the emotion triggered. A positive emotion will be generated when the event facilitates the achievement of a goal; it will be negative when it does not. Therefore, appraisal models are consequentialist: the assessment of the implications of the event and its consequences is central. Roseman (1991) chose the concept of motivation instead of goal[4]; an event is consistent with a motivation when it facilitates its achievement; it is inconsistent when it does not.

Returning to evaluation variables, if we take the example of the OCC model, its main evaluation variable is desirability; the event is desirable if it achieves a goal and is undesirable otherwise.

Another major assessment model, proposed by Lazarus (2001), postulates that an individual continuously and sequentially assesses all the variables in his or her environment. In its most recent version (Sander and Scherer 2014), there are four of these variables, known as stimulus evaluation checks (SEC), which are divided into subcriteria:

– criterion 1: relevance assessment (how relevant is this event to me? Will it affect me directly or my reference social group?); subcriteria of novelty, intrinsic appeal, relevance to goals and needs;

– criterion 2: assessing the implications (what are the implications or consequences of this event and how will it affect my well-being, and my immediate or longer term goals?); subcriterion of causal attribution, probability of consequences, difference from consequences, facilitation/obstruction to goals, needs and urgency;

4 The concepts of goal and motivation are inseparable, as a motivation is a psychological state that pushes one to act in the direction of a desired goal ((https://www.universalis.fr/encyclopedie/motivation-psychologie/1-motivation-et-atteinte-d-un-but//).

– criterion 3: assessment of mastery potential (how well will I be able to adapt or adjust to the consequences?); subcriteria of control, power and adjustment;

– criterion 4: evaluation of normative significance (what is the significance of this event for my internal standards – self-concept – values and social norms?); subcriteria of internal and external standards.

In this model, emotions are triggered according to a particular combination of SEC.

Specifically, the differentiation of emotions depends on the "evaluation profile" of an emotion, that combines the values of the evaluation variables generating that emotion. For example, again in the OCC model, the evaluation profile of fear is defined by the combination of the values of the undesirability and uncertainty variables. The emotion of fear is triggered when a stimulus is assessed as undesirable and uncertain. The association between emotions and combinations of assessment variable values depends on theory (Ortony *et al.* 1988; Roseman 2001; Scherer *et al.* 2001).

In the same way, the intensity of the emotions evoked is defined by the values taken on by the "intensity variables", which themselves depend on the variable that triggered the event.

Let us add that emotion, the result of the appraisal, can be understood in two ways: the discreet approach or the continuous approach. The first one is the most commonly used in models; the emotions are made explicit and their number is finite. Examples include joy, anger, and desire. The continuous approach assigns three dimensions to the emotions: valence, control capacity and level of activation. Valence distinguishes positive emotions from negative emotions, the level of activation measures their intensity and control is the individual's control over the situation. The PAD model by Mehrabian and Russel (1974), which was already mentioned, is a reference for this representation.

As it can be seen, these models lend themselves to computer implementation easily. Scherer (1993) developed an expert system to identify *a priori* the emotion felt by a person, based on answers to SEC evaluation questions. In this experiment, the prediction of the emotional terms, that the subjects would use to describe their feelings, was accurate in 70% of cases. Finally, a stream in the field of artificial research, affective informatics, mobilizes these theories to design systems capable of recognizing and expressing artificial emotions.

2.2.7.4. *From values to emotions*

2.2.7.4.1. Value theory

Schwartz (1996) defined values as:

> desirable, transsituational goals, varying in importance, that serve as guiding. The crucial content aspect that distinguishes among values is the type of motivational goal they express.

We believe that this concept is at the heart of equity crowdfunding investor behavior. Indeed, the literature on entrepreneurial finance reflects the role of values in the context of equity crowdfunding. According to Bessière and Stéphany (2017), the crowd of investors can be analyzed from the perspective of groups made up of individuals who share values and objectives. While at the aggregate level, values are a common denominator for community members, Gerber and Hui (2013) showed that at the individual level, they motivate the investor's action. Investors, in search of projects that resonate with their beliefs, mandate the entrepreneur to carry a cause and achieve objectives that are in line with them.

The motivational dimension of values is established by the literature on social psychology in which they are a determinant of individual behavior, judgments and decisions. According to Rokeach (1973), values are enduring and prescriptive beliefs, that establish a preference for an individual's behavioral patterns (or behaviors) and end states (or goals). Feather (1995) believed that individuals' values, along with their needs, motivate their possible actions. According to Schwartz (2006), values have an influence, often unconscious, on the attention, perception and reading of situations. They produce actions that make it possible to achieve objectives that are themselves, valued attractive. As for Mucchielli (2011), values guide behaviors and are strong beliefs shaped by education and emotional life experiences. Therefore, they are emotionally charged and represent a worthy ideal. These propositions are supported by empirical results establishing causalities between the importance of values and behavioral choices (Feather 1995).

Currently, the dominant value theory is Schwartz's (1992) theory of basic human values. However, it is nothing less than a motivational theory

(Fenouillet 2016). What distinguishes one value from another is the type of objective or motivation it expresses. Schwartz *et al.* (2012) list 19 values organized along a continuum, in its most recent version, defined by a series of six main characteristics based on the definitions of multiple authors (Schwarz 2006). The first characteristic defines them as subjective beliefs inseparably associated with affects. The third indicates the generic nature of values, independent of specific situations. The other four characteristics explain the motivational dimension of values. Characteristics numbers 2 and 4 are eloquent in this respect:

> Characteristic 2: Values relate to desirable goals that motivate action. People for whom social order, justice, and charity are important values are motivated to pursue these goals.
>
> […] Characteristic 4: The values are used as a standard or criteria. Values guide the selection or evaluation of actions, policies, people, and events. Decisions about what is right or wrong, justified or illegitimate, worth doing or avoiding are made on the basis of the possible consequences for the values one holds dear. But the impact of values on everyday decisions is rarely conscious. Values become conscious when the actions or judgements one is contemplating lead to conflicts between different values one holds dear.

Thus, their effect is rarely conscious; it depends on the combination of values activated by a given situation and their relative hierarchical order (characteristic numbers 5 and 6). This mechanism determines an affective evaluation and the selection of desirable actions in regards to a goal, that is, the expression of fundamental values through the individual's behavior.

Let us note that the result of this combination of rules defines the conditions and the intensity of the congruence of the values of an individual facing a situation, a situationist point of view that corresponds quite precisely to a possible implementation of the P-O fit theory, that we presented above.

The search for congruence between personal values and situational behaviors allows the individual to maintain a state of stable cognitive consistency, in accordance with the fundamental hypothesis shared by the various theories of cognitive consistency, which we have also mentioned above. The need to conduct oneself in accordance with fundamental truths integrated by the subject (Mucchielli 2011), or in other words, the need for coherence between one's actions and one's values (Rokeach 1973), is the explanation put forward by Schwartz (2006), to account for the effect of values on behavior. We should note that this motive is of an introspective nature and can be related to "self-image": "the most important values are fundamental to one's self-image. If one feels that there is an opportunity to achieve these values, one sets up an automatic, positive and affective response to actions that go in this direction. If we feel that the attainment of these values is threatened, we react negatively on an emotional level".

A second motive turned towards others is the need for esteem by fellow human beings (Mucchielli 2011).

Applied to equity crowdfunding, the motivational theory, by activation of values, makes it possible to explain the case of the investor, an environmental activist for whom the "universalism" dimension is of prime importance and who, perceiving (consciously or not) this "value activation", is the only one who can explain the "value activation" dimension of their investment value on the campaign page of a Green Tech startup, is driven by the desire to invest. Their motivation is explained by the activation of their primordial value, which arouses emotion and attraction for the company.

It should also be noted that the universal values of this theory can be moral or amoral. Schwartz (2007) distinguishes five basic values (out of the 10 values defined in the original model) that are considered moral by respondents. Moral values promote a positive relationship with others, while amoral values do not express consideration for others, or are the expression of a form of competition with others. Also, it is possible to model the motivation of desire for profitability, natural in finance, by the value named "power-resources" by Schwartz, representing a goal of power through material enrichment, and considered amoral by respondents.

2.2.7.4.2. Link between values and emotions

Section 2.2.7.4.1 established that values, whether moral or amoral, are a source of motivation and are intimately linked to affect. The first characteristic of values is from Schwartz (2006):

> Characteristic 1: Values are beliefs inseparably associated with affects. When values are 'activated', they combine with feelings. People for whom independence is an important value

are alert when their independence is threatened, desperate when they cannot preserve it, and happy when they can exercise it.

As mentioned earlier, this dependence of affects on values is found in the field of argumentation and discourse analysis. Micheli, quoted by Sukiennik (2013), makes value judgments a cognitive antecedent of emotion. Values are the reason for emotion; they are a tool of rhetorical persuasion. This argument brings us in line with appraisal theory (see above) for which teleological significance (the goal) is a cardinal evaluation variable, i.e. a cognitive antecedent to emotion (Scherer *et al.* 2001). This comparison seems consistent with the name "goal" adopted by Schwartz (1994) to qualify values. Furthermore, let us recall that for Micheli, the reasons for emotions are inseparable from an individual axiology: he relied on Boudon (1999), regarding the logical necessity of a system of reasons as the basis of the affective reaction, the latter being all the stronger as the reasons appear to be solid.

While we have previously discussed the link between emotions and values, in the presentation of the model of persuasive advertising, let us note that in the field of marketing, there is a consensus on the mobilization of values to explain changes in the emotional state and emotional reactions of consumers (Lemoine and Plichon 2000).

In order to explain the link between values and emotions, it seems relevant for us to mobilize cognitive assessment models (or appraisal). In the various cognitive assessment models, subjective assessment relies heavily on the individual's goals, which are the main assessment variable. For Lazarus (2001), an emotion can only be triggered if the event affects one of the individual's goals, and this is therefore a necessary condition. The emotion generated is positive when the consequence of the event facilitates the achievement of the goal, and is negative when it does not.

Thus, the consistency between the event and the individual's personal goals is the main determinant of emotion. Values are precisely desirable goals (Schwartz 1994) that are decisive for behavior. In a more general form, we find the rules and mechanisms for selecting desirable actions through the activation of a subject's values in a given situation (Schwartz 2006), an activation that is itself a source of positive emotion, when the consequence of the event facilitates the attainment of the goal (Lazarus 2001). As Sander and

Scherer (2014) wrote: "We will just feel an emotion in situations that affect our own values or needs, in other words: that are personally important".

These developments enable us to make proposal 2.7.

PROPOSAL 2.7.– Cognitive assessment is based on the values of the individual involved in the situation under consideration.

2.2.7.5. *Emotions, motivations and action tendency*

Over the past 20 years or so, a series of works have begun to bring together two distinct fields of psychology that had previously been ignored: the psychology of emotions and the psychology of motivation.

Individuals have ongoing goals, values, plans and needs. When an event occurs, we judge the situation in terms of these motivational factors. If the event interferes with one of these motivational factors, then our priorities can immediately be changed; an emotional process is triggered that will subsequently produce a specific action tendency. This is a preparation for appropriate behavioral reactions adjusted to the context. Many researchers consider that the function of emotions is to motivate behavior, in order to achieve goals and satisfy the needs of the individual. This perspective goes back to Darwin's evolutionary theory (1872), which states that the functional dimension of emotions, characterized by facial and body expressions, are adaptive behaviors useful for the survival of the species. Moreover, this body expression reflects a tendency to action that can be interpreted by others, making them capable of adapting to interact appropriately. Scherer (2000) gave the following illustration: suppose you are walking in a deserted park, suddenly a man appears and blocks your way, a knife in hand. The ensuing interaction will depend to a large extent on the emotional signals you send; if you are paralyzed by fear, the man may push you away without hesitation, while if you scream angrily, signaling that you want to physically fight, the man may change his mind and reassess the situation. It is important to distinguish between action tendencies and the resulting actions, because the latter depend to a large extent on the assessment of the situational constraints of individuals. According to Ekman, quoted by Sander and Scherer (2014), in a normative social context, for example in the world of work, it would be unwise, in the case of anger, to show an action tendency, such as a verbal or physical attack on one's employer, so the resulting action is controlled and adapted.

Let us recall that while motivation follows emotion, it also precedes it: according to Scherer (2014), emotion has an antecedent motivation and a consequent motivation, with these two motivations being logically linked (see Figure 2.9). For example, when visiting a friend's house, if you feel hungry at lunchtime (antecedent motivation) and your host does not invite you to eat, you will probably feel angry or at least dissatisfied (emotion), which will lead you to leave the place early to eat elsewhere (consequent motivation).

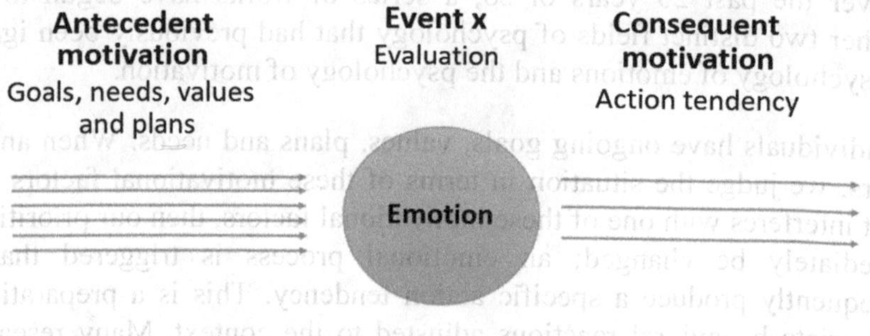

Figure 2.9. *Motivation as an antecedent and consequence of the emotional process, adapted from Sander and Scherer (2014)*

The (antecedent motivation → emotion) link is explained by the appraisal theories already presented, whereas this section focuses on the (emotion → consequent motivation) link. Several theories take emotion as a motivational factor (Sander and Scherer 2014; Fenouillet 2016); without claiming to be exhaustive, we mention below a selection of theories, which are interesting for our research.

First of all, let us recall that Lazarus's (2001) model of component processes combines antecedent and consequent emotions. This model proposes a conceptual framework explaining the differentiation of emotions resulting from a stimulus or event (through the cognitive assessment process that is integrated), and making predictions about the activation patterns of the different interconnected subsystems of the organism: cognitive assessment, peripheral physiology, action tendency, motor expression and subjective feeling. Antecedent motivations are described by the stimulus assessment criteria of the cognitive assessment process, consequent motivations appear in the motivational component, with a function of preparation for action.

On the basis of these theoretical elements, we formulate proposal 2.8.

PROPOSAL 2.8.– An action tendency is associated with affective reaction, which is itself generated by a cognitive assessment process.

According to Lang (1994), behavior is organized around a bipolar appetitive–aversive dimension. Two motivational systems would correspond to appetitive (pleasant) and aversive (unpleasant) stimuli leading to approach, attachment or consumption behavior, and avoidance, flight or defense behavior. These two systems are activated according to the valence and the excitement felt (arousal) in relation to an event.

According to Davidson (1998), humans, like other living beings with less complex nervous systems, have been able to adapt to their environment due to two action tendencies: approach and withdrawal. In this theory, emotions play a role in coordinating perceptions, cognitions and action tendencies. As with Lang, this perspective incorporates only emotional avoidance and withdrawal factors.

From an evolutionary perspective, in line with Darwin's seminal book on natural selection, Plutchik (1970) conceptualized emotion as a hypothetical construct present in humans and animals, with several components such as subjective feeling, expressive behavior and physiological reactions. Plutchik identified eight basic emotions (fear, anger, joy, sadness, acceptance, disgust, anticipation and surprise) associated with particular types of events, cognitions, physiological reactions and adaptive behaviors.

In his differential theory of fundamental emotions, Izard (1977) considered that one of the main functions of emotions is motivational: "Ten fundamental emotions […] constitute the principal motivational system for human beings". Based on Darwin's evolutionary work, Izard (1977) believed that a reduced list of emotions is universally shared by all human beings, which would indicate a genetic explanation. This theory distinguishes drives, based on a biological substrate whose objective is survival, from emotions, which are a sensational expression (not limited to the perceptive senses) that motivate, organize, orient perceptions, thoughts and behaviors.

In his theory of the constructive expansion of positive emotions, Fredrickson (2001) focused on the positive emotions (five in number: joy, interest, satisfaction, pride and love) that motivate an individual to interact with their environment in order to control and explore it, and they therefore act (along with negative emotions) as specific action tendencies. This approach is consistent with evolutionary theory and the adaptive perspective of emotions. Let us note that for this author, the emotion of interest encourages the individual to explore, seek new information, live new experiences and get involved in activities; we will talk about interest in the second part of this book.

According to Frijda (1988, 2006), emotions respect laws, and their consequences are clear, stable and predictable. Frijda proposed a theory "of realizing interests", in which emotions are identified with action tendencies; in other words, emotions and action tendencies are one and the same thing. In this theory, interest is a disposition of the subject, to prefer certain states of the environnement or themselves. Emotions modify the preparation of action for the realization of the individual's interests. As with previous theorists of emotions, an individual's conception of emotions is discrete, i.e. emotions are finite in number and distinct from each other, and each emotion corresponds a specific tendency to action. For example, "desire" is associated with the tendency to action "approach" that predisposes to consumption, or in our case, to investment, while "fear" is associated with "avoidance" and the search for protection.

It seems appropriate for us to link these theories associating emotion and motivation, particularly that of Frijda, with the psychological models of decision-making integrating emotions, as mentioned above. Indeed, some of the authors of these models rely on these theories, notably Zeelenberg *et al.* (2008): "[…] we conceptualize emotions as motivational processes […]. We propose that emotions commit decision makers to certain courses of action by providing control precedence (Frijda 1986), which means that the experience of an emotion brings forward an associated goal that may overrule other goals".

Or Loewenstein *et al.* (2001):

> The idea that emotions have a direct and powerful influence on behavior is widely supported in the psychological literature on emotions. […] (Frijda 1986) has been a major proponent of the idea that a change in readiness for action is at the heart of emotion and has shown that qualitatively distinct emotional states can be distinguished, not only on the basis of the

cognitive assessments that give rise to them, but also in terms of the states of readiness for action that they create.

Let us also note that despite their differences, the theories linking emotions and motivations agree on the categorization of emotions in the two cardinal classes of "pleasure" and "unpleasure". These orient behaviors toward the attraction or repulsion of objects, people, actions, ideas, etc. (Loewenstein *et al.* 2001). This dichotomy of emotions corresponds to the two modalities of the valence attribute of affective reactions, a general class previously defined that groups emotions, moods, feelings, preferences, etc. (Loewenstein *et al.* 2001). Other finer taxonomies were proposed, such as the one proposed by Garcia-Prieto *et al.* (2005), grouping four classes, including that of approach emotions (relief, interest, hope and surprise) and that of antagonistic emotions (jealousy, envy, disgust, contempt, anger, etc.). Nevertheless, these groupings generally show the two basic classes of "pleasure" and "unpleasure". Neurobiology, moreover, attests to the importance of these two classes of emotion, according to Dantzer (2002): "The emotions also play an important organizing role in the evaluation of the world around us. Among the categorizations we make of the external world, it is difficult to find anything more fundamental than the pleasant-unpleasant or beneficial-harmful dichotomy. This categorization motivates and guides action".

2.3. Toward a concise theoretical framework

Following this literature review, which complements the review of equity crowdfunding in the field of entrepreneurial finance (Chapter 1), we have selected the concepts and theories that seemed most appropriate to our problem. In section 2.3.1, we present the selected theoretical framework, the articulation of its components using the proposals established during the literature review, and an overview grouping the theoretical components by parent discipline.

2.3.1. *Theoretical framework*

The focus of this research is on understanding the role of emotional responses and values on the choices of equity crowdfunding investors. The theories and concepts used (see Figure 2.10) are mainly in the field of psychology.

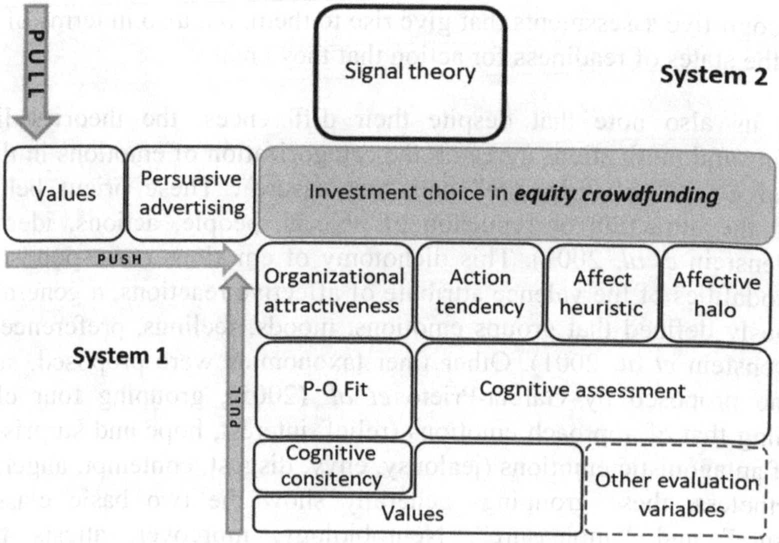

Figure 2.10. *The theoretical framework*

Moreover, our postpositivist epistemological posture has led us to exclude rational choice theory and its multiple developments. Nor do we retain the explanatory psychological models integrating the affective reactions presented, for two reasons: either they derive from the theory of expected utility, or their formulation is not sufficiently precise to envisage an operationalization. In addition, we wish to propose an explanatory model specific to the situation of equity crowdfunding investment. Nevertheless, it is certain that the models, theories and concepts that have been discarded have inspired us. From our point of view, the situation of the crowdfunding equity investor has singular characteristics. The importance of the image, the video and the persuasive narrative of platforms and startup managers, make the role of emotional reactions, their antecedents (values and other variables at the input of the cognitive assessment) and consequences (tendency to act, affectivity heuristic and affective halo), as well as the marketing influence (push) dimension that finds a translation in the model of advertising persuasion, very important.

We have also retained the P-O fit theory, as well as the upstream (cognitive consistency) and downstream (organizational attractiveness) theories, which we find singularly relevant because of the situational analogy between the investor and the job candidate, as well as the fact that they are based on the values of the individual. Signal theory is present, since we wish to quantify the relative weights of influence of the cognitive (with which signal theory is associated) and the affect (with which other theories and concepts are associated). Let us add that the very object of our research explains the imbalance between the number of components of system 2 of the decision (analytical deliberative system) and of system 1 of the decision (affective experiential system).

2.3.2. *Articulation of concepts and theories*

Figure 2.11 links the theories, concepts and models that make up system 1, through eight propositions made in this chapter. The representation of affective responses is reminiscent of their presence at the core or periphery (input or output) of all components of the experiential system.

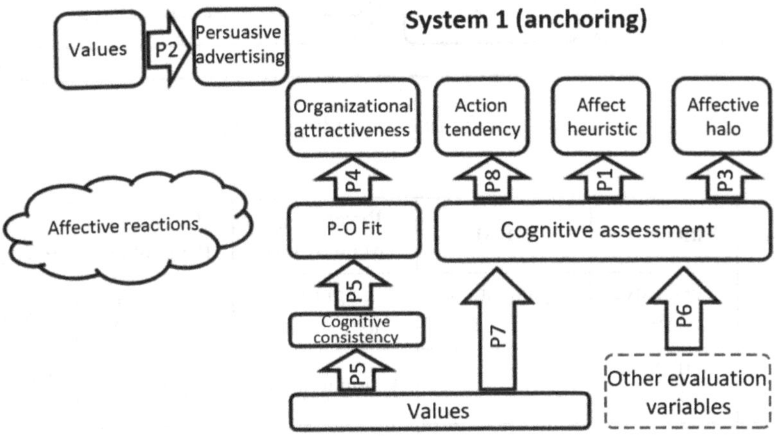

Figure 2.11. *Proposals linking the components of the theoretical framework*

2.3.3. *Disciplinary breakdown of concepts and theories*

While Figure 2.12 shows the disciplines mobilized in this work, Table 2.2 complements it, by providing a breakdown of the theories and concepts of the theoretical framework in the different disciplines mobilized.

It should be noted that this disciplinary division is relatively artificial, in that the disciplines of management sciences often overlap with other human and social sciences, with behavioral finance being by nature, at the crossroads between finance, on one hand, and the fields of psychology and sociology, on the other hand. Thus, while the affective halo is associated with marketing because it is studied in this discipline, the original concept has its roots in psychosociology (Aurifeille 1991).

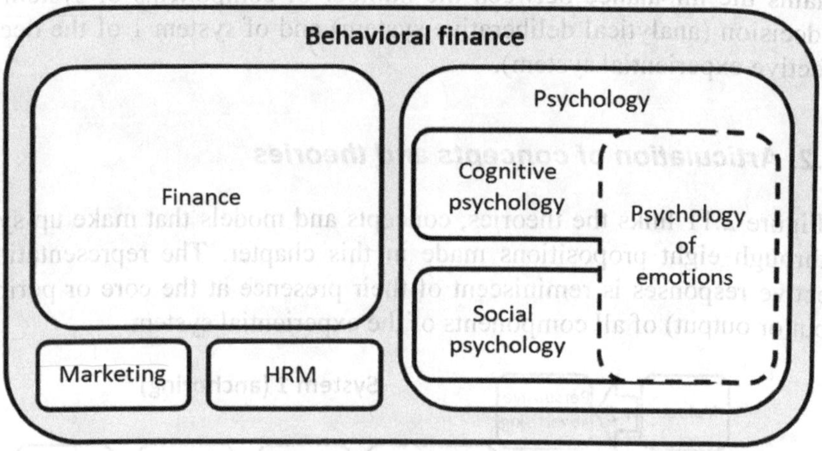

Figure 2.12. *Disciplinary fields for anchoring the theories and concepts retained*

Finance	Marketing	HRM	Psychology of emotions	Cognitive Psychology	Social Psychology
Signal theory	Persuasive advertising	Organizational attractiveness	Cognitive assessment	System 1/ system 2	Values
	Affective halo		Action tendency	P-O fit	Cognitive consistency
			Affect heuristics		

Table 2.2. *Disciplinary breakdown of selected concepts and theories*

2.3.4. *Conclusion*

In Chapter 1, an initial literature review enabled us to review research in the field of corporate finance, focused on the decisions of equity crowdfunding investors. Because of this first stage, we have refined and justified our research focus. We found that the theoretical approach mainly invoked in the literature, to account for investors' choice of projects, is signal theory, i.e. a cognitivist and utilitarian approach that presupposes an individual driven by instrumental rationality. The affective dimension of choice is largely ignored, with the exception of recent research in the field of entrepreneurship. In this chapter, the objective of the second phase of the literature review was presented; the aim was to construct a theoretical framework by exploring knowledge relating to decisions and the affect, in a gradual move away from finance to psychology, as well as the management sciences, more specifically marketing and HRM. This state of the art begins with a presentation of the theory of expected utility, as this remains the essential reference when we are interested in the decisions of economic agents. The normative decision models derived from it are discarded for the development of our theoretical framework, as they are not adapted to our essentially explanatory positioning. Although inspiring, the psychological models and theories of decision-making based on affects are not explicitly retained, either because they are part of a risk context (the theory of perspectives, risk-as-feeling), while equity crowdfunding is in a context of uncertainty (refer to Chapter 1 of Volume 2 for more details on this subject), they are too imprecise to be operationalized (choosing by liking, affect-as-information) or their approach is strictly utilitarian (choices and relative pleasure of consequences). The theory of somatic markers and the heuristic hypothesis of affectivity are very close and implement system 1, or the intuitive system. Although its form is imprecise, we retain the affect heuristic hypothesis because it has already shown its relevance in explaining the behavior of financial actors. The main affective experiences are then specified, we retain the affective reactions, an encompassing class defined essentially by the pleasure/unpleasure bipolarity found in the majority of theories and decision models based on affects. The section on affects in finance deals with issues related to ours, in particular with the choices of BA (screening phase) based on intuition. The field of marketing, and more precisely, of the affective in consumer behavior, proposes a model of persuasive advertising that seems particularly adapted to our problem. It distinguishes two causal routes (affective and cognitive) to explain the attitudes of consumers subjected to the exposure of affective drivers, the first of which is advertising videos, just as the equity crowdfunding investor can be subjected to with the pitch videos of projects. The affective halo is also retained because its effects are linked to those of the affect heuristic. The concept of organizational attractiveness borrowed from HRM, and the theories on which it is based (P-O fit and cognitive consistency), are also retained because of the situational analogy that can be logically established between the crowdfunding investor and the job candidate, both of whom wish to establish a lasting contractual relationship with an organization, on the basis of imprecise information. The cognitive appraisal model offers an explanation for the triggering of affective reactions; it allows us to link the variables at the basis of our modeling (Chapter 1 of Volume 2) and the subsequent effects of affective reactions (affect heuristic, affective halo, anchoring and action tendency). Values form the basis of several theories (cognitive assessment, P-O fit and persuasive advertising) and are in themselves a motivational antecedent. Moreover, the use of values to justify behavior calls for reflection on another form of rationality: axiological, non-consecutive rationality (refer to Chapter 1 of Volume 2 for more details on this subject). The action tendency is another motivational antecedent relevant to choice, resulting from affective reactions. Finally, the first phase of the literature review highlighted the importance of signal theory, which we retain since the model we propose combines cognitive and affective dimensions. However, the signals will be circumscribed and will not result from real or virtual interactions as we set out in the delimitation of our research object.

At the end of the chapter, Figures 2.10 and 2.11 organize the theoretical "building blocks" selected for our framework and link them, two by two, with the help of the proposals formulated, as this state of the art is developed. A third supplementary Figure 2.12 proposes a disciplinary breakdown of the mobilized theories.

References

Ackert, L.F., Church, B.K. (2006). Firm image and individual investment decisions. *Journal of Behavioral Finance*, 7(3), 155–167.

Agrawal, A., Catalini, C., Goldfarb, A. (2011). The geography of crowdfunding. Working paper, NBER, Cambridge.

Agrawal, A., Catalini, C., Goldfarb, A. (2014). Some simple economics of crowdfunding. *Innovation Policy and the Economy*, 14(1), 63–97.

Agrawal, A., Catalini, C., Goldfarb, A. (2015). Crowdfunding: Geography, social networks, and the timing of investment decisions. *Journal of Economics & Management Strategy*, 24(2), 253–274.

Agrawal, A., Catalini, C., Goldfarb, A. (2016). Are syndicates the killer app of equity crowdfunding? *California Management Review*, 58(2), 111–124.

Ahlers, G.K.C., Cumming, D., Günther, C., Schweizer, D. (2015). Signaling in equity crowdfunding. *Entrepreneurship Theory and Practice*, 39(4), 955–980.

Aiman-Smith, L., Bauer, T.N., Cable, D.M. (2001). Are you attracted? Do you intend to pursue? A recruiting policy-capturing study. *Journal of Business and Psychology*, 16(2), 219–237.

Aïte, A.A. (2013). Processus émotionnels et cognitifs dans le développement des capacités de prise de décision sous ambiguïté. PhD Thesis, Paris Descartes University, Paris.

Akerlof, G.A. (1970). The market for "lemons": Quality uncertainty and the market mechanism. *Quarterly Journal of Economics*, 84(3), 488–500.

Akili-Goglin, C. (2018). Financer les jeunes entreprises innovantes. *Centraliens*, 657.

Alba, J.W., Hutchinson, J.W. (1987). Dimensions of consumer expertise. *Journal of Consumer Research*, 13(4), 411–454.

Allais, M. (1953). Le comportement de l'homme rationnel devant le risque : critique des postulats et axiomes de l'École américaine. *Econometrica*, 21(4), 503–546.

Allison, T.H., Davis, B.C., Webb, J.W., Short, J.C. (2017). Persuasion in crowdfunding: An elaboration likelihood model of crowdfunding performance. *Journal of Business Venturing*, 32(6), 707–725.

Andrieu, G., Groh, P. (2018). Specialist versus generalist investors: Trading off support quality, investment horizon and control rights. *European Economic Review*, 101, 459–478.

Arrow, K.J. (1974). *The Limits of Organization*. W.W. Norton & Company, New York.

Ashforth, B.E., Mael, F. (1989). Social identity theory and the organization. *Academy of Management Review*, 14(1), 20–39.

Aspara, J., Tikkanen, H. (2011). Individuals' affect-based motivations to invest in stocks: Beyond expected financial returns and risks. *Journal of Behavioral Finance*, 12(2), 78–89.

Aspara, J., Olkkonen, R., Tikkanen, H., Moisander, J. (2008). A theory of affective self-affinity: Definitions and application to a company and its business. *AMS Review*, 12(3), 40.

Aurifeille, J.-M. (1991). Proposition d'une méthode de mesure du halo affectif en marketing. *Recherche et application en marketing*, 6(4), 59–77.

Baker, H.K., Nofsinger, J.R. (2010). *Behavioral Finance: Investors, Corporations, and Markets*. John Wiley & Sons, New York.

Baker, M., Pan, X., Wurgler, J. (2009). The psychology of pricing in mergers and acquisitions. Working paper, Harvard Business School, Boston.

Baker, W., Hutchinson, J.W., Moore, D., Nedungadi, P. (1986). Brand familiarity and advertising: Effects on the evoked set and brand preference. *ACR North American Advances*, 13, 637–642.

Bammens, Y., Collewaert, V. (2014). Trust between entrepreneurs and angel investors: Exploring positive and negative implications for venture performance assessments. *Journal of Management*, 40(7), 1980–2008.

Barber, B.M., Heath, C., Odean, T. (2003). Good reasons sell: Reason-based choice among group and individual investors in the stock market. *Management Science*, 49(12), 1636–1652.

Bargh, J.A. (1997). The automaticity of everyday life. In *The Automaticity of Everyday Life: Advances in Social Cognition*, Wyer Jr., R.S. (ed.). Psychology Press, Hove.

Bechara, A., Damasio, A.R. (2005). The somatic marker hypothesis: A neural theory of economic decision. *Games and Economic Behavior*, 52(2), 336–372.

Bechara, A., Damasio, A.R., Damasio, H., Anderson, S.W. (1994). Insensitivity to future consequences following damage to human prefrontal cortex. *Cognition*, 50(1–3), 7–15.

Bechara, A., Damasio, H., Damasio, A.R., Lee, G.P. (1999). Different contributions of the human amygdala and ventromedial prefrontal cortex to decision-making. *Journal of Neuroscience*, 19(13), 5473–5481.

Bechter, C., Jentzsch, S., Frey, M. (2011). From wisdom to wisdom of the crowd and crowdfunding. *Journal of Communication and Computer*, 8(11), 951–957.

Becker, J.-M., Rai, A., Ringle, C.M., Völckner, F. (2013). Discovering unobserved heterogeneity in structural equation models to avert validity threats. *MIS Quarterly*, 37(3), 665–694.

Bell, D.E. (1985). Disappointment in decision making under uncertainty. *Operations Research*, 33(1), 1–27.

Belleflamme, P., Lambert, T., Schwienbacher, A. (2014). Crowdfunding: Tapping the right crowd. *Journal of Business Venturing*, 29(5), 585–609.

Bentham, J. (1789). An introduction to the principles of morals and legislation. In *The Collected Works of Jeremy Bentham: An Introduction to the Principles of Morals and Legislation*, Burns, J.H., Hart, H.L.A. (eds). Oxford University Press, Oxford.

Bentler, P.M., Chou, C.-P. (1987). Practical issues in structural modeling. *Sociological Methods & Research*, 16(1), 78–117.

Bernoulli, D. (1954). Exposition of a new theory on the measurement of risk. *Econometrica*, 22(1), 22–36.

Bessière, V., Stéphany, É. (2014). Le financement par crowdfunding. Quelles spécificités pour l'évaluation des entreprises ? *Revue française de gestion*, 40(242), 149–161.

Bessière, V., Stéphany, É. (2015). Financement et gouvernance des start-ups en equity crowdfunding. *Finance Contrôle Stratégie* [Online]. Available at: https://journals.openedition.org/fcs/1684.

Bessière, V., Stéphany, É. (2017). *Le crowdfunding : fondements et pratiques*, 2nd ed. De Boeck, Louvain-la-Neuve.

Bhaskar, R. (1998). The logic of scientific discovery. In *Critical Realism: Essential Readings (Critical Realism: Interventions)*, Archer, M., Bhaskar, R., Collier, A., Lawson, T., Norrie, A. (eds). Routledge, London and New York.

Bickart, B.A. (1993). Carryover and backfire effects in marketing research. *Journal of Marketing Research*, 30(1), 52–62.

Billot, A.B. (1987). *Préférence et utilité floues*. PUF, Paris.

Bleichrodt, H., Wakker, P.P. (2015). Regret theory: A bold alternative to the alternatives. *The Economic Journal*, 125(583), 493–532.

Bonnet, C. (2005). La confiance entre capital-investisseurs et dirigeants : conséquences comportementales et influence sur la performance financière. *Finance Contrôle Stratégie*, 8(2), 99–132.

Bornstein, R.F. (1989). Exposure and affect: Overview and meta-analysis of research, 1968–1987. *Psychological Bulletin*, 106(2), 265–289.

Boudon, R. (1999). La "rationalité axiologique" : une notion essentielle pour l'analyse des phénomènes normatifs. *Sociologie et sociétés*, 31(1), 103.

Boudon, R. (2004). Théorie du choix rationnel ou individualisme méthodologique ? *Revue du MAUSS*, 24(2), 281–309.

Boudon, R. (2011). La théorie générale de la rationalité, base de la sociologie cognitive. In *La sociologie cognitive*, Kaufmann, L., Clément, F. (eds). Ophrys, Paris.

Boyle, G.J. (1989). Sex differences in reported mood states. *Personality and Individual Differences*, 10(11), 1179–1183.

Bretschneider, U., Knaub, K., Wieck, E. (2014). Motivations for crowdfunding: What drives the crowd to invest in start-ups? *European Conference on Information Systems*. ECIS, Tel Aviv.

Brody, L., Hall, J.A. (2008). Gender and emotion in context. In *Handbook of Emotions*, Lewis, M., Haviland-Jones, J.M., Barret, L.F. (eds). 3rd ed. Guilford Press, New York.

Broihanne, M.-H., Merli, M., Roger, P. (2004). *Finance comportementale*. Economica, Paris.

Brown, B., Perry, S. (1994). Removing the financial performance halo from fortune's "most admired" companies. *Academy of Management Journal*, 37(5), 1347–1359.

Browne, M.W. (1984). Asymptotically distribution-free methods for the analysis of covariance structures. *British Journal of Mathematical and Statistical Psychology*, 37(1), 62–83.

Bryan, M. (2013). *Histoire illustrée de la philosophie*. Le Pré aux Clercs, Paris.

Bugg-Levine, A., Emerson, J. (2011). Impact investing: Transforming how we make money while making a difference. *Innovations*, 6(3), 9–18.

Burke, L.A., Miller, M.K. (1999). Taking the mystery out of intuitive decision making. *Academy of Management Executive*, 13(4), 91–99.

Burtch, G., Ghose, A., Wattal, S. (2014). Cultural differences and geography as determinants of online prosocial lending. *MIS Quarterly*, 38(3), 773–794.

Buttard, A., Gadreau, M. (2008). D'une rationalité instrumentale à une rationalité interprétative de l'agent. Working paper, Université de Bourgogne, Dijon.

Calvet, L., Campbell, J., Sodini, P. (2009). Measuring the financial sophistication of households. *American Economic Review*, 99(2), 393–398.

Camerer, C., Loewenstein, G., Prelec, D. (2005). Neuroeconomics: How neuroscience can inform economics. *Journal of Economic Literature*, 43(1), 9–64.

Cannon, W.B. (1927). The James-Lange theory of emotions: A critical examination and an alternative theory. *The American Journal of Psychology*, 39(1–4), 106.

Capelli, S., Guillot-Soulez, C., Sabadie, W. (2015). Engagement RSE et attractivité organisationnelle : la communication protège-t-elle en cas de crise ? *Revue de gestion des ressources humaines*, 96(2), 3–23.

Capraro, R.M., Capraro, M.M. (2002). Myers-Briggs type indicator score reliability across studies: A meta-analytic reliability generalization study. *Educational and Psychological Measurement*, 62(4), 590–602.

Carontini, E. (1990). Le rôle de l'abduction dans le processus d'interprétation. In *Technologies et symboliques de la communication*, Sfez, L., Coutlée, G. (eds). PUG, Grenoble.

Cassel, C., Hackl, P., Westlund, A.H. (1999). Robustness of partial least-squares method for estimating latent variable quality structures. *Journal of Applied Statistics*, 26(4), 435–446.

Cattell, R.B. (1966). The scree test for the number of factors. *Multivariate Behavioral Research*, 1(2), 245–276.

Cauffman, E., Shulman, E.P., Steinberg, L., Claus, E., Banich, M.T., Graham, S., Woolard, J. (2010). Age differences in affective decision making as indexed by performance on the Iowa Gambling Task. *Developmental Psychology*, 46(1), 193–207.

Chalmers, A.F. (1987). *Qu'est-ce que la science ? Popper, Kuhn, Lakatos, Feyrabend.* Livre de Poche, Paris.

Chamberlin, E.H. (1948). An experimental imperfect market. *Journal of Political Economy*, 56(2), 95–108.

Chapman, D.S., Uggerslev, K.L., Carroll, S.A., Piasentin, K.A., Jones, D.A. (2005). Applicant attraction to organizations and job choice: A meta-analytic review of the correlates of recruiting outcomes. *Journal of Applied Psychology*, 90(5), 928–944.

Charreaux, G. (1998). Le rôle de la confiance dans le système de gouvernance des entreprises. *Économie et Société, Sciences de gestion*, 8–9, 47–65.

Charreaux, G. (2002). Au-delà de l'approche juridico-financière : le rôle cognitif des actionnaires et ses conséquences sur l'analyse de la structure de propriété et de la gouvernance. Paper, University of Burgundy, Dijon.

Charreaux, G. (2011). Quelle théorie pour la gouvernance ? De la gouvernance actionnariale à la gouvernance cognitive et comportementale. *Cahier du FARGO*, 1110402.

Chataigné, C. (2014). *Psychologie des valeurs*. De Boeck, Louvain-la-Neuve.

Chatman, J.A. (1989). Improving interactional organizational research: A model of person-organization fit. *Academy of Management Review*, 14(3), 333–349.

Chin, W.W., Newsted, P.R. (1999). Structural equation modeling analysis with small samples using partial least squares. In *Statistical Strategies for Small Sample Research*, Hoyle, R. (ed.). Sage Publication, London.

Chin, W.W., Marcolin, B.L., Newsted, P.R. (2003). A partial least squares latent variable modeling approach for measuring interaction effects: Results from a Monte Carlo simulation study and an electronic-mail emotion/adoption study. *Information Systems Research*, 14(2), 189–217.

Cholakova, M., Clarysse, B. (2015). Does the possibility to make equity investments in crowdfunding projects crowd out reward-based investments? *Entrepreneurship Theory & Practice*, 39(1), 145–172.

Churchill, J.J. (1979). A paradigm for developing better measures of marketing constructs. *Journal of Marketing Research*, 16(1), 64–73.

Cloren, G.L., Gasper, K., Garvin, E. (2001). Affect as information. In *Handbook of Affect and Social Cognition*, Forgas, J.P. (ed.). Lawrence Erlbaum Associates, Mahwah.

Coget, J.-F., Haag, C., Bonnefous, A.-M. (2009). Le rôle de l'émotion dans la prise de décision intuitive : zoom sur les réalisateurs-décideurs en période de tournage. *M@n@gement*, 12(2), 118–141.

Cohen, J. (1992). A power primer. *Psychological Bulletin*, 112(1), 155–159.

Cohen, J. (2009). *Statistical Power Analysis for the Behavioral Sciences*, 2nd ed. Psychology Press, New York.

Cohen, J.B., Pham, M.T., Andrade, E.B. (2008). The nature and role of affect in consumer behavior. In *Handbook of Consumer Psychology*, Haugtvedt, C.P., Herr, P., Kardes, F. (eds). Taylor & Francis, London.

Coley, A., Burgess, B. (2003). Gender differences in cognitive and affective impulse buying. *Journal of Fashion Marketing and Management*, 7(3), 282–295.

Collins, L., Pierrakis, Y. (2012). The venture crowd: Crowdfunding equity investment into business. Project report, NESTA, London.

Connelly, B.L., Certo, S.T., Ireland, R.D., Reutzel, C.R. (2011). Signaling theory: A review and assessment. *Journal of Management*, 37(1), 39–67.

Cortina, J.M. (1993). What is coefficient alpha? An examination of theory and applications. *Journal of Applied Psychology*, 78(1), 98–104.

Cox, E.P. (1980). The optimal number of response alternatives for a scale: A review. *Journal of Marketing Research*, 17(4), 407–422.

Crié, D. (2005). De l'usage des modèles de mesure réflectifs ou formatifs dans les modèles d'équations structurelles. *Recherche et Applications en Marketing*, 20(2), 5–27.

Cronbach, L. (1951). Coefficient alpha and the internal structure of tests. *Psychometrika*, 16(3), 297–334.

Cuin, C.-H. (2001). Émotions et rationalité dans la sociologie classique : les cas de Weber et Durkheim. *European Journal of Social Sciences*, XXXIX(120), 77–100.

Cumming, D. (2007). Government policy towards entrepreneurial finance: Innovation investment funds. *Journal of Business Venturing*, 22(2), 193–235.

Cummings, L., Bromiley, P. (1996). The Organizational Trust Inventory (OTI): Development and validation. In *Trust in Organizations – Frontiers of Theory and Research*, Kramer, R., Tyler, T. (eds). Sage Publications, Thousand Oaks.

Damasio, A.R. (2006). *L'Erreur de Descartes*. Odile Jacob, Paris.

Damasio, A.R., Tranel, D., Hanna, D. (1990). Individuals with sociopathic behavior caused by frontal damage fail to respond autonomically to social stimuli. *Behavioural Brain Research*, 41(2), 81–94.

Dane, E., Pratt, M.G. (2007). Exploring intuition and its role in managerial decision making. *Academy of Management Review*, 32(1), 33–54.

Dantzer, R. (2002). *Les émotions*, 3rd ed. PUF, Paris.

Dantzer, R. (2010). *Les émotions*. PUF, Paris.

Darwin, C. (1872). *The Expression of the Emotions in Man and Animals*. John Murray, London.

Dasgupta, P. (2000). Trust as a commodity. In *Trust: Making and Breaking Cooperative Relations*, Gambetta, D. (ed.). Basil Blackwell, Oxford.

David, A. (1999). Logique, épistémologie et méthodologie en sciences de gestion. *Conférence de l'AIMS*. Chatenay-Malabry, 1–23.

Davidson, R.J. (1998). Affective style and affective disorders: Perspectives from affective neuroscience. *Cognition & Emotion*, 12(3), 307–330.

Davis, B.C., Hmieleski, K.M., Webb, J.W., Coombs, J.E. (2017). Funders' positive affective reactions to entrepreneurs' crowdfunding pitches: The influence of perceived product creativity and entrepreneurial passion. *Journal of Business Venturing*, 32(1), 90–106.

Day, A.L., Carroll, S.A. (2004). Using an ability-based measure of emotional intelligence to predict individual performance, group performance, and group citizenship behaviours. *Personality and Individual Differences*, 36(6), 1443–1458.

Deci, E.L., Ryan, R.M. (1985). *Intrinsic Motivation and Self-determination in Human Behavior*. Plenum, New York.

Déjean, F. (2002). L'investissement socialement responsable : une revue de la littérature. Technologie et management de l'information : enjeux et impacts dans la comptabilité, le contrôle et l'audit [Online]. Available at: https://halshs.archives-ouvertes.fr/halshs-00584461/document.

Derbaix, C., Filser, M. (2011). *L'affectif dans les comportements d'achat et de consommation*. Economica, Paris.

Derbaix, C., Pham, M.T. (1989). Pour un développement des mesures de l'affectif en marketing : synthèse des prérequis. *Recherche et Applications en Marketing*, 4(4), 71–87.

Derbaix, C., Pham, M.T. (1991). Affective reactions to consumption situations: A pilot investigation. *Journal of Economic Psychology*, 12(2), 325–355.

Derbaix, C., Poncin, I. (2005). La mesure des réactions affectives en marketing : évaluation des principaux outils. *Recherche et Applications en Marketing*, 20(2), 55–75.

Desbrières, P. (2001). Le capital-investissement. *Banque & Marchés*, 51, 40–45.

Desbrières, P., Broye, G. (2000). Critères d'évaluation des investisseurs en capital : le cas français. *Finance Contrôle Stratégie*, 3(3), 5–43.

Dhar, R., Zhu, N. (2006). Up close and personal: Investor sophistication and the disposition effect. *Management Science*, 52(5), 726–740.

Diamantopoulos, A. (2006). The error term in formative measurement models: Interpretation and modeling implications. *Journal of Modelling in Management*, 1(1), 7–17.

Diamantopoulos, A., Winklhofer, H.M. (2001). Index construction with formative indicators: An alternative to scale development. *Journal of Marketing Research*, 38(2), 269–277.

Diamantopoulos, A., Sarstedt, M., Fuchs, C., Wilczynski, P., Kaiser, S. (2012). Guidelines for choosing between multi-item and single-item scales for construct measurement: A predictive validity perspective. *Journal of the Academy of Marketing Science*, 40(3), 434–449.

Dorff, M.B. (2014). The siren call of equity crowdfunding. *Journal of Corporation Law*, 39(3), 493–524.

Dubocage, E. (2006). L'évaluation de la "start-up" par le capital-risqueur entre objectivité, jugement et mimétisme. *Vie & sciences de l'entreprise*, 173(4), 9–18.

Dumez, H. (2011). Faire une revue de littérature : pourquoi et comment ? *Le Libellio d'Aegis*, 7(2–summer), 15–27.

Dumez, H. (2012). Qu'est-ce que l'abduction, et en quoi peut-elle avoir un rapport avec la recherche qualitative ? *Le Libellio d'Aegis*, 8(3), 3–9.

Eber, N., Willinger, M. (2012). *L'économie expérimentale*. La Découverte, Paris.

Efron, B. (1987). Better bootstrap confidence intervals. *Journal of the American Statistical Association*, 82(397), 171.

Epstein, S. (1994). Integration of the cognitive and the psychodynamic unconscious. *American Psychologist*, 49(8), 709.

Ericsson, K.A., Simon, H.A. (1980). Verbal reports as data. *Psychological Review*, 87(3), 215–251.

Feather, N.T. (1995). Values, valences, and choice: The influences of values on the perceived attractiveness and choice of alternatives. *Journal of Personality and Social Psychology*, 68(6), 1135–1151.

Fehle, F.R., Tsyplakov, S., Zdorovtsov, V.M. (2005). Can companies influence investor behavior through advertising? Super Bowl commercials and stock returns. *European Financial Management*, 11(5), 625–647.

Fenouillet, F. (2016). *Les théories de la motivation*, 2nd ed. Dunod, Paris.

Fernandes, V. (2012). En quoi l'approche PLS est-elle une méthode à (re)-découvrir pour les chercheurs en management ? *M@n@gement*, 15(1), 102–123.

Festinger, L. (1954). A theory of social comparison processes. *Human Relations*, 7(2), 117–140.

Festinger, L. (1957). *A Theory of Cognitive Dissonance.* Stanford University Press, Redwood City.

Filbeck, G., Smith, L.L. (1997). Team building and conflict management: Strategies for family businesses. *Family Business Review*, 10(4), 339–352.

Filbeck, G., Hatfield, P., Horvath, P. (2005). Risk aversion and personality type. *Journal of Behavioral Finance*, 6(4), 170–180.

Filser, M. (2015). Vers une consommation plus affective ? *Revue Française de gestion*, 41(253), 173–187.

Finucane, M., Alhakami, A., Slovic, P., Johnson, S.M. (2000). The affect heuristic in judgments of risks and benefits. *Journal of Behavioral Decision Making*, 13(1), 17.

Fischhoff, B., Slovic, P., Lichtenstein, S., Read, S., Combs, B. (1978). How safe is safe enough? A psychometric study of attitudes towards technological risks and benefits. *Sciences*, 9, 127–152.

Fornell, C., Larcker, D.F. (1981). Evaluating structural equation models with unobservable variables and measurement error. *Journal of Marketing Research*, 18(1), 39.

Frederick, S. (2002). Automated choice heuristics. In *Heuristics and Biases: The Psychology of Intuitive Judgment*, Gilovich, T., Griffin, D., Kahneman, D. (eds). Cambridge University Press, Cambridge.

Fredrickson, B.L. (2001). The role of positive emotions in positive psychology. *The American Psychologist*, 56(3), 218–226.

Freedman, S., Jin, G.Z. (2014). The signaling value of online social networks: Lessons from peer-to-peer lending. Paper, Indiana University and University of Maryland.

Fried, V.H., Hisrich, R.D. (1994). Toward a model of venture capital investment decision making. *Financial Management*, 23(3), 28.

Frieder, L., Subrahmanyam, A. (2005). Brand perceptions and the market for common stock. *The Journal of Financial and Quantitative Analysis*, 40(1), 57–85.

Frijda, N.H. (1986). *The Emotions*. Cambridge University Press, Cambridge.

Frijda, N.H. (1988). The laws of emotion. *American Psychologist*, 43(5), 349–358.

Frijda, N.H. (2006). *The Laws of Emotion*. Lawrence Erlbaum Associates, Mahwah.

Füller, J. (2006). Why consumers engage in virtual new product developments initiated by producers. *ACR North American Advances, Association for Consumer Research*, 33, 639–646.

Ganesan, S., Hess, R. (1997). Dimensions and levels of trust: Implications for commitment to a relationship. *Marketing Letters*, 8(4), 439–448.

Ganzach, Y. (2000). Judging risk and return of financial assets. *Organizational Behavior and Human Decision Processes*, 83(2), 353–370.

Garcia-Prieto, P., Tran, V., Wranik, T. (2005). Les théories de l'évaluation cognitive et de la différenciation des émotions : une clé pour comprendre le vécu émotionnel au travail. In *Comportement organisationnel (Vol. 1) – Contrat psychologique, émotions au travail, socialisation organisationnelle*, Delobbe, N., Herrbach, O., Lacaze, D., Migonac, K. (eds). De Boeck, Louvain-la-Neuve.

Gavard-Perret, M.-L., Gotteland, D., Haon, C., Jolibert, A. (2013). *Méthodologie de la recherche en sciences de gestion*. Pearson Education France, Paris.

Gayant, J.-P. (2017). *Risque et décision*. Vuibert, Paris.

Gefen, D. (2000). E-commerce: The role of familiarity and trust. *Omega*, 28(6), 725–737.

Geisser, S. (1974). A predictive approach to the random effect model. *Biometrika*, 61(1), 101.

Gerber, E.M., Hui, J. (2013). Crowdfunding: Motivations and deterrents for participation. *ACM Transactions on Computer-Human Interaction (TOCHI)*, 20(6), 34.

Germon, R., Maalaoui, A. (2014). Le crowdfunding, une nouvelle voie de financement pour les PME. In *Le grand livre de l'économie PME 2015*, Lecointre, G. (ed.). Gualino, Paris.

Gil, S. (2009). Comment étudier les émotions en laboratoire. *Revue électronique de psychologie sociale*, 4, 15–24.

Glaser, B.G., Strauss, A.L. (1967). *The Discovery of Grounded Theory: Strategies for Qualitative Research*. Aldine Publishing Company, London.

Glöckner, A., Witteman, C. (2010). Beyond dual-process models: A categorisation of processes underlying intuitive judgement and decision making. *Thinking & Reasoning*, 16(1), 1–25.

Goglin, C. (2020). *Emotions and Values in Equity Crowdfunding Investment Choices 2*. ISTE Ltd, London, and Wiley, New York.

Gond, J.-P., El-Akremi, A., Igalens, J., Swaen, V. (2010). Corporate social responsibility influence on employees. *International Center for Corporate Social Responsibility*, 54, 1–47.

Graillot, L. (1996). Segmentation, choix de cibles et positionnement des produits touristiques : une approche méthodologique. PhD Thesis, University of Burgundy, Dijon.

Grinblatt, M., Keloharju, M., Linnainmaa, J. (2011). IQ and stock market participation. *The Journal of Finance*, 66(6), 2121–2164.

Grullon, G., Kanatas, G., Weston, J.P. (2004). Advertising, breadth of ownership, and liquidity. *Review of Financial Studies*, 17(2), 439–461.

Gully, S.M., Phillips, J.M., Castellano, W.G., Han, K., Kim, A. (2013). A mediated moderation model of recruiting socially and environmentally responsible job applicants. *Personnel Psychology*, 66(4), 935–973.

Gurviez, P., Korchia, M. (2002). Proposition d'une échelle de mesure multidimensionnelle de la confiance dans la marque. *Recherches et Applications en Marketing*, 17(3), 41–61.

Gutman, J. (1982). A means-end chain model based on consumer categorization processes. *Journal of Marketing*, 46(2), 60–72.

Hackman, J., Oldham, G. (1980). *Work Redesign*. Addison-Wesley, Reading.

Hadouni, L., Mesnildrey, L., Lesueur, M., Gouin, S. (2009). Étude des attentes des consommateurs de produits de la mer frais et de leurs produits de la mer frais et de leurs comportements selon les circuits de distribution. *Analyse des dissonances cognitives*, 4, 1–38.

Hahn, C., Johnson, M.D., Herrmann, A., Huber, F. (2002). Capturing customer heterogeneity using a finite mixture PLS approach. *Schmalenbach Business Review*, 54(3), 243–269.

Hair Jr., J.F., Black, W.C., Babin, B.J., Anderson, R.E. (2010). *Mutivariate Data Analysis*, 7th ed. Pearson, London.

Hair, J.F., Ringle, C.M., Sarstedt, M. (2011). PLS-SEM: Indeed a silver bullet. *Journal of Marketing Theory and Practice*, 19(2), 139–152.

Hair, J.F., Sarstedt, M., Pieper, T.M., Ringle, C.M. (2012). The use of partial least squares structural equation modeling in strategic management research: A review of past practices and recommendations for future applications. *Long Range Planning*, 45(5–6), 320–340.

Hair Jr., J.F., Hult, G.T.M., Ringle, C.M., Sarstedt, M. (2017). *A Primer on Partial Least Squares Structural Equation Modeling (PLS-SEM)*, 2nd ed. Sage Publications, Thousand Oaks.

Hall, J., Hofer, C.W. (1993). Venture capitalists' decision criteria in new venture evaluation. *Journal of Business Venturing*, 8(1), 25–42.

Harrison, G.W., List, J.A. (2004). Field experiments. *Journal of Economic Literature*, 42(4), 1009–1055.

Harrison, R.T., Dibben, M.R., Mason, C.M. (1997). The role of trust in the informal investor's investment decision: An exploratory analysis. *Entrepreneurship Theory and Practice*, 21(4), 63–81.

Hatfield, E., Cacioppo, J.T., Rapson, R.L. (1993). Emotional contagion. *Current Directions in Psychological Science*, 2(3), 96–99.

Heath, C., Tversky, A. (1991). Preference and belief: Ambiguity and competence in choice under uncertainty. *Journal of Risk and Uncertainty*, 14(1), 5–28.

Heider, F. (1946). Attitudes and cognitive organization. *The Journal of Psychology*, 21, 107–112.

Heider, F. (1958). *The Psychology of Interpersonal Relations*. Wiley, New York.

Hemer, J. (2011). A snapshot on crowdfunding. Paper, Fraunhofer ISI, Karlsruhe.

Henderson, J.C., Nutt, P.C. (1980). The influence of decision style on decision making behavior. *Management Science*, 26(4), 371–386.

Hendrickx, M. (2014). *Crowdfunding : mode d'emploi*. di Pro 2, Liège.

Hendrickx, L., Vlek, C., Oppewal, H. (1989). Relative importance of scenario information and frequency information in the judgment of risk. *Acta Psychologica*, 72(1), 41–63.

Henseler, J. (2010). PLS-MGA: A non-parametric approach to partial least squares-based multi-group analysis. In *Challenges at the Interface of Data Analysis, Computer Science, and Optimization*, Gaul, W.A., Geyer-Schulz, A., Schmidt-Thieme, L., Kunze, J. (eds). Springer, Berlin.

Henseler, J., Ringle, C.M., Sarstedt, M. (2012). Using partial least squares path modeling in international advertising research: Basic concepts and recent issues. In *Handbook of Research on International Advertising*, Okazaki, S. (ed.). Edward Elgar, Cheltenham.

Henseler, J., Ringle, C.M., Sarstedt, M. (2015). A new criterion for assessing discriminant validity in variance-based structural equation modeling. *Journal of the Academy of Marketing Science*, 43(1), 115–135.

Henseler, J., Ringle, C.M., Sarstedt, M. (2016). Testing measurement invariance of composites using partial least squares. *International Marketing Review*, 33(3), 405–431.

Hervé, F., Manthé, E., Sannajust, A., Schwienbacher, A. (2016). Investor motivations in investment-based crowdfunding. *SSRN*, 2746398.

Hidi, S. (2000). An interest researcher's perspective: The effects of extrinsic and intrinsic factors on motivation. In *Intrinsic and Extrinsic Motivation*, Sansone, C., Hrackiewicz, J.M. (eds). Academic Press, San Diego.

Hidi, S., Baird, W. (1986). Interestingness: A neglected variable in discourse processing. *Cognitive Science*, 10(2), 179–194.

Hidi, S., Baird, W. (1988). Strategies for increasing text-based interest and students' recall of expository texts. *Reading Research Quarterly*, 23(4), 465.

Hidi, S., Renninger, K.A. (2006). The four-phase model of interest development. *Educational Psychologist*, 41(2), 111–127.

Holbrook, M.B. (1986). Emotion in the consumption experience: Toward a new model of the human consumer. In *Consumer Behavior: Emerging Theories and Applications*, Peterson, R.A., Hoyer, W.D., Wilson, W.R. (eds). Lexington Books, Lanham.

Holbrook, M.B., O'Shaughnessy, J. (1984). The role of emotion in advertising. *Psychology & Marketing*, 1(2), 45–64.

Holland, J.L. (1985). *Making Vocational Choices: A Theory of Vocational Personalities and Work Environments*, 2nd ed. Prentice-Hall, Englewood Cliffs.

Hornuf, L., Schwienbacher, A. (2015a). Portal design and funding dynamics in equity crowdfunding [Online]. Available at: http://ssrn.com/abstract=2612998.

Hornuf, L., Schwienbacher, A. (2015b). The emergence of crowdinvesting in Europe: With an in-depth analysis of the German market. Discussion paper no. 2014-43, Department of Economics, University of Munich.

Hornuf, L., Schwienbacher, A. (2016). Portal design and funding dynamics in equity crowdfunding. Paper, 30.

Howard, R.A. (1988). Decision analysis: Practice and promise. *Management Science*, 34(6), 679–695.

Hu, L., Bentler, P.M. (1998). Fit indices in covariance structure modeling: Sensitivity to underparameterized model misspecification. *Psychological Methods*, 3(4), 424–453.

Huang, L., Pearce, J.L. (2015). Managing the unknowable: The effectiveness of early-stage investor gut feel in entrepreneurial investment decisions. *Administrative Science Quarterly*, 60(4), 634–670.

Huberman, G. (2001). Familiarity breeds investment. *Review of Financial Studies*, 14(3), 659–680.

Hull, C.L. (1943). *Principles of Behavior: An Introduction to Behavior Theory*. Appleton-Century-Crofts, New York.

Hutcheson, F. (1726). *An Inquiry into the Original of Our Ideas of Beauty and Virtue*. Liberty Fund, Indianapolis.

Iizuka, M. (2014). *Le crowdfunding : les rouages du financement participatif*. Edubanque Editions, Saint Andre de Cubzac.

Izard, C.E. (1977). *Human Emotions*. Kluwer Academic/Plenum Publishers, Amsterdam.

James, W. (1884). What is an emotion? *Mind*, 9(34), 188–205.

Jarvis, C.B., MacKenzie, S.B., Podsakoff, P.M. (2003). A critical review of construct indicators and measurement model misspecification in marketing and consumer research. *Journal of Consumer Research*, 30(2), 199–218.

Jevons, W.S. (1871). *The Theory of Political Economy*. Macmillan, London.

Jöreskog, K.G. (1971). Statistical analysis of sets of congeneric tests. *Psychometrika*, 36(2), 109–133.

Josue, R., Bahm, C. (2016). Crowdfunding: Applying collective indexing of emotions to campaign videos. *Proceedings of the Conference on Computer Supported Cooperative Work and Social Computing*. ACM, San Francisco, 385–388.

Judge, T.A., Cable, D.M. (1997). Applicant personality, organizational culture, and organization attraction. *Personnel Psychology*, 50(2), 359–394.

Jung, C.G. (1923). *Psychological Types*. Routledge Kegan Paul, London.

Junghans, P. (2016). Le Big data pour construire une information d'anticipation. *I2D – Information, données & documents*, 53(4), 12–14.

Kahneman, D. (2003). A perspective on judgment and choice: Mapping bounded rationality. *American Psychologist*, 58(9), 697–720.

Kahneman, D. (2012). *Thinking, Fast and Slow*. Penguin, London.

Kahneman, D., Frederick, S. (2002). Representativeness revisited: Attribute substitution in intuitive judgement. In *Heuristics and Biases: The Psychology of Intuitive Judgment*, Gilovich, T., Griffin, D., Kahneman, D. (eds). Cambridge University Press, Cambridge.

Kahneman, D., Thaler, R. (2006). Anomalies: Utility maximization and experienced utility. *The Journal of Economic Perspectives*, 20(1), 221–234.

Kahneman, D., Tversky, A. (1979). Prospect theory: An analysis of decision under risk. *Econometrica*, 47(2), 263–292.

Kaiser, H.F. (1960). The application of electronic computers to factor analysis. *Educational and Psychological Measurement*, 20(1), 141–151.

Kaiser, H.F., Rice, J. (1974). Little Jiffy, Mark IV. *Educational and Psychological Measurement*, 34(1), 111–117.

Kast, R. (2002). *La théorie de la décision*. La Découverte, Paris.

Kenny, D.A. (2015). Moderator variables: Effect size and power [Online]. Available at: http://davidakenny.net/cm/moderation.htm.

Keynes, J.M. (1936). *The General Theory of Employment, Interest, and Money*. Palgrave Macmillan, London.

Kim, K., Viswanathan, S. (2016). The experts in the crowd: The role of reputable investors in a crowdfunding market. *TPRC 41: The 41st Research Conference on Communication, Information and Internet Policy*. *SSRN*. Available at: http://ssrn.com/abstract=2258243.

Kinder, P.D. (2005). *"Socially Responsible Investing": An Evolving Concept in a Changing World*. KLD Research & Analytics, Boston.

Kleemann, F., Voß, G.G., Rieder, K. (2008). Un(der)paid innovators: The commercial utilization of consumer work through crowdsourcing. *Science, Technology & Innovation Studies*, 4(1), 5–26.

Knight, F.H. (1921). *Risk, Uncertainty and Profit*. Houghton Mifflin, Boston.

Korchia, M. (2004). Connaissances de la marque : définition et mesures. *Congrès de l'AFM*. AFM, Saint-Malo.

Krapp, A. (2005). Basic needs and the development of interest and intrinsic motivational orientations. *Learning and Instruction*, 15, 381–395.

Kristof, A.L. (1996). Person-organization fit: An integrative review of its conceptualizations, measurement and implications. *Personnel Psychology*, 49(1), 1–49.

Kumar, A. (2009). Who gambles in the stock market? *The Journal of Finance*, 64(4), 1889–1933.

Kuppuswamy, V., Bayus, B.L. (2015). Crowdfunding creative ideas: The dynamics of project backers in kickstarter. *SSRN*, 5, 1–37.

La Porta, R., Lopez-de-Silanes, F., Shleifer, A. (1998). Law and finance. *Journal of Political Economy*, 106(6), 1113–1155.

Labreuche, J. (2010). Les principaux tests statistiques de l'analyse univariée : quand et comment les utiliser ? *Sang Thrombose Vaisseaux*, 22(10), 544–553.

Laciana, C.E., Weber, E.U. (2008). Correcting expected utility for comparisons between alternative outcomes: A unified parameterization of regret and disappointment. *Journal of Risk and Uncertainty*, 36(1), 1–17.

Lacroux, A. (2011). Les avantages et les limites de la méthode "Partial Least Square" (PLS) : une illustration empirique dans le domaine de la GRH. *Revue de gestion des ressources humaines*, 2, 45–64.

Lainé, M. (2016). Incertitude, probabilités et esprits animaux. Ontologie, épistémologie et théorie de la décision d'investissement productif chez Keynes. *Œconomia. History, Methodology, Philosophy*, 6–3, 403–439.

Lajante, M. (2013). Contribution des neurosciences à l'étude de l'émotion en persuasion publicitaire : concepts, méthodes et mesures. PhD Thesis, Université de Rennes, Rennes.

Lambert, T., Schwienbacher, A. (2010). An empirical analysis of crowdfunding [Online]. Available at: http://ssrn.com/abstract=1578175.

Lang, P.J. (1994). The motivational organization of emotions: Affect-reflex connections. In *Emotions: Essays on Emotion Theory*, van Goozen, S.H.M., Van de Poll, N.E., Sergeant, J.A. (eds). Psychology Press, Abingdon.

Lange, C. (1885). *Om Sinsbevaegelster: Et psyko-fysiologiske Studie*. Rasmussen, Copenhagen.

Lavison, C. (2011). L'investissement socialement responsable. Report, École Polytechnique – Sciences Po Paris, Paris.

Lazarus, R.S. (1966). *Psychological Stress and the Coping Process*. McGraw-Hill Book Company, New York.

Lazarus, R.S. (1982). Thoughts on the relations between emotion and cognition. *American Psychologist*, 37(9), 1019–1024.

Lazarus, R.S. (1984). On the primacy of cognition. *American Psychologist*, 39(2), 124–129.

Lazarus, R.S. (2001). Relational meaning and discrete emotions. In *Appraisal Processes in Emotion: Theory, Methods, Research*, Scherer, K.R., Schorr, A., Johnstone, T. (eds). Oxford University Press, Oxford.

Le Heron, E. (2012). Formaliser la décision en incertitude radicale ? *Conférence CEPN*. CEPN, Université Paris XIII, Paris.

Lebart, L., Salem, A. (1994). *Statistique Textuelle*. Dunod, Paris.

Lebraty, J., Lobre-Lebraty, K. (2013). *Crowdsourcing: One Step Beyond*. ISTE Ltd, London, and Wiley, New York.

Lebrun, A.-M. (2002). Le rôle de la familiarité du contexte d'achat sur la tendance exploratoire et à la recherche de variété. *Revue Française du Marketing*, 186, 53.

Ledoux, J. (1998). *The Emotional Brain: The Mysterious Underpinnings of Emotional Life*. Simon and Schuster, New York.

Lefèvre, F., Popescu, B.F. (2015). *Le Crowdfunding à la française*. Transvalor – Presses des mines, Paris.

Lejeune, C. (2010). Montrer, calculer, explorer, analyser. Ce que l'informatique fait (faire) à l'analyse qualitative. *Logiciels pour l'analyse qualitative*, 9, 15–32.

Lelart, M. (2014). De la finance éthique à l'éthique dans la finance. Research paper, Orleans Economics Laboratory, Orleans.

Lemoine, J.-F., Onnée, S. (2003). Vers une analyse des enjeux et des pratiques de la gestion de la relation avec l'actionnaire individuel. *Décisions Marketing*, 31, 25–37.

Lemoine, J.-F., Plichon, V. (2000). Le rôle des facteurs situationnels dans l'explication des réactions affectives du consommateur à l'intérieur d'un point de vente. *LEG – CERMAB/Centre de Recherche en Marketing de Bourgogne – Cahier de recherche*, LEG-CERMAB, CNRS UMR 5118, University of Burgundy.

Lesage, C. (2000). L'expérimentation de laboratoire en sciences de gestion. *21ème congrès de l'AFC*. AFC, Angers.

Lesourne, J. (1965). *Technique économique et gestion industrielle*. Dunod, Paris.

Lewis, A. (2001). A focus group study of the motivation to invest: "Ethical/green" and "ordinary" investors compared. *The Journal of Socio-Economics*, 30(4), 331–341.

Li, J., Chen, X.-P., Kotha, S., Fisher, G. (2017). Catching fire and spreading it: A glimpse into displayed entrepreneurial passion in crowdfunding campaigns. *Journal of Applied Psychology*, 102(7), 1075–1090.

Lichtenstein, S., Slovic, P., Fischhoff, B., Layman, M., Combs, B. (1978). Judged frequency of lethal events. *Journal of Experimental Psychology: Human Learning and Memory*, 4(6), 551–578.

Lin, M., Viswanathan, S. (2015). Home bias in online investments: An empirical study of an online crowdfunding market. *Management Science*, 62(5), 1393–1414.

Lin, M., Prabhala, N.R., Viswanathan, S. (2013). Judging borrowers by the company they keep: Friendship networks and information asymmetry in online peer-to-peer lending. *Management Science*, 59(1), 17–35.

Lin, Y., Boh, W.F., Goh, K.H. (2014). How different are crowdfunders? Examining archetypes of crowdfunders and their choice of projects. *SSRN* [Online]. Available at: https://ssrn.com/abstract=2397571.

Lindeman, M., Verkasalo, M. (2005). Measuring values with the short Schwartz's value survey. *Journal of Personality Assessment*, 85(2), 170–178.

Linnenbrink-Garcia, L., Durik, A.M., Conley, A.M., Barron, K.E., Tauer, J.M., Karabenick, S.A., Harackiewicz, J.M. (2010). Measuring situational interest in academic domains. *Educational and Psychological Measurement*, 70(4), 647–671.

Lis, B. (2012). The relevance of corporate social responsibility for a sustainable human resource management: An analysis of organizational attractiveness as a determinant in employees' selection of a (potential) employer. *Management Revue*, 23(3), 279–295.

Lo, A.W., Repin, D.V. (2002). The psychophysiology of real-time financial risk processing. *Journal of Cognitive Neuroscience*, 14(3), 323–339.

Loewenstein, G. (1987). Anticipation and the valuation of delayed consumption. *The Economic Journal*, 97(387), 666–684.

Loewenstein, G. (1999). Experimental economics from the vantage-point of behavioural economics. *The Economic Journal*, 109(453), 25–34.

Loewenstein, G.F., Weber, E.U., Hsee, C.K., Welch, N. (2001). Risk as feelings. *Psychological Bulletin*, 127(2), 267–286.

Loomes, G., Sudgen, R. (1982). Regret theory: An alternative theory of rational choice under uncertainty. *The Economic Journal*, 92, 805–824.

Loomes, G., Sudgen, R. (1987). Testing for regret and disappointment in choice under uncertainty. *The Economic Journal*, 97, 118–129.

Lopes, H. (2005). Utilité, normes et sentiments moraux. *Revue du MAUSS*, 25(1), 404–427.

Luhmann, N. (2001). Confiance et familiarité. *Réseaux*, 108(4), 15–35.

Lynn, D. (2012). The crowdfunding provisions of the JOBS act. *Financial Executive*, 28(4), 42–44.

Lynn, D., Sabbagh, H. (2012). The JOBS act open door for crowdfunding offerings, *Morrison & Forrester Social Media Newsletter*, 4(11), 6–8.

Maalaoui, A., Conreaux, P. (2014). *Crowdfunding : les clés du financement participatif*. Ellipses Marketing, Paris.

MacGregor, D.G., Slovic, P., Dreman, D., Berry, M. (2000). Imagery, affect, and financial judgment. *The Journal of Psychology and Financial Markets*, 1(2), 104–110.

Macmillan, I.C., Siegel, R., Narasimha, P.N.S. (1985). Criteria used by venture capitalists to evaluate new venture proposals. *Journal of Business Venturing*, 1(1), 119–128.

Macmillan, I.C., Kulow, D.M., Khoylian, R. (1989). Venture capitalists' involvement in their investments: Extent and performance. *Journal of Business Venturing*, 4(1), 27–47.

MacMullen, R. (2004). *Les Émotions dans l'Histoire, ancienne et moderne*. Les Belles Lettres, Paris.

Magron, C.-E. (2014). Approches comportementales de la gestion individuelle de portefeuille. PhD Thesis, University of Strasbourg, Strasbourg.

Maio, G.R., Olson, J.M. (1998). Values as truisms: Evidence and implications. *Journal of Personality and Social Psychology*, 74(2), 294–311.

Mangot, M. (2008). *Psychologie de l'investisseur et des marchés financiers*, 2nd ed. Dunod, Paris.

Mangot, M. (2013). 25 ans de finance comportementale ou l'émergence d'un nouveau paradigme. In *Grandeur et misère de la finance moderne*, Chambon, J.-L., Pluchart, J.-J. (eds). Eyrolles, Paris.

Manigart, S., Wright, M., Robbie, K., Desbrières, P., De Waele, K. (1997). Venture capitalists' appraisal of investment projects: An empirical European study. *Entrepreneurship: Theory & Practice*, 21(4), 29–43.

Marshall, A. (1890). *Principles of Economics*. Prometheus Books, New York.

Martinez, F. (2012). L'individu face au risque : l'apport de Kahneman et Tversky. *Idées économiques et sociales*, 161, 15–23.

Mason, C., Stark, M. (2004). What do investors look for in a business plan? A comparison of the investment criteria of bankers, venture capitalists and business angels. *International Small Business Journal*, 22(3), 227–248.

Maxwell, A.L., Jeffrey, S.A., Lévesque, M. (2011). Business angel early stage decision making. *Journal of Business Venturing*, 26(2), 212–225.

Mayer, J.D., Caruso, D.R., Salovey, P. (1999). Emotional intelligence meets traditional standards for an intelligence. *Intelligence*, 27(4), 267–298.

McAllister, D.J. (1995). Affect- and cognition-based trust as foundations for interpersonal cooperation in organizations. *Academy of Management Journal*, 38(1), 24–59.

Mehrabian, A., Russel, J.A. (1974). *An Approach to Environmental Psychology*. MIT Press, Cambridge.

Mellers, B.A. (2000). Choice and the relative pleasure of consequences. *Psychological Bulletin*, 126(6), 910–924.

Menger, C. (1871). *Principles of Economics*. CreateSpace Independent Publishing Platform, Scotts Valley.

Meyer, J.P., Allen, N.J. (1991). A three-component conceptualization of organizational commitment. *Human Resource Management Review*, 1(1), 61–89.

Michinov, E. (2001). L'attraction interpersonnelle : un concept en évolution. *Les Cahiers Internationaux de Psychologie Sociale*, 50, 11–26.

Mill, J.S. (1882). *A System of Logic, Ratiocinative and Inductive*, 8th ed. Harper & Brothers, New York.

Miller, G.A. (1955). The magical number seven, plus or minus two: Some limits on our capacity for processing information. *Psychological Review*, 101(2), 343–352.

Miller, J. (2015). *Spinoza and the Stoics*. Cambridge University Press, Cambridge.

Millette, V., Gagné, M. (2008). Designing volunteers' tasks to maximize motivation, satisfaction and performance: The impact of job characteristics on volunteer engagement. *Motivation and Emotion*, 32(1), 11–22.

Milovac, M., Sanchez-Burks, J., Baron, R.A. (2015). The psychology of crowdfunding: How mood, passion, and emotion make or break a pitch. *Academy of Management Proceedings*, 1(1), 1.

Mollick, E. (2013). The dynamics of crowdfunding: An exploratory study. *Journal of Business Venturing*, 29(1), 1–16.

Mollick, E., Nanda, R. (2015). Wisdom or madness? Comparing crowds with expert evaluation in funding the arts. Working paper, Harvard Business School.

Moorman, C., Zaltman, G., Deshpande, R. (1992). Relationships between providers and users of market research: The dynamics of trust within and between organizations. *Journal of Marketing Research*, 29(3), 314.

Morgan, R.M., Hunt, S.D. (1994). The commitment-trust theory of relationship marketing. *Journal of Marketing*, 58(3), 20.

Mucchielli, A. (2005). Émotions, normes sociales, décisions et jugements. *Revue internationale de psychosociologie*, XI(25), 11–19.

Mucchielli, A. (2011). *Les motivations*. PUF, Paris.

Murnieks, C.Y., Sudek, R., Wiltbank, R. (2015). The role of personality in angel investing. *The International Journal of Entrepreneurship and Innovation*, 16(1), 19–31.

Neumann, V.J., Morgenstern, O. (1944). *Theory of Games and Economic Behavior*. Princeton University Press, Princeton.

Neveu, V. (2004). La confiance organisationnelle : définition et mesure. Document, Congrès de l'Association Française des Ressources Humaines.

Nisbett, R.E., Wilson, T.D. (1977). The halo effect: Evidence for unconscious alteration of judgments. *Journal of Personality and Social Psychology*, 35(4), 250–256.

Nivoix, S. (2008). L'aversion au risque : pourquoi est-ce si difficile à mesurer ? *Management & Avenir*, 15, 65–78.

Nofsinger, J.R. (2001). *The Psychology of Investing*. Pearson Prentice Hall, Upper Saddle River.

Northcraft, G.B., Neale, M.A. (1987). Experts, amateurs, and real estate: An anchoring-and-adjustment perspective on property pricing decisions. *Organizational Behavior and Human Decision Processes*, 39(1), 84–97.

O'Keefe, D.J. (2002). *Persuasion: Theory and Research*. Sage Publications, Thousand Oaks.

Ochs, M. (2007). Modélisation, formalisation et mise en œuvre d'un agent rationnel dialoguant émotionnel empathique. PhD Thesis, Université Paris 8, Paris.

Ola, A.M. (2016). L'identification des opportunités d'investissement en incertitude : le jugement intuitif des Business Angels dans le financement des firmes entrepreneuriales. PhD Thesis, University of Angers, Angers.

Olson, J., Reynold, T. (1983). Understanding consumer's cognitive structures: Implications for advertising strategy, advertising and consumer psychology. In *Advertising and Consumer Psychology*, volume 1, Percy, L., Woodside, A. (eds). Lexington Books, Lanham.

Onnée, S., Renault, S. (2014). Crowdfunding : vers une compréhension du rôle joué par la foule. *Management & Avenir*, 74, 117–133.

Ordanini, A., Miceli, L., Pizzetti, M., Parasuraman, A. (2011). Crowd-funding: Transforming customers into investors through innovative service platforms. *Journal of Service Management*, 22(4), 443–470.

Orléan, A. (2010). L'impossible évaluation du risque. *Prisme*, 18, 1–38.

Ortony, A., Clore, G., Collins, A. (1988). *The Cognitive Structure of Emotions*. Cambridge University Press, Cambridge.

Osgood, C.E., Tannenbaum, P.H. (1955). The principle of congruity in the prediction of attitude change. *Psychological Review*, 62(1), 42–55.

Osgood, C.E., Suci, G.J., Tannenbaum, P.H. (1957). *The Measurement of Meaning*. University of Illinois Press, Champaign.

Overskeid, G. (2000). The slave of the passions: Experiencing problems and selecting solutions. *Review of General Psychology*, 4(3), 284–309.

Pare, J.L., Rédis, J. (2011). Réorienter la recherche en finance entrepreneuriale. *Gestion 2000*, 28(4), 17–31.

Petit, E. (2013). L'expérimentation en économie : méthode et principes fondateurs [Online]. Available at: http://ressources.aunege.fr/nuxeo/site/esupversions/7d01faf2-0582-47bd-af37-a52852812398/co/RESS2-1_1.html.

Petty, R.E., Cacioppo, J.T. (1984). Source factors and the elaboration likelihood model of persuasion. *ACR North American Advances*, NA-11, 668–672.

Petty, R.E., Cacioppo, J.T. (1986). The elaboration likelihood model of persuasion. *Advances in Experimental Social Psychology*, 19, 123–205.

Pfister, H.-R., Böhm, G. (2008). The multiplicity of emotions: A framework of emotional functions in decision making. *Judgement and Decision Making*, 3(1), 5–17.

Pham, M.T. (1998). Representativeness, relevance, and the use of feelings in decision making. *Journal of Consumer Research*, 25(2), 144–159.

Piolat, A., Bannour, R. (2008). Emotions et affects : contribution de la psychologie cognitive. In *Le sujet des émotions au Moyen-Âge*, Nagy, P., Boquet, D. (eds). Beauchesne, Paris.

Plutchik, R. (1970). Emotions, evolution and adaptive processes. In *Feelings and Emotions: The Loyola Symposium*, Arnold, M. (ed.). Academic Press, New York.

Poggi, I., Germani, M. (2003). Emotions at work. *Proceedings of the Conference on Human Aspects of Advanced Manufacturing: Agility and Hybrid Automation*. HAAMAHA, Rome, 461–468.

Poissonnier, A. (2016). *Le financement participatif, un nouvel outil pour les entreprises*. Eyrolles, Paris.

Poncin, I., Derbaix, C. (2009). Commercials as context for other commercials. *Journal of Advertising*, 38(3), 33–49.

Power, T.V. (2012). SEC regulation of crowdfunding intermediaries under Title III of the JOBS act. *Banking & Financial Services Policy Report*, 10(31), 1–7

Quenk, N.L. (2009). *Essentials of Myers-Briggs Type Indicator Assessment*, 2nd ed. John Wiley & Sons, New York.

Quiggin, J. (1982). A theory of anticipated utility. *Journal of Economic Behavior & Organization*, 3(4), 323–343.

Ramsey, Y. (2012). What the heck is crowdfunding? *Business People*, 54–57.

Reinert, A. (1983). Une méthode de classification descendante hiérarchique : application à l'analyse lexicale par contexte. *Les cahiers de l'analyse des données*, 8(2), 187–198.

Rigdon, E.E. (2012). Rethinking partial least squares path modeling: In praise of simple methods. *Long Range Planning*, 45(5–6), 341–358.

Rigdon, E., Ringle, C.M., Sarstedt, M. (2010). Structural modeling of heterogeneous data with partial least squares. *Review of Marketing Research*, 7, 255–296.

Rimé, B. (2009). *Le partage social des émotions*. PUF, Paris.

Rimé, B. (2016). L'émergence des émotions dans les sciences psychologiques. *Revue électronique du CRH*, 16.

Rokeach, M. (1973). *The Nature of Human Value*. Free Press, New York.

Roseman, I.J. (1991). Appraisal determinants of discrete emotions. *Cognition & Emotion*, 5(3), 161–200.

Roseman, I.J. (2001). A model of appraisal in the emotion system. In *Appraisal Processes in Emotion: Theory, Methods, Research*, Scherer, K.R., Schorr, A., Johnstone, T. (eds). Oxford University Press, Oxford.

Rosenberg, M.J. (1965). When dissonance fails: On eliminating evaluation apprehension from attitude measurement. *Journal of Personality and Social Psychology*, 1(1), 28–42.

Rosenzweig, P. (2007). Misunderstanding the nature of company performance: The halo effect and other business delusions. *California Management Review*, 49(4), 6–20.

Rousseau, D.M. (1977). Technological differences in job characteristics, employee satisfaction, and motivation: A synthesis of job design research and sociotechnical systems theory. *Organizational Behavior and Human Performance*, 19(1), 18–42.

Roy, B. (1985). *Méthodologie multicritère d'aide à la décision.* Economica, Paris.

Ruffieux, B., Rozan, A., Robin, S. (2008). Mesurer les préférences du consommateur pour orienter les décisions des pouvoirs publics : l'apport de la méthode expérimentale. *Économie & prévision*, 182(1), 113–127.

Russell, J.A. (1980). A circumplex model of affect. *Journal of Personality and Social Psychology*, 39(6), 1161–1178.

Russell, J.A., Pratt, G. (1980). A description of the affective quality attributed to environments. *Journal of Personality and Social Psychology*, 38(2), 311–322.

Rynes, S.L., Barber, A.E. (1990). Applicant attraction strategies: An organizational perspective. *Academy of Management Review*, 15(2), 286–310.

Ryu, S., Kim, Y.-G. (2014). Crowdfunding as a two-sided platform: Development of a crowdfunding participation model. *SSRN*. Available at: https://papers.ssrn.com/sol3/papers.cfm?abstract_id=2423315.

Sadler-Smith, E., Shefy, E. (2004). The intuitive executive: Understanding and applying "gut feel" in decision-making. *Academy of Management Executive*, 18(4), 76–91.

Salem Khalifa, A. (2004). Customer value: A review of recent literature and an integrative configuration. *Management Decision*, 42(5), 645–666.

Salichs, M.A., Malfaz, M. (2012). A new approach to modeling emotions and their use on a decision-making system for artificial agents. *IEEE Transactions on Affective Computing*, 3(1), 56–68.

Sander, D., Scherer, K.R. (2014). *Traité de psychologie des émotions*. Dunod, Paris.

Sapienza, H.J., Korsgaard, M.A. (1996). Procedural justice in entrepreneur-investor relations. *Academy of Management Journal*, 39(3), 544–574.

Sarstedt, M., Becker, J.-M., Ringle, C.M., Schwaiger, M. (2011a). Uncovering and treating unobserved heterogeneity with FIMIX-PLS: Which model selection criterion provides an appropriate number of segments? *Schmalenbach Business Review*, 63(1), 34–62.

Sarstedt, M., Henseler, J., Ringle, C.M. (2011b). Multigroup analysis in partial least squares (PLS) path modeling: Alternative methods and empirical results. In *Advances in International Marketing*, Sarstedt, M., Schwaiger, M., Taylor, C.R. (eds). Emerald Group Publishing Limited, Bingley.

Sarstedt, M., Wilczynski, P., Melewar, T.C. (2013). Measuring reputation in global markets: A comparison of reputation measures' convergent and criterion validities. *Journal of World Business*, 48(3), 329–339.

Savage, L.J. (1951). The theory of statistical decision. *Journal of the American Statistical Association*, 46(253), 55–67.

Savage, L.J. (1954). *The Foundations of Statistics*. John Wiley & Sons, New York.

Scarbrough, H., Swan, J., Amaeshi, K., Briggs, T. (2013). Exploring the role of trust in the deal-making process for early-stage technology ventures. *Entrepreneurship Theory and Practice*, 37(5), 1203–1228.

Schachter, S. (1964). The interaction of cognitive and physiological determinants of emotional state. *Advances in Experimental Social Psychology*, 1, 49–80.

Scherer, K.R. (1993). Studying the emotion-antecedent appraisal process: An expert system approach. *Cognition & Emotion*, 7(3–4), 325–355.

Scherer, K.R. (2000). Emotion. In *Introduction to Social Psychology: A European Perspective*, Hewstone, M., Stroebe, W. (eds). Blackwell, Oxford.

Scherer, K.R. (2005). What are emotions? And how can they be measured? *Social Science Information*, 44(4), 695–729.

Schiefele, U. (1991). Interest, learning, and motivation. *Educational Psychologist*, 26(3–4), 299–323.

Schiefele, U. (2009). Situational and individual interest. In *Handbook of Motivation at School*, Wentzel, K., Wigfield, A. (eds). Routledge, New York.

Schiefele, U., Krapp, A., Wild, K.-P., Winteler, A. (1993). Der "Fragebogen zum Studieninteresse" (FSI). *Diagnostica*, 39(4), 335–351.

Schmidt, C. (2010). *Neuroéconomie*. Odile Jacob, Paris.

Schneider, B. (1987). The people make the place. *Personnel Psychology*, 40(3), 437–453.

Schram, A. (2005). Artificiality: The tension between internal and external validity in economic experiments. *Journal of Economic Methodology*, 12(2), 225–237.

Schwartz, N., Clore, G.L. (2003). Mood as information: 20 years later. *Psychological Inquiry*, 14(3–4), 296–303.

Schwartz, S.H. (1992). Universals in the content and structure of values: Theoretical advances and empirical tests in 20 countries. *Advances in Experimental Social Psychology*, 25, 1–65.

Schwartz, S.H. (1994). Are there universal aspects in the structure and contents of human values? *Journal of Social Issues*, 50(4), 19–45.

Schwartz, S.H. (1996). Value priorities and behavior: Applying a theory of integrated value systems. In *The Psychology of Values: The Ontario Symposium*, Celigman, C., Olson, J.M., Zana, M.P. (eds). Psychology Press, Abingdon.

Schwartz, S.H. (2006). Les valeurs de base de la personne : théorie, mesures et applications. *Revue française de sociologie*, 47(4), 929–968.

Schwartz, S.H. (2007). Universalism values and the inclusiveness of our moral universe. *Journal of Cross-cultural Psychology*, 38(6), 711–728.

Schwartz, S.H., Cieciuch, J., Vecchione, M., Davidov, E., Fischer, R., Beierlein, C., Ramos, A., Verkasalo, M., Lönnqvist, J.-E., Demirutku, K., Dirilen-Gumus, O., Konty, M. (2012). Refining the theory of basic individual values. *Journal of Personality and Social Psychology*, 103(4), 663–688.

Schwienbacher, A. (2015). Le Crowdinvesting : une nouvelle forme de finance entrepreneuriale. In *Le Financement de l'innovation : nouvelles perspectives théoriques & pratiques*, Bessière, V., Stéphany, É. (eds). De Boeck, Paris.

Schwienbacher, A., Larralde, B. (2010). Crowdfunding of small entrepreneurial ventures. In *The Oxford Handbook of Entrepreneurial Finance*, Cumming, D. (ed.). Oxford University Press, Oxford.

Shapiro, S., Spence, M.T. (1997). Managerial intuition: A conceptual and operational framework. *Business Horizons*, 40(1), 63–68.

Sharma, D., Borna, S., Stearns, J.M. (2009). An investigation of the effects of corporate ethical values on employee commitment and performance: Examining the moderating role of perceived fairness. *Journal of Business Ethics*, 89(2), 251–260.

Shefrin, H., Statman, M. (1985). The disposition to sell winners too early and ride losers too long: Theory and evidence. *The Journal of Finance*, 40(3), 777–790.

Shefrin, H., Statman, M. (2000). Behavioral portfolio theory. *Journal of Financial and Quantitative Analysis*, 35(2), 127–151.

Shiller, R.J. (2000). *Irrational Exuberance*. Princeton University Press, Princeton.

Sigar, K. (2012). Fret no more: Inapplicability of crowdfunding concerns in the internet age and the JOBS acts safeguards. *Administrative Law Review*, 2(64), 474–505.

Signol, A. (2011). La psychanalyse est-elle une science ? *Le Journal des psychologues*, 291, 54–58.

Signori, A., Vismara, S. (2016). Returns on investments in equity crowdfunding. *SSRN* [Online]. Available at: https://ssrn.com/abstract=2765488.

Silvia, P.J. (2006). *Exploring the Psychology of Interest*. Oxford University Press, Oxford.

Simon, H.A. (1955). A behavioral model of rational choice. *The Quarterly Journal of Economics*, 69(1), 99.

Simon, H.A. (1956). Rational choice and the structure of the environment. *Psychological Review*, 63(2), 129–138.

Simon, H.A. (1987). Making management decisions: The role of intuition and emotion. *Academy of Management Executive*, 1(1), 57–64.

Simon, É. (2007). La confiance dans tous ses états. *Revue française de gestion*, 175, 83–94.

Sinclair, M., Ashkanasy, N. (2005). Intuition: Myth or a decision making tool? *Management Learning*, 36(3), 353–370.

Skoglund, E., Stiernblad, M. (2013). The future of equity crowdfunding – Is "the crowd" capable of good investment? [Online]. Available at: http://lup.lub.lu.se/luur/download?func=downloadFile&recordOId=3814918&fileOId=3814919/.

Slovic, P. (2001). Cigarette smokers, rational actors or rational fools? In *Smoking: Risk, Perception, and Policy*. Sage Publications, Thousand Oaks.

Slovic, P., Layman, M., Kraus, N., Flynn, J., Chalmers, J., Gesell, G. (1991). Perceived risk, stigma, and potential economic impacts of a high-level nuclear waste repository in Nevada. *Risk Analysis*, 11(4), 683–696.

Slovic, P., Finucane, M., Peters, E., MacGregor, D.G. (2002). The affect heuristic. In *The Psychology of Intuitive Judgment*, Gilovich, T., Griffin, D., Kahneman, D. (eds). Cambridge University Press, New York.

Smith, A. (1822). *The Theory of Moral Sentiments*. J. Richardson, London.

Smith, V.L. (1962). An experimental study of competitive market behavior. *The Journal of Political Economy*, 70(2), 111–137.

Spence, M. (1973). Job market signaling. *The Quarterly Journal of Economics*, 87(3), 355–374.

Stanovich, K.E., West, R.F. (2000). Individual differences in reasoning: Implications for the rationality debate? *Behavioral and Brain Sciences*, 23(5), 82.

Statman, M. (2002). Lottery players/stock traders. *Financial Analysts Journal*, 58(1), 14–21.

Stone, M. (1974). Cross-validatory choice and assessment of statistical predictions. *Journal of the Royal Statistical Society*, 36(2), 111–147.

Stucki, D. (2014). Financer une entreprise par le crowdfunding. *La Revue Banque*. RB Edition/Eyrolles, Paris.

Sugden, R. (1991). Rational choice: A survey of contributions from economics and philosophy. *The Economic Journal*, 101(407), 751–785.

Sukiennik C. (2013). Plantin, Christian. 2011. Les bonnes raisons des émotions. Principes et méthode pour l'étude du discours émotionné (Berne : Peter Lang) ; Micheli, Raphaël. 2010. L'émotion argumentée. L'abolition de la peine de mort dans le débat parlementaire français (Paris : Le Cerf). *Argumentation et Analyse du Discours*. [Online], Available at: http://journals.openedition.org/aad/1566.

Taffler, R. (2014). Emotional finance: Theory and application. Paper, Warwick Business School.

Thaler, R., Sustein, C. (2012). *Nudge*. Pocket, Paris.

Thorndike, E.L. (1920). A constant error in psychological ratings. *Journal of Applied Psychology*, 4(1), 25–29.

Thurstone, L.L. (1931). The indifference function. *The Journal of Social Psychology*, 2(2), 139–167.

Tieger, P., Barron, B., Tieger, K. (2014). *Do What You Are: Discover the Perfect Career for You through the Secrets of Personality Type*. Little, Brown Spark, New York.

Tirole, J. (2017). *Economics for the Common Good*, translated by Steven Rendall. Princeton University Press, Princeton and Oxford.

Tom, V.R. (1971). The role of personality and organizational images in the recruiting process. *Organizational Behavior and Human Performance*, 6(5), 573–592.

Tomczak, A., Brem, A. (2013). A conceptualized investment model of crowdfunding. *Venture Capital*, 15(4), 335–359.

Tomkins, S. (1962). *Affect Imagery Consciousness: Volume I: The Positive Affects*. Springer, Berlin.

Trouilloud, D., Sarrazin, P. (2003). Note de synthèse – les connaissances actuelles sur l'effet Pygmalion : processus, poids et modulateurs. *Revue française de pédagogie*, 145(1), 89–119.

Turban, D.B., Hendrickson, C., Forret, M.L. (1998). Applicant attraction to firms: Influences of organization reputation, job attributes, and recruiter behaviors. *Journal of Vocational Behavior*, 52(1), 24–44.

Tversky, A., Kahneman, D. (1974). Judgment under uncertainty: Heuristics and biases. *Sciences*, 185(4157), 1124–1131.

Tversky, A., Kahneman, D. (1992). Advances in prospect theory: Cumulative representation of uncertainty [Online]. Available at: http://cemi.ehess.fr/docannexe/file/2780/tversjy_kahneman_advances.pdf, 27.

Tyebjee, T.T., Bruno, A.V. (1984). A model of venture capitalist investment activity. *Management Science*, 30(9), 1051–1066.

Vaidis, D., Halimi-Falkowicz, S. (2007). La théorie de la dissonance cognitive : une théorie âgée d'un demi-siècle. *Revue électronique de Psychologie sociale*, 1, 9–18.

Valette-Florence, P. (1994). Introduction aux chaînages cognitifs. *Recherche et Applications en Marketing*, 9, 93–117.

Verplanken, B., Holland, R.W. (2002). Motivated decision making: Effects of activation and self-centrality of values on choices and behavior. *Journal of Personality and Social Psychology*, 82(3), 434–447.

Vinzi, E.V., Chin, W.W., Henseler, J., Wang, H. (2010). *Handbook of Partial Least Squares: Concepts, Methods and Applications in Marketing and Related Fields*. Springer, Berlin.

Viviani, J.-L. (1994). Incertitude et rationalité. *Revue française d'économie*, 9(2), 105–146.

Voorbraak, K.J.P. (2011). Crowdfunding for financing new ventures consequences of the financial model on operational decisions. Paper, Eindhoven University of Technology, Eindhoven.

Walrass, L. (1874). *Éléments d'économie politique pure : ou théorie de la richesse sociale*. Kessinger Publishing, Whitefish.

Wang, M., Keller, C., Siegrist, M. (2011). The less you know, the more you are afraid of – A survey on risk perceptions of investment products. *Journal of Behavioral Finance*, 12(1), 9–19.

Wash, R. (2013). The value of completing crowdfunding projects. *Proceedings from the Seventh International AAAI Conference on Weblogs and Social Media*. ICWSM, Cambridge.

Weber, M. (2003). *Économie et société, tome 1 : les catégories de la sociologie*. Pocket, Paris.

Weber, S.J., Cook, T.D. (1972). Subject effects in laboratory research: An examination of subject roles, demand characteristics, and valid inference. *Psychological Bulletin*, 77(4), 273–295.

Wechsler, J. (2013). Know your crowd: The drivers of success in reward based crowdfunding. Paper, University of Fribourg, Fribourg.

Weiner, B., Graham, S. (1989). Understanding the motivational role of affect: Life-span research from an attributional perspective. *Cognition & Emotion*, 3(4), 401–419.

Wetzer, C. (2008). La finance comportementale, régulation des marchés financiers. Master's Thesis, Université Paris II Panthéon Assas, Paris.

Wheat, R.E., Wang, Y., Byrnes, J.E., Ranganathan, J. (2013). Raising money for scientific research through crowdfunding. *Trends in Ecology & Evolution*, 28(2), 71–72.

Wilkie, W.L. (1990). *Consumer Behavior*. John Wiley & Sons, New York.

Wold, H. (1985). Partial least squares. In *Encyclopedia of Statistical Sciences*, volume 6, Kotz, S., Johnson, N.L. (eds). John Wiley & Sons, New York.

Wright, P. (1975). Consumer choice strategies: Simplifying vs. optimizing. *Journal of Marketing Research*, 12(1), 60–67.

Wright, M., Robbie, K. (1996). Venture capitalists, unquoted equity investment appraisal and the role of accounting information. *Accounting and Business Research*, 26(2), 153–168.

Wuillaume, A., Jacquemin, A., Janssen, F. (2016). L'influence du contenu émotionnel de la narration entrepreneuriale sur l'attitude et la prise de décision des contributeurs en crowdfunding. *13ème Congrès International Francophone en Entrepreneuriat et PME*. CIFEPME, Trois-Rivières.

Wuillaume, A., Jacquemin, A., Janssen, F. (2017). "Cher crowd, laisse-moi te raconter une histoire… " : l'influence du contenu émotionnel, du sentiment d'appartenance à la communauté et de l'authenticité de la narration entrepreneuriale sur le succès à lever des fonds via le crowdfunding. Paper, Louvain Research Institute in Management and Organizations, Louvain.

Yennek, N. (2014). Contribution de l'intérêt situationnel à une reconsidération de la satisfaction dans la formation pour adultes. PhD Thesis, Paris Nanterre University, Nanterre.

Yin, R.K. (2009). *Case Study Research: Design and Methods. Applied Social Research Methods*, 4th ed. Sage Publications, Los Angeles.

Zajonc, R.B. (1968). Attitudinal effects of mere exposure. *Journal of Personality and Social Psychology*, 9(2), 1–27.

Zajonc, R.B. (1980). Feeling and thinking. *American Psychologist*, 1S1, 35(2), 151–175.

Zajonc, R.B. (2001). Mere exposure: A gateway to the subliminal. *Current Direction in Psychological Science*, 10(6), 224–228.

Zaleski, P.A. (2011). Start-ups and external equity: The role of entrepreneurial experience. *Business Economics*, 46(1), 43–50.

Zeelenberg, M., Pieters, R. (1999). Comparing service delivery to what might have been. *Journal of Service Research*, 2(1), 86–99.

Zeelenberg, M., Nelissen, R.M., Breugelmans, S.M., Pieters, R. (2008). On emotion specificity in decision making: Why feeling is for doing. *Judgment and Decision Making*, 3(1), 18.

Zhao, X., Lynch, J.G., Chen, Q. (2010). Reconsidering Baron and Kenny: Myths and truths about mediation analysis. *Journal of Consumer Research*, 37(2), 197–206.

Zidi, A. (2009). Analyse de la fidélité des échelles mesurant la confiance entre le capital risqueur et l'entrepreneur et son impact dans la création de valeur : cas du contexte tunisien. Paper, CERAM Business School and IAE d'Aix-en-Provence, Sophia-Antipolis.

Index

H, I

L, M

N, O, P

R

S

U

V

Other titles from

iSTE

in

Innovation, Entrepreneurship and Management

2020

ANDREOSSO-O'CALLAGHAN Bernadette, DZEVER Sam, JAUSSAUD Jacques, TAYLOR Robert
Sustainable Development and Energy Transition in Europe and Asia (Innovation and Technology Set – Volume 9)

BEN SLIMANE Sonia, M'HENNI Hatem
Entrepreneurship and Development: Realities and Future Prospects (Smart Innovation Set – Volume 30)

CHOUTEAU Marianne, FOREST Joëlle, NGUYEN Céline
Innovation for Society: The P.S.I. Approach (Smart Innovation Set – Volume 28)

CORON Clotilde
Quantifying Human Resources: Uses and Analysis (Technological Changes and Human Resources Set – Volume 2)

CORON Clotilde, GILBERT Patrick
Technological Change (Technological Changes and Human Resources Set – Volume 1)

CERDIN Jean-Luc, PERETTI Jean-Marie
The Success of Apprenticeships: Views of Stakeholders on Training and Learning
(Human Resources Management Set – Volume 3)

DELCHET-COCHET Karen
Circular Economy: From Waste Reduction to Value Creation
(Economic Growth Set – Volume 2)

DIDAY Edwin, GUAN Rong, SAPORTA Gilbert, WANG Huiwen
Advances in Data Science
(Big Data, Artificial Intelligence and Data Analysis Set – Volume 4)

DOS SANTOS PAULINO Victor
Innovation Trends in the Space Industry
(Smart Innovation Set – Volume 25)

GUILHON Bernard
Venture Capital and the Financing of Innovation
(Innovation Between Risk and Reward Set – Volume 6)

LATOUCHE Pascal
Open Innovation: Human Set-up
(Innovation and Technology Set – Volume 10)

MAKRIDES Andreas, KARAGRIGORIOU Alex, SKIADAS Christos H.
Data Analysis and Applications 3: Computational, Classification, Financial, Statistical and Stochastic Methods
(Big Data, Artificial Intelligence and Data Analysis Set – Volume 5)
Data Analysis and Applications 4: Financial Data Analysis and Methods
(Big Data, Artificial Intelligence and Data Analysis Set – Volume 6)

MASSOTTE Pierre, CORSI Patrick
Complex Decision-Making in Economy and Finance

MICHAUD Thomas
Science Fiction and Innovation Design (Innovation in Engineering and Technology Set – Volume 6)

MONINO Jean-Louis
Data Control: Major Challenge for the Digital Society
(Smart Innovation Set – Volume 29)

MORLAT Clément
Sustainable Productive System: Eco-development versus Sustainable Development
(Smart Innovation Set – Volume 26)

SAULAIS Pierre, ERMINE Jean-Louis
Knowledge Management in Innovative Companies 2: Understanding and Deploying a KM Plan within a Learning Organization
(Smart Innovation Set – Volume 27)

2019

AMENDOLA Mario, GAFFARD Jean-Luc
Disorder and Public Concern Around Globalization

BARBAROUX Pierre
Disruptive Technology and Defence Innovation Ecosystems
(Innovation in Engineering and Technology Set – Volume 5)

DOU Henri, JUILLET Alain, CLERC Philippe
Strategic Intelligence for the Future 1: A New Strategic and Operational Approach
Strategic Intelligence for the Future 2: A New Information Function Approach

FRIKHA Azza
Measurement in Marketing: Operationalization of Latent Constructs

FRIMOUSSE Soufyane
Innovation and Agility in the Digital Age
(Human Resources Management Set – Volume 2)

GAY Claudine, SZOSTAK Bérangère L.
Innovation and Creativity in SMEs: Challenges, Evolutions and Prospects
(Smart Innovation Set – Volume 21)

GORIA Stéphane, HUMBERT Pierre, ROUSSEL Benoît
Information, Knowledge and Agile Creativity
(Smart Innovation Set – Volume 22)

HELLER David
Investment Decision-making Using Optional Models
(Economic Growth Set – Volume 2)

HELLER David, DE CHADIRAC Sylvain, HALAOUI Lana, JOUVET Camille
The Emergence of Start-ups
(Economic Growth Set – Volume 1)

HÉRAUD Jean-Alain, KERR Fiona, BURGER-HELMCHEN Thierry
Creative Management of Complex Systems
(Smart Innovation Set – Volume 19)

LATOUCHE Pascal
Open Innovation: Corporate Incubator
(Innovation and Technology Set – Volume 7)

LEHMANN Paul-Jacques
The Future of the Euro Currency

LEIGNEL Jean-Louis, MÉNAGER Emmanuel, YABLONSKY Serge
Sustainable Enterprise Performance: A Comprehensive Evaluation Method

LIÈVRE Pascal, AUBRY Monique, GAREL Gilles
Management of Extreme Situations: From Polar Expeditions to Exploration-Oriented Organizations

MILLOT Michel
Embarrassment of Product Choices 2: Towards a Society of Well-being

N'GOALA Gilles, PEZ-PÉRARD Virginie, PRIM-ALLAZ Isabelle
Augmented Customer Strategy: CRM in the Digital Age

NIKOLOVA Blagovesta
The RRI Challenge: Responsibilization in a State of Tension with Market Regulation
(Innovation and Responsibility Set – Volume 3)

PELLEGRIN-BOUCHER Estelle, ROY Pierre
Innovation in the Cultural and Creative Industries
(Innovation and Technology Set – Volume 8)

PRIOLON Joël
Financial Markets for Commodities

QUINIOU Matthieu
Blockchain: The Advent of Disintermediation

RAVIX Joël-Thomas, DESCHAMPS Marc
Innovation and Industrial Policies
(Innovation between Risk and Reward Set – Volume 5)

ROGER Alain, VINOT Didier
Skills Management: New Applications, New Questions
(Human Resources Management Set – Volume 1)

SAULAIS Pierre, ERMINE Jean-Louis
Knowledge Management in Innovative Companies 1: Understanding and Deploying a KM Plan within a Learning Organization
(Smart Innovation Set – Volume 23)

SERVAJEAN-HILST Romaric
Co-innovation Dynamics: The Management of Client-Supplier Interactions for Open Innovation
(Smart Innovation Set – Volume 20)

SKIADAS Christos H., BOZEMAN James R.
Data Analysis and Applications 1: Clustering and Regression, Modeling-estimating, Forecasting and Data Mining
(Big Data, Artificial Intelligence and Data Analysis Set – Volume 2)
Data Analysis and Applications 2: Utilization of Results in Europe and Other Topics
(Big Data, Artificial Intelligence and Data Analysis Set – Volume 3)

UZUNIDIS Dimitri
Systemic Innovation: Entrepreneurial Strategies and Market Dynamics

VIGEZZI Michel
World Industrialization: Shared Inventions, Competitive Innovations and Social Dynamics
(Smart Innovation Set – Volume 24)

2018

BURKHARDT Kirsten
Private Equity Firms: Their Role in the Formation of Strategic Alliances

CALLENS Stéphane
Creative Globalization
(Smart Innovation Set – Volume 16)

CASADELLA Vanessa
Innovation Systems in Emerging Economies: MINT – Mexico, Indonesia, Nigeria, Turkey
(Smart Innovation Set – Volume 18)

CHOUTEAU Marianne, FOREST Joëlle, NGUYEN Céline
Science, Technology and Innovation Culture
(Innovation in Engineering and Technology Set – Volume 3)

CORLOSQUET-HABART Marine, JANSSEN Jacques
Big Data for Insurance Companies
(Big Data, Artificial Intelligence and Data Analysis Set – Volume 1)

CROS Françoise
Innovation and Society
(Smart Innovation Set – Volume 15)

DEBREF Romain
Environmental Innovation and Ecodesign: Certainties and Controversies
(Smart Innovation Set – Volume 17)

DOMINGUEZ Noémie
SME Internationalization Strategies: Innovation to Conquer New Markets

ERMINE Jean-Louis
Knowledge Management: The Creative Loop
(Innovation and Technology Set – Volume 5)

GILBERT Patrick, BOBADILLA Natalia, GASTALDI Lise,
LE BOULAIRE Martine, LELEBINA Olga
Innovation, Research and Development Management

IBRAHIMI Mohammed
Mergers & Acquisitions: Theory, Strategy, Finance

LEMAÎTRE Denis
Training Engineers for Innovation

LÉVY Aldo, BEN BOUHENI Faten, AMMI Chantal
Financial Management: USGAAP and IFRS Standards
(Innovation and Technology Set – Volume 6)

MILLOT Michel
Embarrassment of Product Choices 1: How to Consume Differently

PANSERA Mario, OWEN Richard
Innovation and Development: The Politics at the Bottom of the Pyramid
(Innovation and Responsibility Set – Volume 2)

RICHEZ Yves
Corporate Talent Detection and Development

SACHETTI Philippe, ZUPPINGER Thibaud
New Technologies and Branding
(Innovation and Technology Set – Volume 4)

SAMIER Henri
Intuition, Creativity, Innovation

TEMPLE Ludovic, COMPAORÉ SAWADOGO Eveline M.F.W.
Innovation Processes in Agro-Ecological Transitions in Developing Countries
(Innovation in Engineering and Technology Set – Volume 2)

UZUNIDIS Dimitri
Collective Innovation Processes: Principles and Practices
(Innovation in Engineering and Technology Set – Volume 4)

VAN HOOREBEKE Delphine
The Management of Living Beings or Emo-management

2017

AÏT-EL-HADJ Smaïl
The Ongoing Technological System
(Smart Innovation Set – Volume 11)

BAUDRY Marc, DUMONT Béatrice
Patents: Prompting or Restricting Innovation?
(Smart Innovation Set – Volume 12)

BÉRARD Céline, TEYSSIER Christine
Risk Management: Lever for SME Development and Stakeholder Value Creation

CHALENÇON Ludivine
Location Strategies and Value Creation of International Mergers and Acquisitions

CHAUVEL Danièle, BORZILLO Stefano
The Innovative Company: An Ill-defined Object
(Innovation between Risk and Reward Set – Volume 1)

CORSI Patrick
Going Past Limits To Growth

D'ANDRIA Aude, GABARRET Inés
Building 21st Century Entrepreneurship
(Innovation and Technology Set – Volume 2)

DAIDJ Nabyla
Cooperation, Coopetition and Innovation
(Innovation and Technology Set – Volume 3)

FERNEZ-WALCH Sandrine
The Multiple Facets of Innovation Project Management
(Innovation between Risk and Reward Set – Volume 4)

FOREST Joëlle
Creative Rationality and Innovation
(Smart Innovation Set – Volume 14)

GUILHON Bernard
Innovation and Production Ecosystems
(Innovation between Risk and Reward Set – Volume 2)

HAMMOUDI Abdelhakim, DAIDJ Nabyla
Game Theory Approach to Managerial Strategies and Value Creation
(Diverse and Global Perspectives on Value Creation Set – Volume 3)

LALLEMENT Rémi
Intellectual Property and Innovation Protection: New Practices and New Policy Issues
(Innovation between Risk and Reward Set – Volume 3)

LAPERCHE Blandine
Enterprise Knowledge Capital
(Smart Innovation Set – Volume 13)

LEBERT Didier, EL YOUNSI Hafida
International Specialization Dynamics
(Smart Innovation Set – Volume 9)

MAESSCHALCK Marc
Reflexive Governance for Research and Innovative Knowledge
(Responsible Research and Innovation Set – Volume 6)

MASSOTTE Pierre
Ethics in Social Networking and Business 1: Theory, Practice and Current Recommendations
Ethics in Social Networking and Business 2: The Future and Changing Paradigms

MASSOTTE Pierre, CORSI Patrick
Smart Decisions in Complex Systems

MEDINA Mercedes, HERRERO Mónica, URGELLÉS Alicia
Current and Emerging Issues in the Audiovisual Industry
(Diverse and Global Perspectives on Value Creation Set – Volume 1)

MICHAUD Thomas
Innovation, Between Science and Science Fiction
(Smart Innovation Set – Volume 10)

PELLÉ Sophie
Business, Innovation and Responsibility
(Responsible Research and Innovation Set – Volume 7)

SAVIGNAC Emmanuelle
The Gamification of Work: The Use of Games in the Workplace

SUGAHARA Satoshi, DAIDJ Nabyla, USHIO Sumitaka
Value Creation in Management Accounting and Strategic Management: An Integrated Approach
(Diverse and Global Perspectives on Value Creation Set –Volume 2)

UZUNIDIS Dimitri, SAULAIS Pierre
Innovation Engines: Entrepreneurs and Enterprises in a Turbulent World
(Innovation in Engineering and Technology Set – Volume 1)

2016

BARBAROUX Pierre, ATTOUR Amel, SCHENK Eric
Knowledge Management and Innovation
(Smart Innovation Set – Volume 6)

BEN BOUHENI Faten, AMMI Chantal, LEVY Aldo
Banking Governance, Performance And Risk-Taking: Conventional Banks Vs Islamic Banks

BOUTILLIER Sophie, CARRÉ Denis, LEVRATTO Nadine
Entrepreneurial Ecosystems (Smart Innovation Set – Volume 2)

BOUTILLIER Sophie, UZUNIDIS Dimitri
The Entrepreneur (Smart Innovation Set – Volume 8)

BOUVARD Patricia, SUZANNE Hervé
Collective Intelligence Development in Business

GALLAUD Delphine, LAPERCHE Blandine
Circular Economy, Industrial Ecology and Short Supply Chains
(Smart Innovation Set – Volume 4)

GUERRIER Claudine
Security and Privacy in the Digital Era
(Innovation and Technology Set – Volume 1)

MEGHOUAR Hicham
Corporate Takeover Targets

MONINO Jean-Louis, SEDKAOUI Soraya
Big Data, Open Data and Data Development
(Smart Innovation Set – Volume 3)

MOREL Laure, LE ROUX Serge
Fab Labs: Innovative User
(Smart Innovation Set – Volume 5)

PICARD Fabienne, TANGUY Corinne
Innovations and Techno-ecological Transition
(Smart Innovation Set – Volume 7)

2015

CASADELLA Vanessa, LIU Zeting, DIMITRI Uzunidis
Innovation Capabilities and Economic Development in Open Economies
(Smart Innovation Set – Volume 1)

CORSI Patrick, MORIN Dominique
Sequencing Apple's DNA

CORSI Patrick, NEAU Erwan
Innovation Capability Maturity Model

FAIVRE-TAVIGNOT Bénédicte
Social Business and Base of the Pyramid

GODÉ Cécile
Team Coordination in Extreme Environments

MAILLARD Pierre
Competitive Quality and Innovation

MASSOTTE Pierre, CORSI Patrick
Operationalizing Sustainability

MASSOTTE Pierre, CORSI Patrick
Sustainability Calling

2014

DUBÉ Jean, LEGROS Diègo
Spatial Econometrics Using Microdata

LESCA Humbert, LESCA Nicolas
Strategic Decisions and Weak Signals

2013

HABART-CORLOSQUET Marine, JANSSEN Jacques, MANCA Raimondo
VaR Methodology for Non-Gaussian Finance

2012

DAL PONT Jean-Pierre
Process Engineering and Industrial Management

MAILLARD Pierre
Competitive Quality Strategies

POMEROL Jean-Charles
Decision-Making and Action

SZYLAR Christian
UCITS Handbook

2011

LESCA Nicolas
Environmental Scanning and Sustainable Development

LESCA Nicolas, LESCA Humbert
Weak Signals for Strategic Intelligence: Anticipation Tool for Managers

MERCIER-LAURENT Eunika
Innovation Ecosystems

2010

SZYLAR Christian
Risk Management under UCITS III/IV

2009

COHEN Corine
Business Intelligence

ZANINETTI Jean-Marc
Sustainable Development in the USA

2008

CORSI Patrick, DULIEU Mike
The Marketing of Technology Intensive Products and Services

DZEVER Sam, JAUSSAUD Jacques, ANDREOSSO Bernadette
Evolving Corporate Structures and Cultures in Asia: Impact of Globalization

2007

AMMI Chantal
Global Consumer Behavior

2006

BOUGHZALA Imed, ERMINE Jean-Louis
Trends in Enterprise Knowledge Management

CORSI Patrick *et al.*
Innovation Engineering: the Power of Intangible Networks

Printed in the USA/Agawam, MA
September 16, 2026

910661.021